What he himself characteristically called 'his idiosyncratic mode of regard' is a factor few readers of Hardy's novels can overlook and one with which all serious students of his fiction must come to terms. The fact that there is nevertheless little final agreement about the nature of his achievement has prompted Miss Vigar to make a fresh study of Hardy's own notes and essays on the art of the novel and to analyse his fictional technique in the light of these unduly neglected observations. Her approach centres on Hardy's pervasive theme of the contrast between appearance and reality and on his frequent use of 'pictorial' devices to express his imaginative vision. She is able to develop a critical account of Hardy's work that can convincingly explain, by reference to the same criteria, both its strengths and its weaknesses, its successes and failures.

THE NOVELS OF THOMAS HARDY:
ILLUSION AND REALITY

THE NOVELS OF THOMAS HARDY: ILLUSION AND REALITY

by
PENELOPE VIGAR

UNIVERSITY OF LONDON
THE ATHLONE PRESS
1974

Published by
THE ATHLONE PRESS
UNIVERSITY OF LONDON
at 4 Gower Street London WC1

*Distributed by Tiptree Book Services Ltd
Tiptree, Essex*

*USA and Canada
Humanities Press Inc*

© *Penelope Vigar* 1974

ISBN 0 485 11147 0

Printed in Great Britain by
T. & A. CONSTABLE LTD
EDINBURGH

Coleridge says, aim at *illusion* in audience or readers—
i.e., the mental state when dreaming, intermediate
between complete *delusion* . . . and a clear perception
of falsity.

Thomas Hardy

PREFACE

In recent years, there has been a great deal of interest, both public and academic, in the novels of Thomas Hardy. A massive amount of criticism on his work has appeared, notably over the last three decades, and with it an equal variety of opinion. However, it seems to me that critics still tend to judge Hardy's work by attempting to fit it into a preconceived esoteric or fashionable mould, and that they have unduly neglected most of his personal comments on the subject of novel-writing.

My aim in this book is to analyse the concepts on which Hardy based his literary style, and to show how profoundly these elemental principles affected his artistic vision as it is projected in the novels. His is a view of life which I see as being essentially less complicated, although perhaps more skilfully contrived, than has often been assumed.

My concern is primarily with Hardy's technique as a novelist, and to this end I have intentionally left out of my examination any detailed discussion of his so-called philosophy. It may also be noted that I avoid any specific reference to his moral and religious convictions, his poetry, or his private life. Again, for such omissions I offer no apology save the above explanation.

P.E.S.V.

PUBLISHERS' NOTE

Extracts from Thomas Hardy's works are reprinted by permission of the Trustees of the Hardy Estate, Macmillan, London and Basingstoke and The Macmillan Company of Canada.

CONTENTS

Introduction: Hardy's Concept of his Art   I

I   The Technique of the Novels   13

II   Experiments and Mistakes   58

III   *Under the Greenwood Tree* and
The Trumpet-Major   85

IV   *Far from the Madding Crowd*   101

V   *The Return of the Native*   125

VI   *The Mayor of Casterbridge*   146

VII   *Tess of the d'Urbervilles*   169

VIII   *Jude the Obscure*   189

Conclusion   213

Notes   217

Index   223

Hardy's Concept of his Art

All writers necessarily say what they say at the expense of not saying what they do not say, but only the unsatisfactory writer reminds us of this.

David Lodge, *The Language of Fiction*, p. 69

Public and critical opinions of Thomas Hardy as a novelist (scarcely less as a poet) have always been kaleidoscopic. He has been idolized and denigrated, tolerated and scorned, earnestly inter-preted in a hundred different ways. Some choose to see him simply as a primitive but inspired rustic with an eye for a good story; others, more hopefully, find in him a primitive but inspired precursor to D. H. Lawrence. Lovers of Henry James frequently consider him boring or inadequate, and point out the obviousness of his symbolism and the simplicity of his charac-terization. There seems to be no special method for understanding him. One approach leaves him in the twilit ranks of the once popular romantic novelette writers, another credits him with a profound philosophy which he himself probably never dreamed of. He has been indiscriminately and vaguely termed 'Victorian' and 'modern', a realist and a creator of allegorical fables. In the end, one must agree with John Wain, who wrote of 'The Novel' in its abstract form that 'when discussing [it] one has the sense of punching at a fog-bank; anything can be said, and it will be true of some novel, somewhere'.[1]

What *is* interesting, and indisputable, is that Hardy's novels, regardless of their chronological position, show enormous varia-tions in intention and execution—so much so that it is sometimes hard to believe that *The Hand of Ethelberta* and *A Laodicean* could have anything in common with *The Return of the Native* or *Tess of the d'Urbervilles*. Similarly, within each individual novel there are

I

surprising fluctuations, not only in quality but also, seemingly, in the author's own attitude. Why, for example, should scenes of great power and sensibility be followed up by lengthy passages of pedantic, apparently irrelevant 'explanation' or philosophizing?

Several critics have tried, with varying success, to demonstrate that Hardy's weaknesses simply add to his strength. Ian Gregor, for example, argues convincingly that this is the case: 'Had he possessed a greater sophistication, a greater mastery of "the art of the novel", *Tess* and *Jude* would not have caused the stir they did. Looking back, we can see the gaucheness as an intrinsic part of the power.'[2] However, this train of thought is seldom pursued at length, and its most coherent explication is still (to my mind) contained in M. D. Zabel's essay, 'Hardy in Defense of His Art: The Aesthetic of Incongruity', which was published in 1940.[3] More often (though less frequently in recent years), the final summation of his worth is one which is faintly apologetic or less faintly condescending. David Lodge, for instance, has obviously a sympathetic appreciation of Hardy's work, but feels obliged to call him an ' "in-spite-of" novelist' ('That is, he figures in literary criticism and literary history as a great novelist "in spite of" gross defects').[4] In an earlier assessment, Frank Chapman, after roundly denouncing the author's skill and reputation, makes a final grudging qualification: 'But, whatever its faults, Hardy's medium is individual, and unlike that of any of his contemporaries'.[5]

On the surface, at least, Hardy himself was remarkably detached about his prowess as a novelist, and those who consider his novels relatively unimportant have seized on his comment that he was quite content to be considered merely as being a good hand at a serial. His own general comments on the novel were not copious nor particularly original. 'Good fiction', he says,

may be defined as that kind of imaginative writing which lies nearest to the epic, dramatic or narrative masterpieces of the past. One fact is certain: in fiction there can be no intrinsically new thing at this stage of the world's history.[6]

So dogmatic a comment would appear to reveal nothing more

than a deliberately obtuse conservatism, and we are scarcely illuminated by his subsequent quotation of the Bible as proof that a revelation of life does not need to be 'set off by a finish of phraseology or incisive sentences of subtle definition', or by his declaration that Scott's *Bride of Lammermoor* is 'an almost perfect specimen of form'.

Nevertheless, he was himself peculiarly sensitive to criticism, and felt often that he was misunderstood and misrepresented. It is perhaps because of this that in his critical writings he so frequently appeals to the reader to make an effort to see what the author is trying to project. At one stage he even comments, rather facetiously, that the reader's aim should be

the exercise of a generous imaginativeness, which shall find in a tale not only all that was put there by the author, put he it never so awkwardly, but which shall find there what was never inserted by him, never foreseen, never contemplated. Sometimes these additions which are woven around a work of fiction by the intensitive power of the reader's own imagination are the finest parts of the scenery. (*PRF*, p. 112)

In spite of this, however, Hardy lived to regret the fact that his critics 'read between the lines'; they frequently did so to his own disadvantage. Even today, with all the mass of well-informed critical material that has been written on the novels, the communication gap is still there and many writers on Hardy have tended of late to concentrate their energies more specifically on the recently unearthed details of his private life. On Hardy's actual achievement as a novelist there would seem to be little more to say; and yet some element of dissatisfaction with what has been said still remains. Several years ago, Philip Larkin commented that 'Hardy doesn't seem to attract the best modern critics':

This must be due to one of two reasons: either Hardy's work is not good enough to warrant their attention, or it is not of a kind that interests them. To choose the second of these as more likely, as we surely must, is not to get much further towards enlightenment. We can say that modern criticism thrives on the difficult . . . and that Hardy is simple; his work contains little in thought or reference that needs elucidation, his language is unambiguous, his themes readily comprehensible. A typical role of the modern critic is to demonstrate that the author has said something other than he intended . . . but when this is tried on Hardy, as in the case of Dr. Kettle and his celebrated contention that *Tess of the d'Urbervilles* symbolizes the decline of the peasantry, the reader feels uncomfortable rather than illuminated.[7]

Clearly, the easiest way to approach the apparent mystery of Hardy's art is to study his own aims and methods as a novelist. His special form of presentation will encompass most of his faults as well as his virtues, and an examination of his work should begin, as a matter of course, with his own theories—however rudimentary—about the craft of fiction. Hardy himself urges the reader to search out the pattern of thought, the inspiration behind the apparent imperfections. It is surely with his own work in mind that he writes:

> In [the] scarcity of excellence in novels as wholes the reader must content himself with excellence in parts . . . In this process he will go with the professed critic so far as to inquire whether the story forms a regular structure of incident, accompanied by an equally regular development of character—a composition based on faithful imagination, less the transcript than the similitude of material fact. But the appreciative, perspicacious reader will do more than this. He will see what his author is aiming at, and by affording full scope to his own insight, catch the vision which the writer has in his eye, and is endeavouring to project upon the paper even while it half eludes him. (*PRF*, p. 115)

So far, with the exception of Zabel's essay, comparatively little attention has been paid to Hardy's three main treatises on the novel: 'The Profitable Reading of Fiction' (1888), 'Candour in English Fiction' (1890) and 'The Science of Fiction' (1891). These essays together with the prefaces to his novels and the notes in *The Early Life* and *The Later Years* (now shown to be autobiographical)[8] comprise the total of his literary philosophy. Many of his notes were destroyed at his own direction, so we may conclude that what remains (although he rarely suppressed anything once it had been printed) is what he wished to remain as his ultimate statement concerning his craft. It is important to notice, however, that the major essays do not relate subjectively to the imaginative world Hardy created in his own novels. Their bias is towards the technique of the novelist and to his role as an instructor and interpreter—one who can 'throw a stronger irradiation' over subjects with which the reader is already familiar. As such, their first editor has described them as 'deliberate, considered self-exposures'.[9] Certainly they reveal, in their thoughtful considera-tion of the relationship between life and art, that Hardy's attitude towards the novel as an artistic form was not that of a clumsy or an indifferent hack-writer. However simple it may ultimately appear, what Hardy calls his 'idiosyncratic mode of regard' must be valued for its own sake as the essential basis of each of his novels.

The communication of any viewpoint necessarily rests on the success or failure of the writer's technique, the way in which he imposes a pattern on the unordered flow of real experience. As Hardy describes it,

. . . in looking at a carpet, by following one colour a certain pattern is suggested, by following another colour, another; so in life the seer should watch that pattern among general things which his idiosyncracy moves him to observe, and describe that alone. This is, quite accurately, a going to Nature; yet the result is no mere photograph, but purely the product of the writer's own mind. (*Life*, p. 153)[10]

The writer, in selecting and manipulating his impressions to give his own individual view of life, must inevitably make use of the technical appurtenances of his trade—style, patterns of imagery and symbolism, character definition, working out of plot—yet none of these, taken in isolation, is an effective guide to the novel's worth. This can only lie in its effect as a whole in which all these separate parts have a special role and significance. For this reason, says David Lodge, 'Confusion about the novelist's art is likely to persist as long as we think of his use of language (or "style") as a skill that can be distinguished from, and on occasion weighed against, his ability to create characters and actions'.[11] In this sense, the study of a novelist's technique must evolve into an appreciation of the total form of his novel, its existence as a work of art which seeks to convey the ideas of the artist to his audience. As such, the novel has no independent physical existence as a mass of words on paper: it exists only in the mind of the reader. Its individual importance can only lie in the success with which it imprints on the receptive mind the particular concept of life which its author has formed, while style and structure are simply the means by which the writer creates and orders his impressions.

It is difficult to pinpoint a consistent 'form' in Hardy's novels, but comparison of his methods with those of other contemporary authors can give some enlightenment. The works of Henry James, for example, develop via an elaborate and subtle network of detail with 'total relevance' to the entire organism. In Hardy's writing there seems to be no such order, and despite the vividness of his prose it shows variations in style and quality such as James abhorred. The pattern of his best work is intuitive rather than academic. With James, the opposite is true. For him,

strenuous selection and comparison are ... the very essence of art, and ... Form *is* substance to that degree that there is absolutely no substance without it. Form alone *takes*, and holds and preserves, substance—saves it from the welter of helpless verbiage that we swim in as in a sea of tasteless tepid pudding ...[12]

But the bias in his position is indicated by Barbara Hardy when she notes that

James did more than anyone to define the aesthetic status of fiction, and it seems apparent from his various discussions of narrative form, that he became more interested in giving the novel a strong and conspicuous aesthetic interest than in telling a good story, or working out a moral argument, or making a representation of life as it feels when we live it. He did all these things, usually did them supremely well, and was by no means unaware of their existence and importance ... But he was chiefly concerned with praising and publicizing a conspicuously aesthetic and intensely concentrated form.[13]

Those who attempt to judge and analyse Hardy's works by Henry

James's standards are doomed to the failure of misrepresentation, for Hardy's novels are nothing like what Barbara Hardy calls the 'Jamesian streamlined beast'. For Hardy, she asserts, 'form' depends on 'fitting the complexity and contradictoriness of life into a pre-determined dogmatic pattern'. More crudely put, in the words of E. M. Forster, 'Hardy arranges the events with emphasis on causality, the ground plan is the plot, and the characters are ordered to acquiesce in its requirements'.[14]

Hardy himself plainly did not feel that a strict aesthetic system should predetermine the writer's approach to his subject, and wrote of James that 'It is remarkable that a writer who has no grain of poetry, or humour, or spontaneity in his productions, can yet be a good novelist'. In the light of this attitude, and in the absence of any more obvious or consistent formal patterning in his work, critical discussions have tended to dwell on Hardy's plots, and their seemingly uncompromising application of certain dogmatic principles, as being the most important features of his novels. One of Hardy's most influential modern critics, A. J. Guerard, decries this misleading conception of the formalistic qualities of his work: '. . . they have tried to find . . . a minute and subtle craftsman . . . it is hard to understand . . . why they should have singled out for praise what today seems one of Hardy's gravest weaknesses; his tendency to shape and plan his novels according to some obvious architectural principle and his failure to conceal the blueprint'.[15] Yet Guerard himself, having dismissed the 'obvious' in Hardy's artistic method, is reluctant to search any deeper. He continues: 'Hardy did think of "beauty of shape" in fiction in external and diagrammatic terms, but he had little to say, in his three brief critical essays, about . . . subtler aspects of form', and later, as a final damnation, he remarks that 'Hardy even thought of form as a superadded ornament, as a decorative addition to content'.

For me, this does not do justice to Hardy. Any novel must have 'form'; this is its being, and it remains only to find out the essential individuality of each work and the unifying elements which give it its particular shape and impact. Both Barbara Hardy

B

and A. J. Guerard, the one in maintaining and the other in dismissing the relevance of his predetermined structural 'blue-prints', seem to me to have neglected those qualities of form which Hardy himself thought essential to a literary work. He saw that 'to a masterpiece in story there appertains a beauty of shape, no less than to a masterpiece in pictorial or plastic art . . .' (*PRF*, p. 120). This beauty of shape lies in 'construction', 'the well-knit interdependence of parts', but also in the perception of a fidelity to life which Hardy himself can only explain by metaphorical equa-tion: 'Every intelligent reader can perceive truth to nature in some degree, but a great reduction must be made for those who can trace in narrative the quality which makes the Apollo and the Aphrodite a charm in marble'. This quality is the constructive art which brings to the reader the novelist's apprehension of *truth*: truth which is drawn from 'the heart of things', not just an imitation of reality. It is not the form of realism or of overt dogmatism, but rather an impressionistic art, which makes one able 'to see in half and quarter views the whole picture, to catch from a few bars the whole tune'. This, says Hardy, is 'the intuitive power that supplies the would-be story-teller with the scientific bases for his pursuit'.[16]

Intuition, 'a sight for the finer qualities of existence', is far more important than the possession of 'a keen eye to the superficial' (*SF*, p. 137). Those critics who find fault with his plot-structures simply on the grounds of their improbability are making the mistake of judging Hardy on the grounds of orthodox realism, which he likewise emphatically rejected. To him, the plot is not to be composed of a succession of ordinary credible events; neither is it to serve primarily as a chart or ground-plan on which to demonstrate a preconceived didactic viewpoint. ('Let me repeat', he wrote in the preface to the fifth and later editions of *Tess of the d'Urbervilles*, 'that a novel is an impression, not an argument; and there the matter must rest . . .'). Rather, he sees the plot as a thread on which to display his pictures of life, his 'seemings' or glimpses into 'the heart of the matter'; and the suspense and twists of fortune are important to him chiefly in so far as they serve to gratify 'the love of the uncommon in human experience' (*Life*, p. 150). The essential form of Hardy's novels is of an imaginative response to reality.

At its most basic level, in Hardy's view, a novel must be entertaining. Late in life he wrote:

Thoughts on the recent school of novel-writers. They forget in their insistence on life, and nothing but life, in a plain slice, that a story *must be worth the telling*, that a good deal of life is not worth any such thing, and that they must not occupy a reader's time with what he can get at first hand anywhere around him. (*Life*, p. 362)

The love of the bizarre and grotesque is an interesting and an integral part of his intention as a novelist, and one which he treated at length. 'The whole secret of fiction and the drama', he wrote, '. . . lies in the adjustment of things unusual to things eternal and universal. The novelist who knows exactly how exceptional, and how non-exceptional, his events should be made, possesses the key to the art' (*Life*, p. 252). Hardy's 'Gothic'-flavoured episodes, his frequent portrayal of the macabre and other-worldly add, at their best, yet another dimension to the 'truth' of the novels as he sees it, an intensification of the imaginary world they present. For the same reason, he often sets his tales in an historical perspective, even if it is only 'some years before the present' or 'within living memory'. All these methods help him to create a world at once uncommon and yet credible because, being distanced from reality, it is more easily imaginable as fact.

Perhaps the greatest incongruity in Hardy's work is the enormous disparity between his presentation of what he sees as the essential reality of existence and his explanation of the same vision. It has often been said of his novels that he fails in them as a philosopher, that his moralizings are laboured and awkward. By the same token, there seems to be a limit beyond which he dare not go. Sometimes he appears to be 'holding back' in episodes where fuller treatment would seem to be imperative. His description of Angel Clare's search for his estranged Tess (*Tess*, Chs liii-lv), or of Jude's life after Sue has left him (*Jude*, Part VI, Chs vi-viii), are cases in point. These scenes, coming as they do at crucial stages in the action of each novel, are full of potential dramatic power; but Hardy does little to show convincingly the full import of such complex psychological situations. Action and reaction are skimmed over in a few bald sentences, or transposed into stylized, highly exclamatory dialogue. Hardy must have been aware to some extent of his limitations: unlike many of his contemporaries, he was reluctant to indulge in the sentimental trap of the death-scene, and moments of supreme agony (Eustacia's, Elfride's, Tess's, Michael Henchard's) are perhaps mercifully spared us. Instead, he more usually presents the aftermath of tragedy as it affects the other characters. Eustacia's final journey into darkness (*The Return of the Native:* Bk v, Chs vii-ix) illustrates well his skill at evading the need for immediate reporting. Suspense is built up through the peripheral anxieties of Clym and Thomasin, and Eustacia's private feelings—apart from her short soliloquy as she fruitlessly awaits her lover—are left largely to the reader's imagination.

It is undeniable, I think, that Hardy is most successful in his presentation of abstracts of thought and emotion when he conveys them indirectly or by analogy. If he attempts to 'explain' an incident, he frequently lapses from clear, direct description into inflated rhetoric. Thus, for example, he pontificates on Tess's predicament after her unlucky confession to Angel:

> Tess's feminine hope—shall we confess it?—had been so obstinately recuperative as to revive in her surreptitious visions of a domiciliary intimacy continued long enough to break down his coldness even against his judgment. Though unsophisticated in the usual sense, she was not incomplete; and it would have denoted deficiency of woman-hood if she had not instinctively known what an argument lies in propinquity. (Ch. xxxiv)

John Holloway, in *The Victorian Sage*, sees Hardy as belonging to a tradition of writers who use language emotively rather than logically; in his best prose, the words 'evoke' rather than state their meaning. In Hardy's opinion, the important thing about style is that it reveals the writer's unique vision of his subject, and thus becomes an integral part of his theme:

> ... it is too commonly viewed as being some independent, extraneous virtue or varnish with which the substance of the narrative is artificially overlaid. Style ... can only be treatment, and treatment depends upon the mental attitude of the novelist; thus entering into the very substance of the narrative ... A writer who is not a mere imitator looks upon the world with his personal eyes, and in his peculiar moods: thence grows up his style, in the full sense of the term. (*PRF*, p. 122)

For this reason, he was at great pains to write spontaneously:

> The whole secret of a living style and the difference between it and a dead style, lies in not having too much style—being, in fact, a little careless, or rather seeming to be, here and there. It brings wonderful life into the writing. (*Life*, p. 105)

Yet he frequently seems to abandon his 'Wordsworthian dictum' in an attempt to model his own style on the example of others. Early in his writing career we find him studying everything from Addison to *Times* leaders in a determined effort to discover as nearly as possible the qualities which gave them their literary power. It is apparent that, as a craftsman, Hardy was more intrigued with forms of expression than his remarks on spontaneity would have us believe. Speaking of the construction of any narrative, no matter how unpolished, he says, in 'The Science of Fiction', that 'Directly the constructive stage is entered upon, Art—high or low—begins to exist'. The choice of particular words and expressions 'with an eye to being more truthful than the truth' transforms the narrator into a 'technicist' at once. S. F. Johnson remarks pointedly that 'However important *what* he said was to him, it is obvious that he laboured over *how* to say it'.[17] The paradox is neatly summed up by T. S. Eliot, who comments that 'at times his style touches sublimity without ever having passed through the stage of being good'.[18]

With all these points in mind, it is my intention to explore the complexities of Hardy's impression of life as it is revealed in his novels in an attempt to see where and how it is most successfully communicated—to see, if possible, why the gaps and inconsistencies exist, and whether they are intentional or not. In doing this, there are many factors which must constantly be taken into account. One must remember the period in which he was writing, and the attendant conditions—serialization, censorship, popular taste—which perforce influenced such a writer at that time. It is also important to realize that Hardy considered several of his works to be mere 'bread-and-butter' performances, which do not even pretend to be literary masterpieces, and finally that he himself professed a wish to be remembered not as a novelist, but as a poet. Yet, in spite of all this, there are still a number of questions surrounding Hardy's art. What kind of effect does his erratic style have on the impact of his novels? How directly is this related to the type of subject he is discussing and to his own attitude? Is he, as Eliot claims, too intensely personal a novelist, allowing his own awkwardnesses and shortcomings to mar his aesthetic vision? Or is this awkwardness in treatment an integral part of his 'idiosyncratic mode of regard'? How far is he a 'conscious' and how far an 'unconscious' writer? His intention and his method often seem to be strangely at variance with each other. Only by detailed analysis of his craft can Hardy's enigmatic individuality be appreciated, and the reasons for his success and failure be made clear.

I

The Technique of the Novels

The novel must strenuously aspire to the plasticity of sculpture, to the colour of painting, and to the magic suggestiveness of music—which is the art of arts.

Joseph Conrad, Preface to *The Nigger of the 'Narcissus'*

(i)

Virginia Woolf, on being asked by Thomas Hardy how she had enjoyed *The Mayor of Casterbridge*, stammered in reply that she 'could not stop reading it, which was true, but sounded wrong'.[1] Many readers have felt this peculiarly ambiguous and confused reaction to Hardy's work. Afterwards, the impression of his novels tends to 'settle' in one's brain. The story, which grips the imagination at the time of reading, fades into secondary importance and the characters (unlike the 'living' characters in Dickens or George Eliot or Tolstoy) become more or less fixed in static positions: yet the flavour of the whole is not lost, and many scenes remain in the memory as being vast and magnificently real. Katherine Anne Porter puts the matter succinctly:

... That celebrated first scene on Egdon Heath ... Who does not remember it? And in actual re-reading, what could be duller? ... Except for this; in my memory of that episode, as in dozens of others in many of Hardy's novels, I have seen it, I was there. When I read it, it almost disappears from view, and afterwards it comes back, phraseless, living in its sombre clearness, as Hardy meant it to do, I feel certain ...[2]

The strange thing about Hardy is that even though he is often apparently a clumsy, even an indifferent writer, his work is *memorable*. In retrospect, the actual machinery of the novel seems to matter very little; it is obvious that he labours to construct and extend the action of his stories, crudely organizing ordinary lives to bring out startling 'moments of truth'. Similarly, Hardy seldom

13

completely convinces us that the tale he is telling is illustrative of any great moral concept, and the fact is that his novels are often, at least on the surface, just good stories—stories, as Donald Davidson convincingly argues,[3] in the ballad tradition, of lovers and ruined maids, ghosts and witches, soldiers and mysterious villains. We accept, for the most part, the world he is showing us, but it does not attain for us a living, independent existence. The same is true of his characters; we can see Henchard or Bathsheba or the Dewy family while we are reading about them, but afterwards they tend to become fixed like pictures in the mind. Few of Hardy's created men and women can live out of context. They belong to Hardy's mental perspective, in 'the kind of artistic climate and environment which will enable him to handle his traditional story with conviction—a world in which typical ballad heroes and heroines can flourish with a thoroughly rationalized "mythology" to sustain them.'[4] Tess, for all her psychological credibility, can easily be seen as the wronged heroine in a melo-drama, a tragic refinement on, for example, Cytherea Graye, whose destiny (more in accordance with the tradition of the popular romantic novel) is certain bliss.

Yet, despite his rather stylized and conventional plots, Hardy manages to create intensely meaningful incidents, clear precise pictures which can later epitomize a whole work in a single memory. Almost inevitably, one 'sees' what one is reading; the words paint some kind of corresponding image in the mind. Yet with Hardy, often, the 'picture' of the whole novel is strangely intense and at the same time strangely incomplete. This is not, however, entirely due to the fact that he is an 'intermittent genius'. Rather, the gaps and vivid patches form a fairly consistent pattern showing the strength and weakness of his artistic approach to fiction.

Obviously it is possible to take an analogy between plastic art and literature too far. The novel includes, in varying degrees, direct exposition and philosophizing, a moving plot, a time sequence and various other devices that the static picture cannot possibly attain. Nevertheless, both artist and novelist are giving form to an experience or a theme or an impression of the world; the artist creates a tangible representation and the novelist a picture in the mind, a picture compounded of his own and his reader's imaginations. From this point of view, Hardy's novels are, in my opinion, better understood if they are seen as narrative pictures. The author not only employs techniques comparable with those of the painter—chiaroscuro, perspective, effects of distancing and balance, for example—but also relies largely on artistic form in that he seems to present not simply a picture of life, but a picture of a picture of life. Hardy is a writer who literally does show the half, and the quarter view, and it is this which makes him at once an annoyance and a challenge to the critic. In his selection and presentation of material he seems consciously to eliminate all factors which do not directly contribute to the scene which he is describing at a given moment. Many of his most striking scenes—Tess in the fields, for example, or Eustacia on the heath—have a peculiarly static quality; all action is suspended while the subject is examined and expounded on. Life and movement crystallize into one 'felt moment'. If one thinks of a Hardy novel, one does not perhaps immediately recall all the twistings of plot, or the actions of individual characters, or the author's most profound and erudite musings. In my experience, it is the *impression* of the book which remains, a vision of moments which remain distinctly in the mind, a string of outstanding incidents. In *Tess of the d'Urbervilles* there are perhaps thirty clearly remembered visual anecdotes; in *A Laodicean* or *The Well-Beloved* only six or seven, and those not evenly distributed throughout. *Desperate Remedies* is a good example of a novel where action and plot dominate over all but a couple of—for want of a better word —'concrete' impressions. In the lighter novels, *Under the Greenwood Tree* and *The Trumpet-Major*, action and depiction are, I think, almost perfectly balanced, even though they lack the pictorially symbolic power of *Tess of the d'Urbervilles* or *Jude the Obscure* or *Far from the Madding Crowd*.

There is no doubt that Hardy was influenced to a considerable extent by the visual arts. His interests were wide and varied: he refers with equal familiarity to Greek sculpture, Etruscan friezes, Dutch Masters and French Impressionists, and exhibits an easy knowledge of painting techniques. Note has often been made of his sometimes annoying habit of referring to particular pictures or artists—Fitzpiers, for instance, is seen on one occasion as 'a Wouvermans eccentricity', or Mrs Yeobright is said to have a view of life akin to that represented by 'the canvasses of Sallaert, Van Alsloot and others of that school'. Critics have deplored this esoteric tendency with some justification. J. I. M. Stewart, in his article, 'The Integrity of Thomas Hardy', remarks scathingly that Hardy believed that his references to mythology and painting were 'an important means of toning up a literary style', but that, otherwise, 'in all matters relating to the artistry of fiction he remained astonishingly naive to the end.'[5]

Nevertheless, Hardy's use of such references is so consistent that it should not be dismissed lightly. Most obviously, his basic intention is quite simply to clarify the image he is intending to convey. Thus, for example, in *Desperate Remedies* he defines his heroine's attitude as she glances over her shoulder at Miss Aldclyffe by adding that 'Those who remember Greuze's "Head of a Girl" have an idea of Cytherea's look askance at the turning'. In the same fashion, Liddy Smallbury in *Far from the Madding Crowd* is concisely and adequately described for us as having a complexion

which at this winter-time was the softened ruddiness on a surface of high rotundity that we meet with in a Terburg or a Gerard Douw; and, like the presentations of those great colourists, it was a face which kept well back from the boundary between comeliness and the ideal. (Ch. ix)

George Somerset, looking at Charlotte de Stancy, sees 'the dinted nose of the de Stancys outlined with Holbein shadowlessness against the blue-green of the distant wood', and later finds in her

a precious quality ... —a tender affectionateness which might almost be called yearning; such as is often seen in the women of Correggio when they are painted in profile. (Bk I, Ch. iii)

A similar reference in *The Return of the Native* introduces an important character with convincing dramatic effect, when Eustacia Vye first discovers Clym Yeobright as

A face [which] showed itself with marked distinctness against the dark-tanned wood ... The spectacle constituted an area of two feet in Rembrandt's intensest manner. A strange power in the lounger's appearance lay in the fact that, although his whole figure was visible, the observer's eye was only aware of his face. (Bk II, Ch. vi)

It is of course true that Hardy's delighted ingenuity in relating his portrayals with such accuracy is sometimes barely distinguishable from academic pretentiousness. We gain remarkably little from the knowledge that Grace Melbury's eyebrows, 'had her portrait been painted, would probably have been done in Prouts's or Vandyke brown', and the invention, also in *The Woodlanders*, of an artistic metaphor to illustrate the passing seasons can appear rather clumsily contrived:

Now could be beheld that change from the handsome to the curious which the features of a wood undergo at the ingress of the winter months. Angles were taking the place of curves, and reticulations of surfaces—a change constituting a sudden lapse from the ornate to the primitive on Nature's canvas, and comparable to a retrogressive step from the art of an advanced school of painting to that of the Pacific Islander. (Ch. vii)

This specifically 'artistic' aspect of Hardy's writing has often been discussed and at least one critic has made a detailed list of the painters to whom Hardy refers throughout his work.[6] Usually, though, it is seen merely as a superficial mannerism, a decorative quirk. Richard C. Carpenter, for instance, writes that 'When we read ... that as a young man Hardy devoted "for many months" twenty minutes after lunch each day studying the paintings in the National Gallery, we rightly conclude that these and later experiences were not lost on his writings',[7] but he ends his essay tentatively: 'I would not ... wish to over-emphasize the importance of painting techniques to Hardy's art. Many of his greatest scenes ... are not pictorial at all.' It seems to me that Carpenter is missing what is perhaps the most important point of the matter. It is not the technique of painting—though this is indeed striking—which gives the most vital clue to Hardy's method of presentation in the novels; rather, it is the whole approach of plastic art as applied to the medium of literature. The form of pictorial art is basic to Hardy's view of life as he expresses it in his works, and essential to his pervasive theme, which is the contrast between appearance and reality, what life *is like* and what life *is*. As such it is inextricably bound up with his entire thought and expression.

The concept is not by any means a new one. Henry James, for example, proclaimed (in words which apply most aptly to Hardy, who was in many respects his *bête noir*) that

The only reason for the existence of a novel is that it does attempt to represent life . . . and the analogy between the art of the painter and the art of the novelist is, so far as I am able to see, complete. Their inspiration is the same, their process (allowing for the different quality of the vehicle) is the same, their success is the same . . . as the picture is reality, so the novel is history. That is the only general description (which does it justice) that we may give of the novel.[8]

The representation of life, the translation of truth into art, is the aim of the novelist, and the particular quality which gives his work its fidelity and individuality, its unique slant on life, is its organizing form—the same quality which makes the Aphrodite 'a charm in marble' or which enables a painter to make 'vividly visible' the 'heart and inner meaning of things'.

One of the most obvious trends in the art of the mid-nineteenth century novelist is the predilection for displaying, with minute precision, the details of everyday life. In the words of Thackeray,

. . . the Art of the Novel *is* to represent Nature: to convey as strongly as possible the sentiment of reality—in a tragedy or a poem or a lofty drama you aim at producing different emotions; the figures moving, and their words sounding, heroically: but in a drawing-room drama a coat is a coat, and a poker a poker; and must be nothing else, according to my ethics, not an embroidered tunic, nor a great red-hot instrument like the Pantomime weapon.[9]

It is interesting to note, parenthetically, Hardy's early opinion on Thackeray's art. In a letter to his sister, written in 1863, he remarks:

About Thackeray. You must read something of his. He is considered to be the greatest novelist of the day—looking at novel-writing of the highest kind as a perfect and truthful representation of actual life— which is no doubt the proper view to take. Hence, because his novels stand so high as works of Art or Truth, they often have anything but an elevating tendency, and on that account are particularly unfitted for young people—from their very truthfulness. People say that it is beyond Mr. Thackeray to paint a perfect man or woman—a great fault if novels are intended to instruct, but just the opposite if they are to be considered merely as Pictures. *Vanity Fair* is considered one of his best. (*Life*, p. 40)

Mario Praz tries to show that this swing to realistic literary 'painting' in the mid-nineteenth century had its source in the popular Dutch and Flemish *genre* painting, which at its best achieved, through exact and intensely painstaking depiction of ordinary people and objects, a deeper, almost transcendental quality of realism. The effect of this on the literary world was, he says, to subdue literature to the visual image: 'Painters took great pains to load their pictures with meaning and suggestion, story-tellers to convey the living image of things by means of a minute, "picturesque" descriptiveness. *Ut pictura poesis* had become the golden rule. . . .'[10] Thus George Eliot, who finds in many Dutch paintings 'a rare, precious quality of truthfulness' in their presentation of 'monotonous homely existence', declares her intention in *Adam Bede* 'to give a faithful account of men and things as they have mirrored themselves in my mind . . . I feel as much bound to tell you as precisely what that reflection is, as if I were in a witness box, narrating my experience on oath.'[11]

With Hardy, though he has been often compared with George Eliot, and indeed seems to show some affinity with her in his portrayal of rural scenes, the situation is rather more complex. In his own novels he was to find increasing difficulty in the reconciliation of realism and fantasy, didactic purpose and sheer impressionistic 'seemings'. Partly, of course, this was a result of the fact that he was, as Frank O'Connor puts it, the victim of an acute 'historical schizophrenia', standing on the 'frontier of two cultures'.[12] Despite probable early influences, the two watchwords in his writings on the art of the novel are 'illusion' and 'impressionism'. He decries the French realists and quotes H. A. Taine: 'They renounce free invention; they narrow themselves to scrupulous exactness; they paint clothes and places with endless detail' (PRF, p. 119). For him, there is ultimately no such thing as 'realism'. Even Zola, who advocated the merits of photographic exactness in novel-writing should, says Hardy, qualify his theory by saying that the novel must 'keep as close to reality *as it can*; a remark which may be interpreted with infinite latitude, and would no doubt have been cheerfully accepted by Dumas *père* or Mrs Radcliffe' (SF, p. 135). Although perhaps desirable, he goes on, it is absolutely impossible to reproduce 'in all its entirety the phantasmagoria of experience with infinite and atomic truth, without shadow, relevancy, or subordination'. Instead, he makes a plea for 'Creativeness in its full and ancient sense—the making a thing or situation out of nothing that ever was before'. The novelist should 'distinguish truths which are temporary from truths which are eternal, the accidental from the essential' (PRF, p. 118). 'Nothing', he says, 'but the *illusion* of truth can permanently please' (SF, p. 135). And in his notes he writes,

We don't always remember as we should that in getting at the truth, we get only at the true nature of the impression that an object, etc., produces on us . . . (*Life*, pp. 247-8)

In claiming that Hardy's approach to fiction is essentially that of a painter, I do not suggest that he was ever directly 'influenced' by any particular artist or school. He *may* have been, but it would be, I think, impossible to judge the extent or usefulness of the influence. His views on art are distinctly catholic and there is never complete consistency in his application of these views to the various techniques of his fiction. Still, there is a need to explore the relationship as it appears in his novels. A great deal, after all, has been made of the much less important fact that Hardy was an architect; his information about Gothic towers and flying buttresses is happily brought in as support for his supposed building of novels on architectural lines, stone on stone. Yet, as Geoffrey Grigson points out, he was not even a particularly good architect and became one almost by accident: '. . . architecture was not vitally prominent in his work, certainly not in his imagination.'[13] His interest in the profession, Grigson continues, gave him only 'that sense of human history in physical images which architecture needs and so few architects ever possess'. It is true of course that the frequent discussion of 'plinths, corbels and architraves' is seldom related to the novel itself. Hardy the mechanical craftsman is only a rather sterile extension of Hardy the artist. His real interest is not so much in the building as in the men who built it; he dwells with loving care on the strange quirks of man's decorative talent, the twisted designs and gargoyles ornamenting the plain form, or on the marks of man's habitation—the smooth pillars and polished beams, the traces of tool-marks on walls and surfaces. This peculiarly sympathetic point of view is well brought out in his description of St Mark's, Venice:

Well. There is surely some conventional ecstasy, exaggeration—shall I say humbug?—in what Ruskin writes about this, if I remember (though I have not read him lately), when the church is looked at *as a whole*. One architectural defect nothing can get over—its squatness as seen from the natural point of view—the glassy marble pavement of the Grand Piazza. Second, its weak, flexuous, constructional lines. Then, the fantastic Oriental character of its details makes it barbaric in its general impression, in spite of their great beauty.

. . . This being said, see what good things are left to say, of its art, of its history! That floor, of every colour and rich device, is worn into undulations by the infinite multitudes of feet that have trodden it, and *what* feet there have been among the rest!

A commonplace man stoops in a dark corner where he strikes a common match, and shows us—what—a lost article?—a purse, pipe, or tobacco pouch? no; shows us—drags from the depths of time as by a miracle—wonderful diaphanous alabaster pillars that were once in Solomon's temple. (*Life*, p. 193)

Perfection is not beauty:

In a work of art it is the accident which *charms*, not the intention; *that* we only like and admire. Instance the amber tones that pervade the folds of drapery in ancient marbles, the deadened polish of the surfaces, and the cracks and the scratches. (*Life*, p. 191)

Age, usage, even ugliness—these are more important artistically to Hardy than an exquisite formal design or an inhuman mass of supports and masonry. 'To find beauty in ugliness', he wrote in 1888, 'is the province of the poet' (*Life*, p. 213).

(ii)

... not only is there a *partial* and variable mystery thus caused by clouds and vapours throughout great spaces of landscapes; there is a continual mystery caused throughout *all* spaces, caused by the absolute infinity of things. WE NEVER SEE ANYTHING CLEARLY.
                    John Ruskin, *Modern Painters*, Vol. IV, Part v, Chs iv–vi

Hardy always had an interest in the contemporary French painters, not only as technicians (in his earliest published work, *Desperate Remedies*, he describes shadows as 'livid grey shades, like those of the modern French painters', Ch. viii), but also because of the theory behind their work. It was not, however, till 1886 that he formulated a statement directly linking the methods of the school to those of literary art:

The impressionist school is strong. It is even more suggestive in the direction of literature than in that of art. As usual, it is pushed to absurdity by some. But their principle is, as I understand it, that what you carry away with you from a scene is the true feature to grasp, or, in other words, *what appeals to your own individual eye and heart in particular* amid much that does not so appeal, and which you therefore omit to record. (*Life*, p. 184)

Exact truth, photographic reproduction, is 'a student's style'. Instead, he shows particular enthusiasm for 'the much-decried, mad, late-Turner rendering' (*Life*, p. 185). It is necessary to 'translate' qualities in the object contemplated, qualities perhaps unseen but which, when united with the material fact, give a representation of greater truth. Each of Turner's watercolours, he says, is 'a landscape *plus* a man's soul' (*Life*, p. 216) So it is that he describes *Jude the Obscure* as being, like all his other works,

an endeavour to give shape and coherence to a series of seemings, or personal impressions, the question of their consistency or their discordance, of their permanence or their transitoriness, being regarded as not of the first moment. (Preface, 1st edn, August 1895)

It is impossible to reproduce the real, but 'Art is the secret of how to produce by a false thing the effect of a true' (*Life*, p. 216). The idea of imbuing impersonal things with special meanings by presenting them as more than simple visual effects continually fascinates him.

In time one might get to regard every object, and every action, as composed, not of this or that material, this or that movement, but of the qualities pleasure and pain in varying proportions. (*Life*, p. 217)

This is not, of course, a theory unique to Hardy. In effect he merely re-states Wordsworth's poetic formula for the *Lyrical Ballads*, as Coleridge described it in the *Biographia Literaria* (Ch. xiv):

Mr. Wordsworth . . . was to propose to himself as his object to give the charm of novelty to the things of every day, and to excite a feeling analogous to the supernatural by awakening the mind's attention from the lethargy of custom, and directing it to the loveliness and the wonder of the world before us.

Hardy was an avid reader of the Romantic poets, and it is worth noting that he deplored Wordsworth's tendency in later life to record 'convictions' rather than 'impressions' (*Life*, p. 377).

Ruskin said of Turner that 'his work was the true image of his own mind'.[14] So, too, it is with Hardy. T. S. Eliot's remark (intended as severe criticism) that he 'seems . . . to have written as nearly for the sake of "self-expression" as a man well can'[15] is incisively true. In his best work, Hardy is seldom purely objective in his presentation of reality; rather, he selects his detail with an

C

instinctive feeling for the total emotional effect. It is clear, for
example, that Egdon Heath, as it is described in *The Return of the
Native*, is not just a landscape: it is a mental impression of a place.
It is a presence, expressed in abstract terms so that we receive the
effect of a picture. When the description is examined word for
word, it is, as Katherine Anne Porter observed, often ponderous
and sometimes rather clumsy. It does not seem particularly
important to us that Hardy could meditate on the qualities of the
Heath with scholarly detachment:

(It was a spot which returned upon the memory of those who loved it
with an aspect of peculiar and kindly congruity. Smiling champains of
flowers and fruit hardly do this, for they are permanently harmonious
only with an existence of better reputation as to its issues than the
present.) (Bk I, Ch. i)

The power and strange empathy of the place are not conveyed by
incongruously urbane argument nor by faithful portraiture, but
by an accumulation of small touches, scarcely noticed during the
actual reading, but later seen vividly against a background of
vaguely sonorous and impressive prose. It is a huge diffuse impression of blackness, enormity and barrenness, broken only by the
sound of dry heather-bells whispering in the wind, and later by
the shooting red and gold flames of the bonfires. The general
commentary is in effect only a canvas, big, rambling and obscure
enough to accommodate its subject. The picture itself is contained
in a very few words, but the important thing is that we do see it
and we do feel it. In the same way, an Impressionist painting can
convey a whole moving landscape, breeze blowing, water rip-
pling, sunlight flickering; and when one looks closely there are
only crude brush-strokes and strange combinations of colour.

It is a commonplace to say that a writer does with words what
an artist does with paints, but usually this is intended to mean no
more than that the writer creates a picture which we can see in our
minds. What Hardy does is to give a special significance to the
picture which is more than our appreciation of what the words
say. Alistair Smart has summed-up one part of the matter: 'Hardy,

indeed, had the eye of a painter, drawing the outlines of his forms as consciously as he filled them with substance and colour; giving them their proper texture and lighting; fixing them firmly in a definite space; and relating them in scale to their surroundings'.[16] This is in many respects the end result of Hardy's technique; but it is, I think, important to see how these effects are created, and to consider if the process is not rather more complex than Smart suggests. The organization and highlighting of his picture of reality is not simply interesting from an artistic point of view; it also has a direct bearing on the way in which we interpret that picture. As Hardy wrote in 1886: 'My art is to intensify the expression of things, as is done by Crivelli, Bellini, etc., so that the heart and inner meaning is made vividly visible' (*Life*, p. 177).

In some of Hardy's major novels, the 'Impressionistic' effect is a predominant structural element, organizing the meaning of the story on several different levels. This is particularly true of *The Woodlanders*, which is perhaps the most static and most pictorial of his works. It is less tragic, more domestic, less sensational in the melodramatic sense, less symbolic than, say, *Tess* or *Jude*; these aspects of Hardy's art are, in the earlier novel, not nearly as prominent in the all-over pattern. Here, it is the indirect method which is ultimately more important, which gives form and coherence to the story simultaneously as it furthers the action, and gives an 'atmosphere' which holds our attention and partially directs our appreciation of a given situation.

In *The Woodlanders* the background has an unusual importance, but frequently, it seems to me, this is because of its illusive, kaleidoscopic quality. It is a quality which is extraordinarily difficult to describe, being, as it is, contained in so many different aspects of the novel—it lies, in Hardy's own words, almost as much in the imagination of the reader as in the author's writing. Perhaps this results from the initial impression one has of this work, which is that it is full of detail, of exact depiction, colourful, tactile and sensuous. There is a conscientious precision in the description of some things; lengths of timber, for instance, cider-making or the workings of a man-trap; but the settings and situations which seem to be vividly presented as intrinsic parts of the plot are often, in fact, barely suggested. On re-reading the novel it can be seen that Hardy has used in effect the technique of an Impressionist painter. He does not show us the whole of the picture, but subtly indicates or highlights the main points; he isolates, projects or obscures for dramatic effect. It is interesting to note that, when he had nearly completed *The Woodlanders*, he wrote in his journal,

After looking at the landscape ascribed to Bonington in our drawing-room I feel that Nature is played out as a Beauty, but not as a Mystery. I don't want to see landscapes, *i.e.*, scenic paintings of them, because I don't want to see the original realities—as optical effects, that is. I want to see the deeper reality underlying the scenic, the expression of what are sometimes called abstract imaginings. (*Life*, p. 185)

Later, he said that *The Woodlanders* was in some respects his best novel.

At the risk of excluding many of the other techniques which Hardy uses in this work, I want to show specifically how the total structure of the story rests on his manipulation of general effects of light and shade, brightness and dimness, night and day, and all the shades of mistiness and partial light in between; and, too, how these effects relate to the concurrent themes of deception and artificiality. Needless to say, these effects are not unique to *The Woodlanders* and are to be seen, to a greater or lesser degree, in Hardy's other novels—notably in *Far from the Madding Crowd* and *The Return of the Native*, both of which preceded it—but it is worth examining the later work in some detail to see with what skill Hardy uses his technique to give dramatic substance to an essentially simple story.

Perhaps it would be easiest to take as illustration the first five chapters of the book, as these show clearly in a small space the pattern which the rest of the novel is to follow. The story opens on 'the louring evening of a bygone winter's day' and moves on into darkness. (It is important to observe that at least half of the action takes place in darkness or in the hours of early morning or late evening.) Already, in the first chapter, the background is hinted at rather than described. We see, through the eyes of the travelling barber (a convenient, anonymous sort of character), the village of Little Hintock, not as a village but distinguished only by 'a few faint lights winking more or less ineffectually through the leafless boughs'. As we draw closer to the scene, the lights reveal themselves as unshaded windows. Half a dozen dwellings are passed and we come to one cottage which is 'in an exceptional state of radiance, the flickering brightness from the inside shining up the chimney and making a luminous mist of the emerging smoke . . .' The door is partly open and a ribbon of light falls through the opening into the darkness outside, while 'Every now and then a moth . . . would flit for a moment across the outcoming rays and disappear again into the night'. The scene is one of extreme delicacy and stillness, brightness and blackness; nothing distracts from the door ajar and the light-enshrouded dwelling, standing so emphatically apart from the others.

Immediately the second chapter opens, this air of expectancy, which we share with the visitor waiting in the dark, is broken, and straightaway we are taken by Hardy to the interior of the room with its blazing fire. In front of it works a young woman, as yet unknown. Outside the barber still waits, and the light of the fire is reflected by a pair of scissors sticking out of his pocket. Again there is a transference and Hardy skips back into the mind of the barber, in whose eyes the scene

. . . composed itself into an impression-picture of the extremest type, wherein the girl's hair alone, as the focus of observation, was depicted with intensity and distinctness, while her face, shoulders, hands and figure in general, were a blurred mass of unimportant detail, lost in haze and obscurity.

This hair plays an unlikely but significant role in the narrative. We are prepared for its importance by Hardy's focussing of our attention first on the scissors and then, through the perception of the barber, on the hair itself which is isolated and heightened as its owner is made—at least artistically—unimportant. The picture is consistent with the rest of the novel: the hair is last seen flamboyantly adorning the head of Mrs Charmond, on whose life it is to have such an unhappy effect, and our last view of Marty is as completely in harmony with this first impression of her. Always she is seen as if through a mist, undistinguished, almost fleshless, with a quality, as Hardy puts it, of 'abstract humanism'.

From the beginning of the first chapter, one can see how subtly Hardy is preparing to introduce his main characters. The opening scene, which is of a dark countryside, timeless, ageless and impersonal, is suddenly livened by the appearance of the carrier's van. From this conveyance, with its shadowy, unidentified passengers, we move slowly down into greater reality, with places and people less impersonal. There is a continual progression from the vague and obscured and general into the increasingly particular and identifiable: it is a technique of which Hardy was particularly fond, and which he uses in many of his novels. He creates an impression of continually telescoping vision, moving swiftly in a series of illuminated glances while the unimportant fades away into the background. The feeling that we are being shown a picture rather than being told a story is heightened by the fact that there is no direct presentation of character until the moment when Marty starts at the crunch of the barber's boots on the sanded floor.

It is a calculated piece of artistry on Hardy's part that he introduces almost all the major characters of *The Woodlanders* in darkness. Nearly the whole of the action of the first five chapters takes place in obscurity. This establishes the aesthetic milieu for much of the novel and also provides for a series of dramatic and imagistic effects which help to project and later maintain the identity and, indirectly, to reflect the function of each character within the story.

The presentation of Fitzpiers, for instance, is entirely in accord. He is first shown as an unknown, mysterious presence: at the beginning of Chapter iii we are told that the lights of the village go out till there remain only two; one of these, shining from the hillside, belongs to 'the young gentleman in league with the devil', and the other comes from Marty's window. The introduction of Felice Charmond, Fitzpiers' female counterpart, is very similar in effect—she, too, is first heard of by repute and is then discovered at night-time merely as a voice coming from the depths of a dark carriage, a carriage whose lamps, as they draw abreast of Marty, seem to 'penetrate her very pores'.[17] The latter is continually seen as light, transparent, part of her natural environment, while Mrs Charmond revels in glooms and artificial lighting. Significantly, Fitzpiers first sees her by candlelight, and the use of calculated or artificial illumination assumes an almost symbolic prominence in regard to this couple. In one passage, Fitzpiers finds his mistress in her room with the curtains shut; when he draws them the red glow of the lamp and the two candles becomes 'almost invisible' under the flood of sunlight. A second later, we are told, he regrets that he has killed 'the rosy passionate lamplight by opening the curtains and letting in the garish day' (Ch. xxvii). He and Mrs Charmond alike are diminished by the simple honesty of night and day and can only retain their romantic auras in a mysterious, delusive atmosphere of semi-darkness. Ironically, we are told in Chapter vii that Grace, who has been intrigued by the late-burning light from Fitzpiers' window, finds that 'somehow, in the broad practical daylight, that unknown and lonely gentleman seemed to be shorn of much of the interest which had invested his personality and pursuits in the hours of darkness'. Similar, too, is the vacillating Fitzpiers' reaction to the willing Suke Damson, as he sees her on Midsummer's Eve after the Maidens' rites: 'In the moonlight Suke looked very beautiful, the scratches and blemishes incidental to her outdoor occupation being invisible under these pale rays' (Ch. xx).

Grace, on the other hand, is introduced in broad daylight, stepping daintily over a muddy square; later, she is seen illuminated by firelight, her face and hands, thus, 'wonderfully smooth and fair', and the glow shining through her hair 'as sunlight through a brake' (Ch. vi). Grace is continually shown in bright sunshine or moonlight; like a good heroine, she is frequently silhouetted as a small white-clad figure against a darker

background. The contrast between the three main female characters—Grace, Marty and Felice Charmond—is implicit, and often
ironic.

Sometimes the variously positioned and illuminated presentation of character is functional in an even deeper sense. In Chapter
iii, for example, as Marty goes secretly to the Melburys' home, she
hears a woman calling, and the light of a lantern casts 'a moving
thorn-pattern of shade' on her (Marty's) face before it lights on
George Melbury. It is because of George Melbury, indirectly, that
Marty is to suffer, and though in this passage the shadows on her
face do not constitute a directly symbolic comment, they add a
peculiar depth of fore-knowledge in perspective as the girl
realizes, listening to the conversation of husband and wife, that
Giles Winterborne is 'not for her'. A similar comment is made
with the appearance of Giles himself. He comes to Marty's door
carrying a perforated lantern which casts 'grotesque shapes' on her
walls and ceiling, and as they go out to work together the pattern
of air-holes at the top of the lantern rises to the mist overhead,
where it 'appeared of giant size, as if reaching the tent-shaped
sky'. The picture is of two tiny grey human beings overshadowed
by mist, isolated yet together, like the holes in the lantern—
('And yet their lonely courses formed no detached design at all,
but were part of the pattern in the great web of human doings . . .')
(Ch. iii).

The dramatic emphasis of lighting is also frequently used by
Hardy to illustrate the probable ordering of the narrative. Sometimes the effects are relatively simple; the use of profile, silhouette
and shadow, for example, is often more than merely descriptive,
and may be made to emphasize different stages in the story. As a
case in point, we are shown in succession first the shadow of
Marty's shorn head on the wall, then the premonitory fire
shadows which flicker, one blue, one yellow, before George
Melbury as he ponders the problem of Grace and Giles, then the
silhouettes of the latter couple as they ride home in the gig, with
the heads drawing closer together. The attraction between Grace
and Fitzpiers is advanced by Grammer Oliver, who has sold her

head with its unusually large brain to the young doctor; her misery finally forces Grace to approach him. The situation is made at once grisly and comic by the picture of the old woman's profile which, as she lies in bed, 'casts itself in a coal-black shadow upon the white-washed wall, her large head being still further magnified by an enormous turban, which was really her petticoat wound in a wreath around her temples' (Ch. xvii).

More directly instrumental in furthering the plot are the half-seen events; the white-nightgowned figure of Suke leaving Fitzpiers' house in the early morning; the horse Fitzpiers rides, which makes his illicit journeys visible because of its pale colour against the gloom of the woodlands. Even more obvious and important are the incidents and misunderstandings which take place in complete obscurity: Grace and Mrs Charmond lost together in the woods at night; Fitzpiers' complaints and revelations to George Melbury, whom he does not recognize in the darkness; Giles' determination to show himself to Grace only at night-time so that she cannot see how ill and changed he is. Related to this last incident is that in which Fitzpiers, wounded, struggles to Mrs Charmond's house for help. She sees him as a disembodied face, 'surrounded with the darkness of the night without, corpse-like in its pallor and covered with blood' (Ch. xxxvi). With this macabre illustration, Hardy directly anticipates Giles' actions, and the dramatic contrast is effectively established.

All this goes to show that the obscurity of night-time is an important element in the plot—though *not*, it must be emphasized, as a 'sympathetic' or a 'malignant' influence, but simply because it *is* night, something which follows, naturally and inexorably, after day. We are frequently given instances of the anonymity of the novel's setting. When we are told, for example, just before Giles' death, that the sun, shining through the wet trees, throws 'splotches of such ruddiness on the leaves beneath . . . that they were turned to gory hues' or that the puddles of water appear to Grace to have 'a cold corpse-like luminousness' (Ch. xlii), the metaphors are premonitive, but in no way influence the ensuing action. The moonlight may influence Fitzpiers' attitude towards

Suke, but the description of the night and the countryside at the
moment shows them as passive and supremely indifferent. Again
there is a hint of irony—'the hayfield stretched away into remoteness till it was lost to the eye in a soft mist. It was daybreak
before Fitzpiers and Suke Damson re-entered Little Hintock'
(Ch. xx).

The human characters are distanced and isolated very effectively;
they are seen as small and central, while the landscape is wide,
calm and all-embracing. The dramatic result is largely pictorial.
A similar effect is created by Hardy in his emphasis on the
palpable presence of night, not as simple darkness but as a wide,
living phenomenon. In itself it gives a certain coherence and form
to the whole of the novel. Living presences inside the darkness are
represented by scent and sound—squeaks and rustles; and things
normal in daylight become strange shapes and shadows. It is the
perfect artistic milieu for a novel that depends so much on the
need to distinguish reality from falsity. Throughout the story,
events are seen as being simply part of the normal order of life.
The darkness is a cloak as much for the preying animals and their
victims as for the wandering and unconsciously deluded human
characters.

Other details, seemingly trivial, tend in their cumulative effect
to link the story together with its theme into an artistic whole.
There are, for instance, the continuous references to firelight,
starlight or moonlight—references which may be merely descriptive, or which may help to highlight some object or person
important to the plot, or which may somehow reflect actions, as
does the 'attentuated skeleton of a moon' (Ch. xl) which keeps
Fitzpiers company as he rides to Mrs Charmond. Then, too, there
are the metaphors of light often used by Hardy to describe a
character's state of mind: Mr Melbury, confused with the
intricacies of divorce proceedings, is said to be 'blind to these
subtleties, which he had formerly beheld as in a noontide light'
(Ch. xxxix). Mrs Charmond's heart reveals on her face 'as by a
lightning gleam' her love for Fitzpiers (Ch. xxxiii); Grace and
Giles, forgetting 'the gloomy atmosphere of the past and the still

gloomy horizon of the present', come back to their senses and 'the due balance of shade among the light' is restored (Ch. xxxviii). Such expressions are numerous in *The Woodlanders* and, though it would be too ingenious to place undue importance on each separately, their total effect subtly creates an emotional environment which reflects and interrelates with the material setting.

The combination of all these related elements in *The Woodlanders* results in a picture of kinds of loving, in which characters are grouped into categories which illustrate their states of being. The love of Marty and Giles, which is undeveloped in one sense, is connected with the cold early hours of morning, or seen through a misty haze; the passionate love of Fitzpiers and Mrs Charmond is rosy, warm but artificial, altogether too unreal for the atmosphere of Little Hintock, and ironically tainted by its similarity to the affair of Fitzpiers and Suke. The greatest love, that of Grace and Giles, is a simple daylight love which dies in complete darkness when it is at its fullest and most futile, and the love which completes the circle, the final coming together of Grace and Fitzpiers, has in retrospect a rather grey and disillusioned aspect.

It can be seen from all this that Hardy's technique in this novel is supremely pictorial in an impressionistic sense while, additionally, it fulfils an important structural function. The interlinking of all the factors and methods I have mentioned creates an enormous frame for the working of the story, not the least element being the role provided for the narrator as spectator and guide. In effect Hardy is leading both his readers and his characters through the darkness, real and metaphorical. It is partially through his use of lighting emphasis that he gives pseudo-symbolic identities to his characters, weaves their lives together, creates suspense and an appropriate atmosphere, and orders his narrative. He works on three levels of consciousness, and reveals, subdues or highlights his subjects as the picture takes shape. Yet it is only when one looks at the total effect of his technique that the strength of the pattern becomes apparent.

(iii)

The artist does not conceive in general mental terms, but in terms of concrete material.

René Wellek and Austin Warren, *Theory of Literature*, p. 129

My task ... is, before all, to make you *see*.

Joseph Conrad, Preface to *The Nigger of the 'Narcissus'*

The subtle accumulative effect which Hardy creates by his use of suggestion and selection contrasts markedly with his method of direct and exact presentation, yet both are essential features of his art and are mutually dependent. The transitions from the general to the particular which are so noticeable in all the novels are most often simply changes in perspective, which can perhaps best be explained as being similar to the techniques now used in the cinema. (I am not going to enlarge on this, but it does help to establish a useful point of reference—Hardy's creative eye is in some ways very like a camera.) His devices of diminution, telescoping, panoramic or microscopic vision have frequently been noticed.[18] We see as if through his eyes, for instance, Eustacia in *The Return of the Native*—first in the distance as 'a spike on a helmet', then, moving, as a drop of water gliding down a bud, before she is described in bold close-up (Bk i, Ch. iii). Or, in *Tess of the d'Urbervilles*, he shows us a generalized picture of women working in a field, and gradually directs our attention to one to whom 'the eye returns involuntarily ... she being the most flexuous and finely-drawn figure of them all' (Ch. xiv). It is this special technique of Hardy's which enables us to see his stories as distant and immediate, his characters as at once impersonal beings submerged in their own world, and as individuals.

In order to present his view of the world as dramatically and emotionally credible, Hardy must also make it appear to be physically real. So it is that his allusive and metaphorical use of language often gives way sharply to concrete, realistic description. The shadowy world of imagination and conjectural truth must be sustained and substantiated in its details.

The skilful conjunction of the two techniques can be seen

clearly in the second chapter of *Far from the Madding Crowd*. Here, firstly, Hardy presents an impression of the natural world based on the multiple and various sounds of the trees and grasses in the wind. Actual visual effects are all but excluded, and the credibility and immediacy of the scene are based entirely on a minute appreciation of sound and sensation within the contrasting darkness and loneliness of night. From this establishment of the apparently familiar within a new and awe-inspiring context, the perspective shifts to the huge mystery of the starry skies, and the immense turning world:

To persons standing alone on a hill during a clear midnight such as this, the roll of the world eastward is almost a palpable movement. The sensation may be caused by the panoramic glide of the stars past earthly objects, which is perceptible in a few minutes of stillness, or by the better outlook upon space that a hill affords, or by the wind, or by the solitude; but whatever be its origin, the impression of riding along is vivid and abiding. The poetry of motion is a phrase much in use, and to enjoy the epic form of that gratification it is necessary to stand on a hill at a small hour of the night, and, having first expanded with a sense of difference from the mass of civilized mankind, . . . long and quietly watch your stately progression through the stars. After such a nocturnal reconnoitre it is hard to get back to earth, and to believe that the consciousness of such majestic speeding is derived from a tiny human frame. (Ch. ii)

Then, suddenly, with no preparation, Hardy weaves into the grandeur and silence of the universe the small distinct notes of Farmer Oak's flute. The connecting thread is drawn between man and his environment, the presence of an individual existence in the enormity of the infinite. So far, the vision has been created for us by suggestion only. Hardy has used words whose connotations are vaguely vast and emotional: 'panoramic', 'epic', 'stately', 'majestic', 'fathomless'. More important, the accumulative effect of these indefinite but impressive adjectives is continually qualified by reference to the specifically tangible and human. Even the stars 'seemed to be but throbs of one body, timed by a common pulse'; the metaphor of 'riding along' is evocative of ordinary physical movement, and we are not allowed to forget the presence of the undefined watcher on the hill. The feeling of space and distance still rules, however. The music of the flute is heard 'up against the sky', and Oak's hut must appear naturally in the hugeness of the night as 'a small Noah's Ark on a small Ararat', a toy thing standing 'on little wheels'. Then, almost as abruptly, complete prosaic 'normality' is established:

The inside of the hut, as it now presented itself, was cosy and alluring, and the scarlet handful of fire in addition to the candle, reflecting its own genial colour upon whatever it could reach, flung associations of enjoyment even over utensils and tools. In the corner stood the sheep-crook, and along a shelf at one side were ranged bottles and canisters of the simple preparations pertaining to ovine surgery and physic; spirits of wine, turpentine, tar, magnesia, ginger, and castor-oil being the chief. On a triangular shelf across the corner stood bread, bacon, cheese, and a cup for ale or cider, which was supplied from a flagon beneath. Beside these provisions lay the flute, whose notes had lately been called forth by the lonely watcher to beguile a tedious hour. The house was ventilated by two round holes, like the lights of a ship's cabin, with wood slides. (Ch. ii)

The important thing to notice is that there is no jarring or falsity in the movement from the transcendental and metaphysical to humble material fact. Neither is there any appreciable change in Hardy's prose style. The reason for this, simply, is that he relates all the processes of the earth and sky to a single unseen human observer, one to whom the gliding stars and rustling trees are an integral part of his own existence. Although the actual perspective is continually altered as it sweeps from ground to sky and back again, the point of reference remains unchanged; every scene, every impression comes to us as if through the consciousness of this impersonal medium. Even the interior of Gabriel's hut, which we know to be distinctively *his*, is not shown to us subjectively. It is a detailed depiction of 'an interior as it ... presented itself', a view passively awaiting detailed commentary and analysis. In each case, the total impact and immediacy of the scene is the result of a complete artistic detachment.

There is consequently a solid interaction between what are, ostensibly, three different exposures: the dark earth, with its sounds and shapes and movements, the vast sky embracing the total world in its place in the universe, and the seemingly minute world of man, whose life and signs of habitation are made in comparison bright and real and important. The vividness and familiarity of Gabriel's hut and its surroundings make the final focal point against which the mysterious processes of the cosmos are at once more credible and more awe-inspiring. Thus the two techniques—of general impressionistic implication and of faithful representation—are part of the same perspective. It is only the vision which is different. The unseen, imagined truth continually impinges on the detailed visible reality, while each contains elements of the other. The consistency of Hardy's all-embracing perspective lies in his mastery of two skills not normally present together: he is able to give the reader a clear sense of the principles underlying events while evoking a scene in vivid detail.

Hardy's continued use of projected visual techniques to replace direct reporting is due, says Frank O'Connor, to

a pictorial imagination of almost unnatural sensitiveness which is not always easy to distinguish from naturalism, a style of writing deeply influenced by painting. But naturalism cannot explain why the observer —the watcher and listener—is so often intruded where no such intrusion is necessary or even desirable . . .

It is not as though Hardy were excluding himself from the scene. Rather, it is as though he were being excluded and returning as a sort of disembodied presence, a *revenant*, someone of a different substance who cannot mix with the human materials he observes . . .[19]

The result is often a strange passivity in the novels, not so much in the portrayal of scene and action (where it is calculated and usually effective) as in the characterization and the presentation of mental processes. Often, it seems, Hardy places a barrier between the flow and movement of real life and what he chooses to select from it as representative. He sees not real people so much as a picture of those people, and our most vivid apprehension of his characters is usually taken at second-hand, as he 'freezes' them for us in characteristic poses. Mostly, even in the physical sense, his men and women are shown as they are *seen*, not as they *exist*. Take, for example, the description of Michael Henchard and his family at the beginning of *The Mayor of Casterbridge*:

What was really peculiar . . . in this couple's progress, and would have attracted the attention of any casual observer otherwise disposed to look over them, was the perfect silence they preserved. They walked side by side in such a way as to suggest afar off the low, easy, confidential chat of people full of reciprocity; but on closer view it could be discerned that the man was reading, or pretending to read, a ballad sheet which he kept before his eyes with some difficulty by the hand that was passed through the basket strap . . . the woman enjoyed no society whatever from his presence. Virtually she walked the highway alone, save for the child she bore. Sometimes the man's bent elbow almost touched her shoulder, for she kept as close to his side as was possible without actual contact . . .

   The chief—almost the only—attraction of the young woman's face was its mobility. When she looked down sideways to the girl she became pretty, and even handsome, particularly that in the action her features caught slantwise the rays of the strongly coloured sun, which made transparencies of her eyelids and nostrils and set fire on her lips. (Ch. i)

Through such a description we gain a fairly detailed impression of what the characters are like, but it is entirely an external impression. Seldom, in any of the novels, do we gain an 'inside' knowledge of what these people think or feel or see. The recording of intangible thought-processes, for instance, is nearly always carried out impersonally or metaphorically, translated into Hardy's own expression and presented as part of the action. There is little attempt to show an abstract idea or emotion as directly belonging to the mind in which it was ostensibly formulated. Thus, in *The Mayor of Casterbridge*, Hardy takes Elizabeth-Jane's feelings about Farfrae, describing them in his own words, without relating them to her individual character or transcribing them into her own vernacular:

As she looked at Farfrae from the back of the settle she decided that his statements showed him to be no less thoughtful than his fascinating

melodies revealed him to be cordial and impassioned. She admired the
serious light in which he looked at serious things . . . He seemed to feel
exactly as she felt about life and its surroundings—that they were a
tragical rather than a comical thing; that though one could be gay on
occasion, moments of gaiety were interludes, and no part of the actual
drama. (Ch. viii)

In the same way, he often demonstrates emotions by the
objective depiction of their outward signs. A village girl expresses
surprise and awe by exhibiting to the unseen observer 'an inhaling
position of the mouth and circular eyes' (*Trumpet-Major*, Ch. ii);
Cainy Ball, in a state of breathlessness, shows 'his mouth red and
open, like the bell of a penny trumpet, from which he coughed
with noisy vigour and a great distension of face' (*Far From the
Madding Crowd*, Ch. xv). In *The Mayor of Casterbridge* the gradual
effects of intoxication at the 'great public dinner' are observed
with a humorously detached eye and a fine awareness of the
dramatic contrast in characterization which may be shown simply
by appearance:

Men were putting their heads together in twos and threes, telling good
stories, with pantomimic laughter which reached convulsive grimace.
Some were beginning to look as if they did not know how they had
come there, what they had come for, or how they were going to get
home again; and provisionally sat on with a dazed smile. Square-built
men showed a tendency to become hunchbacks; men with a dignified
presence lost it in a curious obliquity of figure, in which their features
grew disarranged and one-sided; whilst the heads of a few who had
dined with extreme thoroughness were somehow sinking into their
shoulders, the corners of their mouth and eyes being bent upwards by
the subsidence. Only Henchard did not conform to these flexuous
changes; he remained stately and vertical, silently thinking. (Ch. vi)

On a rather more complex level in *The Return of the Native*,
Eustacia's thoughts, as she hears Clym's voice, are not only shown
through her physical appearance, but also in poetic analogy:

On such occasions as this a thousand ideas pass through a highly charged
woman's head; and they indicate themselves on her face; but the
changes, though actual, are minute. Eustacia's features went through a

D

rhythmical succession of them. She glowed; remembering the mendacity of the imagination, she flagged; then she freshened; then she fired; then she cooled again. It was a cycle of aspects, produced by a cycle of visions. (Bk II, Ch. iii)

Even here, Hardy is obviously as concerned with the artistic expression of the outward signs of emotion as with the feeling itself. By his use of imagery he is reinforcing our predominant conception of Eustacia (throughout the novel she is associated with fire and flames) as well as maintaining the precision and detachment which is necessary to his consistent presentation of her.

In his blending of metaphorical suggestion with exact pictorial representation, Hardy frequently creates in his novels a web of referents which may replace any deeper searching into the realities of social and psychological aspects. Often the structural patterns of these symbols seem to be too direct and obvious, providing facile substitutes for what should at all costs be presented as real and credible. Examples come readily to mind; the pigsticking in *Jude the Obscure*, the significance of blood in *Tess of the d'Urbervilles* or of blindness in *The Return of the Native*. Yet where these images follow a recurrent pattern—for example, in the emphasis on tombs and graves in *Tess*, or on clothing and money in *The Mayor of Casterbridge*—they frequently add immeasurably to the richness and emphasis of the story. Harder to justify, however, is Hardy's wilful ingenuity in suddenly focussing attention on some particular thing, an isolated, often incongruous event—such as the falling church tower in *A Pair of Blue Eyes*, which symbolizes absolutely the destruction of the love that was between Elfride Swancourt and Henry Knight, or the death of 'Little Father Time' in *Jude the Obscure*.

It is easy to claim that Hardy's symbolic devices are sometimes heaped on to the stories to the point of absurdity, that he deliberately pushes the reader without allowing him to form his own opinions and conclusions. Some critics are indulgent; for instance, Dorothy van Ghent writes, of the passage where Tess listens to Angel in the garden at Talbothays: 'Who but Hardy would have dared to give him the name Angel and a harp too? It is Hardy's incorruptible feeling for the actual that allows his symbolism its amazingly blunt privileges.'[20] It is also this aspect of his work which gives rise to such comments as that of A. J. Guerard, whose conclusion is that 'Hardy was a great popular novelist and not a great deliberate artist . . .'[21]

Certainly, to condemn this facet of Hardy's writing out of hand shows a lack of sympathy with his mind and art. Again, it is a result of his marked duality of feeling: prosaic and poetic, didactic and allusive. It is the difference between his depiction of a leaf with the vivid exactness of a Millais, and his rendering of the essence of that leaf. Hardy may show his picture of life by indirect emotive means, or he may resort to the heavily representational method of the Pre-Raphaelite painters, who make their statement and then reiterate it with a mass of minute details which underlie the main theme. I am not suggesting, however, that Hardy imitated the methods of the Pre-Raphaelites, simply that the intention and effect of his moralistic set-pieces are of the same order. We know that Hardy was indeed acquainted with the paintings of Millais, Holman Hunt and Burne-Jones; like them, he was influenced by Wordsworth, read Ruskin and admired Turner; and it is conceivable that their style may have affected his own literary approach, which was by nature 'painterly'.

I have already noted that the Pre-Raphaelites took great pains to load their paintings with meaning and suggestion. Unlike the Dutch and Flemish *genre* painters, whose statement was simple and unforced, they delighted in heaping their domestic scenes with moralistic and didactic overtones, bordering often on the sentimental. For the sake of argument, one could select almost any painting of the school in its earlier stages (with the exception of Rossetti) and examine the means by which every detail reflects and emphasizes the main theme. Take, for instance, the well-known 'Death of Chatterton' (H. Wallis, 1830-1916), which is a good representation, in its skilful mixture of sentimentality and ghoulishness, of the sort of subject so dearly beloved of the romantic Victorians. The cause of death is made clear by the empty phial lying well in the foreground of the painting, and the dingy garret contrasts pointedly with the ethereal, shining vision of St Paul's seen through the open window. The body of the tragic young poet is partly suffused with sunlight, there is a fresh living potplant on the sill, and the smoke from a snuffed candle is drifting towards the open air. (Ruskin, incidentally, described this work as 'faultless and wonderful'.) The same sort of heavily underlined dramatic irony is used often by Hardy—for example, in his description of Fanny Robin's death in *Far from the Madding Crowd*, or, more subtly, in his presentation of Tess burying her child. The visual means of persuasion is the same, even though the picture is not static: we are shown the rough nettle-grown corner of the graveyard, the coffin ('a small deal box under an ancient woman's shawl'), the hand-made cross and the flowers in a little jar of water marked 'Keelwell's Marmalade'. Objects and actions accurately represent thoughts and attitudes; the detail of the marmalade jar suggests and sums up a great deal of what has gone before.

On a lower scale, one might see the later picture of Tess the 'kept woman' as directly related to the kind of moralistic painting epitomized by Holman Hunt's 'Awakening Conscience', which shows a young woman finally ensnared by a man, presumably of doubtful character. (The painting, which shows the captor and his victim in the setting of a wealthy drawing-room, at once gloomy and ornate, includes the detail of a cat eating a bird under the table.) Hardy's picture of Tess's horror at her situation as Alec d'Urberville's mistress is specifically shown to us as a *vignette*, a tableau seen by the landlady through the keyhole:

Only a small space of the room inside was visible, but within that space came a corner of the breakfast table, which was already spread for the meal, and also a chair beside. Over the seat of the chair Tess's face was bowed, her posture being a kneeling one in front of it; her hands were clasped over her head, the skirts of her dressing-gown and the embroidery of her nightgown flowed upon the floor behind her, and her stockingless feet, from which the slippers had fallen, protruded upon the carpet. (Ch. lvi)

She is here merely a study, a symbol of what she has become. It is hardly surprising that her subsequent words, intended to be impassioned and climactic, have the wooden sound of the heroine's lament in a popular melodrama. It is not Tess speaking, it is Hardy vocalizing for the woman in the picture.

Often it seems that Hardy chooses to treat his subjects with a peculiar eye for their pictorial significance, with an eye, even, for making 'visual equivalents to parables'.[22] In the same way, Holman Hunt tells us that Millais, painting 'a bit of nature', would seek for 'a moral idea to tack the nature on to';[23] conversely, the latter writes to his patron, 'I am nightly working my brains for a subject. Some incident to illustrate patience I have a desire to paint.' The same weakness in forcing moral ideas on to simple representation comes through in most of the 'undigested' episodes in Hardy's work; the pictures of life which can be separated and tagged, and which do not gain their special importance from their intrinsic relationship with the rest of the novel. The death of Little Father Time, as I shall show later, fails partly because of its ghastly improbability, but mostly because Hardy saw fit to supply an explanatory note, a legend for the bottom of the picture which is itself carefully arranged as a crucifixion piece. This, like many of the paintings of the Pre-Raphaelites, is heavily orientated towards an audience who liked to be illuminated without too much effort.

Hardy's artistic inclinations, then, fall into two strangely different categories. His approach to reality, his ideas on the concept of art, tally strongly with those of the Impressionists, yet his penchant for depicting thematically meaningful incidents and his frequent reliance on stock emotional effects are more closely akin to the static, 'photographic' art popular in the mid-nineteenth century and later. The two radically opposed methods of approach, and the ways in which they interact in the novels themselves, may help to illuminate Hardy's erratically powerful literary style, and the sometimes curious ways in which he projects his vision of life.

(iv)

... though every good author will confine himself within the bounds of probability, it is by no means necessary that his characters, or his incidents, should be trite, common or vulgar; such as happen in every street, or in every house, or which may be met with in the home articles of a newspaper. Nor must he be inhibited from showing many persons and things, which may possibly have never fallen within the knowledge of a great part of his readers. If the writer strictly observes the rules above-mentioned, he hath discharged his part; and is then entitled to some faith from his reader, who is indeed guilty of critical infidelity if he disbelieves him.

Henry Fielding, Tom Jones (1749) (Bk VIII, Ch. i)

... I have my own idea about art, and it is this: What most people regard as fantastic and lacking in universality, *I* hold to be the inmost essence of truth.

Feodor Dostoevsky, Letter to Nikolay Strachov, (26 February 1869)

To Hardy, art in all its manifestations, whether suggestive or explicit, is essentially an imaginative process,

... a disproportioning ... of realities, to show more clearly the features that matter ... which, if merely copied or reported inventorially, might possibly be observed, but would more probably be overlooked. Hence, 'realism' is not Art. (*Life*, p. 229)

Early in his career as a novelist he writes of his interest in unusual painting techniques, effects of distancing, magnifying and perspective. In 1870 he noted admiringly a picture, 'Jerusalem', by Gérôme, saying: 'The *shadows only* of the three crucified are seen. A fine conception' (*Life*, p. 76). This work obviously made a strong impression on him, for in 1887 he mentions it again, remarking of some religious enthusiasts that, like Gérôme, they 'open fresh views of Christianity by turning it in reverse positions' (*Life*, p. 206). There is more than one approach to reality, so he chooses for preference the odd, the different view. ('If I were a painter', he once observed, 'I would paint a picture of a room as viewed by a mouse from a chink under the skirting') (*Life*, p. 235).

Nearly always the effects of disproportioning and apparent exaggeration in his novels are simply the result of a different angle on actuality, a deliberate contrivance to make us look at something in a new way. An ordinary scene can be suddenly given a new perspective, or it can be metaphorically enlarged or condensed to give us overall a heightened, clearer picture. Thus from a height 'hedgerows appear [as] a network of dark green threads', or Casterbridge seems, from a bird's-eye view, to be 'a mosaic-work of subdued reds, browns, greys and crystals, held together by a rectangular frame of deep green'. On a more dramatic level, the scarlet blot of Alec d'Urberville's blood on an oblong white ceiling has 'the appearance of a gigantic ace of hearts'. Sometimes the vivid pictorial effect can also present a deeper meaning; for example, Eustacia and Wildeve walking across the heath appear to the reddleman as 'two horns which the sluggish heath had put forth from its crown, like a mollusc, and had now again drawn in'. In its particular context, this double diminishing of both landscape and human beings to insect scale is ironically significant as well as artistically arresting. All life, implicitly contrasted with its accepted hierarchy of importance, is reduced to the lowest common factor.

Throughout his novels, Hardy shows a fascinated preoccupation with the strange and marvellous, the unexpected, the ugly and horrifying. Many of his earlier critics deplored his so-called lapses in credibility. S. C. Chew, for example, makes the typical remark that 'Hardy's employment of sensational devices and situations . . . [are] admissible in novels of another sort, but in general they are out of accord with the austere control exhibited by [him] in other respects. Moreover they are in actuality of too rare occurrence to be representative of life; and the novel should reflect the great norm of existence, not the isolated phenomena.'[24] Yet, for Hardy, the mysterious, often repulsive side of life can reveal its essential truth more certainly than the side we normally see. Guerard says that he was 'determined to see a ghost'.[25] It is important to realize, however, that the 'ghost' in Hardy's writing is not there simply as an intriguing decoration to add 'atmosphere' to his stories, but that it is a vital part of his artistic vision. For him there are no absolutes; there is beauty in ugliness, ugliness in beauty. The apparent truth

must be interpreted by the eye of the imagination. So, in his notes
Hardy writes,

... if Nature's defects must be looked in the face and transcribed,
whence arises the *art* in poetry and novel-writing? which must surely
show art, or it becomes mere mechanical reporting. I think the art lies
in making these defects the basis of a hitherto unperceived beauty, by
irradiating them with 'the light that never was' on their surface, but is
seen to be latent in them by the spiritual eye. (*Life*, p. 114)

Ugliness and macabre absurdity are seldom introduced into the
stories gratuitously. They have their logical pattern behind the
sequence of apparent normality, illuminating everyday scenes by
startling and weird juxtaposition. Tess, lying awake in bed, is
suddenly picked up by her sleep-walking husband, carried outside
and deposited in an empty stone coffin; an unperceived gargoyle
neatly ruins Troy's handiwork on Fanny's grave; Knight and
Stephen Smith just happen to travel home on a train bearing the
hearse of their formerly beloved Elfride. Taken in isolation, such
scenes can easily appear ridiculous. That they do not so appear is
largely because Hardy (for the most part) sticks to his principle
that

The uncommonness must be in the events, not in the characters; and
the writer's art lies in shaping that uncommonness while disguising its
unlikelihood, if it be unlikely. (*Life*, p. 150)

Generally, too, we can accept the oddities and coincidences of
Hardy's plotting because behind the glaring illogicalities there is a
subtle network of image and reference in which the mundane is
continually expressed in fantastic or incongruous terms, and the
extreme is shown as ordinary occurrence. Sometimes, for example,
a simple landscape may be described in terms of exaggerated
fantasy, and it is only on closer analysis that one can see how
completely Hardy has *suggested* his grotesque effect. Consider the
clever interweaving of actual and metaphorical in this description
from *Tess of the d'Urbervilles*:

At half-past six the sun settled down upon the levels, with the aspect of
a great forge in the heavens, and presently a monstrous pumpkin-like

moon arose on the other hand. The pollard willows, tortured out of their natural shape by incessant choppings, became spiny-haired monsters as they stood up against it. (Ch. xxviii)

The strongest impressions are obviously created by the three operative images; the sun is 'a great forge', the moon is 'monstrous' and 'pumpkin-like', the trees are 'spiny-haired monsters'. The total effect is (for me, at least) rather like that of a bizarre fairy-tale illustration. Yet, on examination, it is quite apparent that Hardy has grounded his imaginative interpretation in the most prosaic fact. The sun settled precisely 'at half-past six'; the moon rose 'on the other hand'. In Tess's eyes the sun has only 'the aspect of' a forge, the moon is 'pumpkin-like', and the curious shapes of the trees can be explained by the way in which they have been pruned —in any case, they only *look like* monsters in silhouette. Taken like this, of course, the impact of the scene is lost, even though its complete credibility is explained. Hardy has merely exaggerated the qualities of the picture which are 'latent', without sacrificing the apparent and recognizable.

The most normal effects can make something appear (to its poetic advantage) to be what it is not. Tricks of light and shade, for instance, can bring out strange, meaningful resemblances at the most appropriate points in the narrative. In *A Pair of Blue Eyes*, Stephen, anguished at the faithlessness of the fickle Elfride, sees 'a strongly illuminated picture' of her with Henry Knight in the summerhouse:

Their two foreheads were close together, almost touching, and both were looking down. Elfride was holding her watch, Knight was holding the light with one hand, his left arm being round her waist. Part of the scene reached Stephen's eyes through the horizontal bars of the woodwork, which crossed their forms like the ribs of a skeleton. (Ch. xxv)

In *Tess of the d'Urbervilles*, at the stage when Alec is re-entering the story, simple geographical conditions can suggest a sort of hell:

From the west sky a wrathful shine—all that wild March could afford in the way of sunset—had burst forth after the cloudy day, flooding the tired and sticky faces of the threshers, and dyeing them with a coppery light, as also the flapping garments of the women, which clung to them like dull flames. (Ch. xlviii)

If man himself is to be seen as ordinary and believable, his environment, as it reflects his thought and imagination, often appears grotesque and bewildering, the more so as it may incorporate characteristics of humanity in strange distortion. For Hardy, the natural world is important chiefly in so far as it reveals elements of human experience, the essential condition of man as he sees it. On 22 April 1878, he writes:

... the method of Boldini, the painter of 'The Morning Walk' ... (a young lady beside an ugly blank wall on an ugly highway)—of Hobbema, in his view of a road with formal lopped trees and flat tame scenery—is that of infusing emotion into the baldest external objects either by the presence of a human figure among them, or by mark of some human connection with them.
This accords with my feeling ... —as I wrote at the beginning of *The Return of the Native*—that the beauty of association is entirely superior to the beauty of aspect ... (*Life*, p. 120)

Paradoxically, though, this meaningfulness of 'association' also operates in reverse; as the natural world can take on an added spiritual dimension from its connection with humanity, so too humanity can reveal its essential featureless and horrifying conformity with the substratum of life. A distant London crowd is seen imaginatively by Hardy as

... an organic whole, a molluscous black creature having nothing in common with humanity, that takes the shape of the streets along which it has lain itself, and throws out horrid excrescences and limbs into neighbouring alleys; a creature whose voice exudes from its scaly coat, and who has an eye in every pore of its body. The balconies, stands and railway-bridge are occupied by small detached shapes of the same tissue, but of gentler motion, as if they were the spawn of the monster in their midst. (*Life*, p. 131)

This tension of double association is an essential part of Hardy's view of the world. Again, it is almost exclusively pictorial, an extension of his impressionistic technique; half-way between fantasy and normality, he touches his picture with weird half-lights, showing us one thing while we actually see another. Man and the world of nature are shown as inextricably bound together and yet in a state of continual irreconciliation. Hardy uses un-ashamed 'effects' to demonstrate this strange dichotomy. In particular, he employs exaggerated and unexpected images of the grotesque, 'wrenching and twisting the frame of the real to provide a more penetrating vision, a more significant aesthetic experience'.[26] For this reason he frequently attributes human or animal characteristics to non-living things. Trees have faces and hands; a threshing machine is a 'buzzing red glutton' and straw its faeces; the gargoyle in *Far from the Madding Crowd* and the mask on Lucetta's door in *The Mayor of Casterbridge* are both endowed with specifically human features in hideous distortion.

As a characteristic example of this method, one might examine Hardy's treatment of the trees in *The Woodlanders*. We know them instinctively—apple-trees, oaks, hazels, orchards, copses and woods, masses of sunlight and shadow, continually rustling and moaning with their individual sounds. Superficially they are real trees in a real landscape, yet their total effect is only incidentally that of a pleasant tangible background. Like nearly all Hardy's natural images, they define the two kinds of reality. The trees which 'cast green shades, which disagreed with the complexion of the girls who walked there' are the same in which, by night, 'Imagination could trace amid the trunks and boughs swarthy faces and funereal figures' (Ch. xx). They seem to embody the sweetness of Nature (the love of Grace and Fitzpiers 'grew as imperceptibly as the twigs budded on the trees') (Ch. xix) but in their luxuriance and beauty is also the mystery and oldness of death. They are thin spectres in winter and have a magical affinity with the lives of humans; old Mr South must fall dead as his tree falls. Containing human characteristics, they are yet grotesquely inhuman:

They . . . skirted trunks with spreading roots whose mossed rinds made them like hands wearing green gloves, elbowed old elms and ashes with great forks, in which stood pools of water that overflowed on rainy days, and ran down their stems in green cascades. On older trees still than these huge lobes of fungi grew like lungs. Here, as everywhere, the Unfulfilled Intention, which makes life what it is, was as obvious as it could be among the depraved crowds of a city slum. The leaf was deformed, the curve was crippled, the taper was interrupted, the lichen ate the vigour of the stalk, and the ivy slowly strangled to death the promising sapling. (Ch. vii)

The trees caricature humanity not only in their appearance but also in their behaviour. They have an exaggerated nightmare ugliness; beeches have 'vast armpits', rotting stumps rise from the mossy ground 'like black teeth from green gums'. Yet beneath the close-grouped trees, 'wrestling for existence, their branches dis-figured with wounds resulting from their mutual rubbings and blows', is the beauty of the moss, 'dark green and pale green; . . . like little fir trees, like plush, like malachite stars', and of the 'stemless yellow fungi like lemons and apricots' (Ch. xlii). It is by no means solely a world of horror.

Sometimes the grotesque suggestion that a character's situation is reflected, unknown to him, in the inanimate objects surround-ing him, can have a much more specific dramatic effect. A particular image may ramify enormously in meaning. Take, for instance, Hardy's portrayal of Tess as she tells Angel of her past life:

Their hands were still joined. The ashes under the grate were lit by the fire vertically, like a torrid waste. Imagination might have beheld a Last Day luridness in this red-coaled glow, which fell on his face and hand, and on hers, peering into the loose hair about her brow, and firing the delicate skin underneath. A large shadow of her shape rose upon the wall and ceiling. She bent forward, at which each diamond on her neck gave a sinister wink like a toad's . . . (Ch. xxxiv)

By this last subtle touch, Hardy doubly emphasizes the irony of her predicament; the mockery of the precious adornment she is wearing corresponds implicitly with the image of the toad, whose jewelled eyes are incongruous in his hideous body. Conversely, Tess, who will be regarded as loathesome by Angel, is in fact still beautiful; she is as much a part of the innocent natural world as he is formed by convention and artificiality, hard and inhuman like the diamonds which sit so oddly on her. The two are illuminated symbolically by a purgatorial fire, and even this seems insidiously to be attacking Tess; the friendly warming coals become harsh inquisitors, '*peering* at her', and 'firing [her] delicate skin'. The foreboding of the situation, the mockery of its consequences, are more than hinted at in the 'sinister wink' of the jewels. Hardy's attitude here is almost one of savage humour.

Even at its most macabre, though, Hardy's presentation of the grotesque is marked by its detachment. As an ironic comment on man and the universe, it is essentially only another way of looking at things, not necessarily a deep interpretation of them. Often he shows his imaginative perception of the ordinary as the projected vision of one of his characters, whose circumstances or mental state give a peculiar emotional orientation or disproportioning to what he or she sees. When, for example, Mrs Yeobright sees in a dried-out puddle 'the maggoty shapes of innumerable obscene creatures . . . heaving and wallowing with enjoyment', it is her own contrasting disillusionment and weariness which places such clear emotional significance on what is simply *there*. In the same way, Tess, reminded of her own unfortunate history by the dairyman's story, sees the evening sun as 'now ugly to her, like a great inflamed wound in the sky', or to Gabriel Oak, broken in spirit after the destruction of his flock of sheep, a pool of water seems to glitter 'like a dead man's eye'. To Henry Knight, clinging to 'the Cliff without a Name', the blue sea appears to be black like a funeral pall: in such a way, says Hardy, 'We colour according to our moods the objects we survey'.

So it is that Hardy frequently lends credibility to his fantastic images by placing them within a psychological perspective. Throughout his novels, he shows a continued obsession with the figments of the human mind, with its areas of consciousness and blindness and its irrationalities, and, most of all, with its verging into the realms of dream and superstition and fantasy. He draws a clear line between the sensationalism of pure 'Gothic' romance and that which takes its extremes from the natural peculiarities and mysteries of the mind.

A 'sensation-novel' is possible in which the sensationalism is not casualty, but evolution; not physical but psychical ... The difference between the latter kind of novel and the novel of physical sensationalism—*i.e.* personal adventure, etc.,—is this: that whereas in the physical the adventure itself is the subject of interest, the psychical results being passed over as commonplace, in the psychical the casualty or adventure is held to be of no intrinsic interest, but the effect upon the faculties is the important matter to be depicted. (*Life*, p. 204)

It is significant that in 'The Science of Fiction' he speaks of 'the phantasmagoria of experience', and that in his own life he saw himself as 'a spectre not solid enough to influence his environment', one who put on 'the manners of ghosts ... taking their views of surrounding things' (*Life*, p. 210). His view of life often seems as if channelled to us through a sort of dream-consciousness, tinged with a nightmare reality. 'Wessex' becomes real and familiar to us, but it is not a physically real place; rather, it is a closely realized dream of a real place, Hardy's dream or vision of the actual world. (Interestingly, John Morley, in criticizing *The Poor Man and the Lady*—Hardy's earliest literary effort—remarked that some of the scenes 'read like some clever lad's dream'. Otherwise, the

naive realism in circumstantial details that were pure invention was so well assumed that both Macmillan and Morley had been perhaps a little, or more than a little, deceived by its seeming actuality; to Hardy's surprise, when he thought the matter over in later years, that his inexperienced imagination should have created figments that could win credence from such experienced heads.) (*Life*, p. 61)

Within this perspective, the unknown, because, simply, it is unknowable, is effectively transcribed into the strange, the odd or the frightening. Hardy's skill is in the mystic aura with which he surrounds his world, his prophetic showing of actuality. His method is to 'fix' his abstract ideas permanently in impressions and glancings of truth, in strange symbols and images which mean far more to us because of their implication, what they leave *unsaid*. This continual consciousness of something *behind* the apparent suffuses Hardy's whole attitude to life, where the most casual conjunctions of the prosaic and the unexpected can take on the power of symbols. For example, he describes with relish how he watches the children playing in the streets whilst he himself listens to a First Aid lecture:

A skeleton—the one used in these lectures—is hung up inside the window. We face it as we sit. Outside the band is playing, and the children are dancing. I can see their little figures through the window past the skeleton dangling in front. (*Life*, p. 157)

Basically, all such illustrations derive from Hardy's pervasive concern with the contrast between what is really true and what can be simply observed as truth. On 21 December 1885, he writes,

The Hypocrisy of things. Nature is an arch-dissembler. A child is deceived completely; the older members of society more or less according to their penetration; though even they seldom get to realize that *nothing* is as it appears. (*Life*, p. 176)

He himself acknowledged that his own mind was essentially that of a child; childhood memories which remained vivid to him all his life suggest often the sort of imagery he employs in his novels. He remembers how he was taken, while still a small boy, to see the burning in effigy of the Pope and Cardinal Wiseman during the No-Popery riots:

The sight . . . was most lurid, and he never forgot it; and when the cowl of one of the monks in the ghastly procession blew aside and revealed the features of one of his father's workmen his bewilderment was great. (*Life*, p. 21)

Hardy's art is to show the unconscious and half-formed vividness of the dream-world beyond the greyness of philosophy; the imperfect childish point of view contrasts with the external and uncompromising truth of the real world, as shown objectively by the author himself. The characters he creates, often innocent or childlike, are frequently deceived, and believe in life and nature by their outward signs, while Hardy, with his knowledge of both sides, presents the ironic counter to their visions. Throughout his novels credulity and reality are at war. The truth becomes progressively grimmer and the deception more garish till, in *Jude the Obscure*, Hardy shows the culmination of Nature's hypocrisy. Life becomes, for those who exist in a visionary idealistic world, a frightening game, and children's complete deception becomes the reality by which they must act.

Linked with this credulous acceptance of the apparent as absolute truth is Hardy's peculiar featuring of the ghostly as a physical presence attendant upon each human being. Sometimes is appears as a premonitory symbol whose presence is ironically unperceived by the character involved; thus the shadowed profile of Cytherea's head is seen to dance 'like a demon, blue and grim', or Dairyman Crick's 'great knife and fork . . . planted erect on the table' seems to resemble 'the beginning of a gallows'. Sometimes, in a mystical way, those things which are irrationally imagined can become true enough to be an effective influence on the progress of human lives. Henchard sees himself floating dead in a river; Eustacia's love for Clym Yeobright is kindled by a dream; Lucetta is killed by the sight of her own effigy. Appearance becomes reality: daylight neighbours become in the dark scarlet and black demons, or figures from an ancient frieze, or pagan gods and goddesses. In the eyes of a child, the reddleman in *The Return of the Native* is the devil, not because of what he does but because of the way he looks. Fitzpiers is associated with the black arts and Eustacia is accepted as a witch, both merely because they are 'different'. In a life of mundane, natural things, the extraordinary must stand out with particular vividness, but to the eye of the imagination even the apparently ordinary is fantastic and incomprehensible. As Guerard remarks, in Hardy's novels 'the dream-world, with its nightmare conjunctions, impinges suddenly on an until then perfectly sane world of tradesmen, shepherds and furze-cutters; of everyday experiences and daylight desires. The unreal falls like a lash on the prosaic and dull'.[27]

Obviously Hardy's use of the fantastic and grotesque is not

uniform in its aesthetic worth. It is a method of presentation which he developed gradually, and which even in his last and best novels manifests itself sometimes in a clear, profound or ironic symbolism and sometimes in a trivial appeal to the 'thrilling' and 'romantic'. Guerard says that basically he was 'a pure romantic, like Scott, appealing to the surprised child who lingers in us all'.[28] Often his imaginative sensibility expresses itself in a way of writing which is purely and blatantly decorative, in the unashamed romantic tradition of the so-called 'Gothic' novelists. It is with obvious pleasure that, in *Tess of the d'Urbervilles*, he describes 'the notched tips of fir-trees' as appearing 'like battlemented towers crowning black-fronted castles of enchantment' (Ch. xxx). In many of the novels there is an undisguised delight in coffins, crypts and family vaults, ancient monuments and historical associations. The picture of Paula Power's ancient, ivy-covered castle in *A Laodicean* is embellished with loving detail. There are rooks, spiders' webs, suits of armour and gloomy old family portraits. There is even a brood of young owls in the tower. But this sort of imagery is seldom functional in the same sense as the type which I have already described—simply, it provides an 'atmosphere' conducive to tales of adventure and mystery. Often, too, the method of intensification through contrasts of light and shadow is used melodramatically rather than with impressionistic subtlety. There are many scenes whose exaggerated effects are contrived mainly towards a sense of 'romantic' appositeness. In *The Mayor of Casterbridge*, Hardy sets the scene for Michael Henchard's mood after he has discovered that Elizabeth-Jane is not, as he had believed, his own daughter:

The river—slow, noiseless, and dark—the Schwarzwasser of Caster-bridge—ran beneath a low cliff... Here were the ruins of a Franciscan priory, and a mill attached to the same, the water of which roared down the back-hatch like the voice of desolation. Above the cliff, and beyond the river, rose a pile of buildings, and in the front of the pile a square mass cut into the sky. It was like a pedestal lacking its statue. This missing feature... was, in truth, the corpse of a man; for the square mass formed the base of a gallows...

E

The exaggeration which darkness imparted to the glooms of this region impressed Henchard more than he had expected. The lugubrious harmony of the spot with his domestic situation was too perfect for him . . . it reduced his heart-burning to melancholy . . . (Ch. xix)

The ostensible function of such a scene as an emotional referent seems at first, in its conscious presentation, too calculated a piece of artifice. It is important to notice, however, the subtle means by which the deliberate evocation of melodrama is brought down to the reality of its human subject. Henchard was 'impressed . . . more than he had expected'; again, it is Hardy's 'impressive' style of writing, rather than his subject-matter, which creates the illusion.

This idiosyncratic tendency towards mysterious or super-natural decorative effects must inevitably have derived from Hardy's early interest in the tales of the Gothic romanticists. We know that he was familiar with the novels of Harrison Ainsworth and Sir Walter Scott, and that he admired their work. As a child he

loved reading Dumas *père's* romances . . . and Shakespeare's tragedies for the plots only, not thinking much of *Hamlet* because the ghost did not play his part up to the end as he ought to have done. (*Life*, p. 24)

Sometimes it is obvious that in his novels he is consciously striving to achieve effects of pure spectacle and awesome terror. He felt that 'we tale-tellers are all Ancient Mariners, and none of us is warranted in stopping Wedding Guests . . . unless he has some-thing . . . unusual to relate' (*Life*, p. 252). To the end of imbuing even the common event with a sort of poetic intensity, he made a practice of studying Burke's *Enquiry into the Sublime and Beautiful* (1759), using this as a handbook to help him in his aim of achiev-ing a powerful and elevated prose style.[29]

Hardy's use of the grotesque, then, operates on innumerable different levels. As David Cecil puts it, it is 'Sublime, irregular, quaint, mysterious and extravagant, showing itself most typically now in a wild grandeur of conception, now in some vivid particularity of detail'.[30] It merges the known with the unknown or unrecognized, sees linkages in apparently unrelated subjects, and is based on Hartley Coleridge's dictum, which Hardy believed implicitly, that a writer must 'aim at illusion' in his audience. Beginning in his earliest published novel, *Desperate Remedies*, as a tentative and rather crude method of creating suspense and horror, it comes, in his later works, almost to embody his sympathetic and ironic view of life.

Experiments and Mistakes

It was a sort of thing he had never contemplated writing . . .
                                        Thomas Hardy, *Life*, p. 85

(i)

Desperate Remedies shows Hardy's artistic tendency at its obvious worst and at its potential best, with both elements tentatively in solution. The author himself, in his preface to the 1889 edition of the novel, indicates that he considers it to be a supremely uneven work:

The principles involved in its composition are, no doubt, too exclusively those in which mystery, entanglement, surprise and moral obliquity are depended on for exciting interest; but some of the scenes, and at least one of the characters, have been deemed not unworthy of a little longer presentation.

Two radically different styles of writing appear to have evolved from this intriguingly ambivalent first publication, and with them has arisen a dual concept of Hardy's literary status. On the one hand, we have Hardy the Sublime, author of *Far from the Madding Crowd* and *Tess of the d'Urbervilles*; on the other, Hardy the hack-writer, purveyor of lumpish serial 'thrillers' and romances. Naturally, Hardy was himself keenly aware of this dichotomy. In the 'General Preface to the Novels and Poems', written in 1912 for Macmillan's definitive 'Wessex' edition of his works, he claims no high artistic merit for approximately half of his novels in his own final classification of them.[1] The 'Novels of Character and Environment', he says, 'may claim a verisimilitude in general treatment and detail', but the other categories, by their very definition as 'Romances and Fantasies' and 'Novels of Ingenuity', are clearly placed by their author on a rather lower scale of accomplishment. He admits openly that the novels of the latter group

show a not infrequent disregard of the probable in the chain of events, and depend for their interest mainly on the incidents themselves. They might also be characterized as 'Experiments', and were written for the nonce simply; though despite the artificiality of their fable some of their scenes are not without fidelity to life.

Many of Hardy's less distinguished works have been partially excused for their comparative lack of merit on practical or circumstantial grounds. *Desperate Remedies* is, after all, mere apprentice-work; *A Pair of Blue Eyes* is understandably marred by the author's lack of maturity and his self-involvement with the autobiographical elements of the romance; *The Hand of Ethelberta* was ruined by commercial pressures and inexperience. Hardy himself complained afterwards that his publishers hurried him into the latter production

before he was aware of what there had been of value in his previous one [*i.e.*, *Far from the Madding Crowd*]: before learning, that is, not only what had attracted the public, but what was of true and genuine substance on which to build a career as a writer with a real literary message. (*Life*, p. 102)

Yet this chronological means of justification inevitably breaks down in the end. It is reasonable to expect, for example, that despite Hardy's determination not to produce another volume of 'sheep and shepherds', *The Hand of Ethelberta* might have benefited at least technically from the successful method of its forerunner. *A Laodicean* and *Two on a Tower* are similarly placed between two acknowledged 'masterpieces', *The Return of the Native* and *The Mayor of Casterbridge*; while *The Well-Beloved*, though conceived earlier, was written and published in its original form only two years before the serialization of *Jude the Obscure*. Such lack of consistency is in itself bewildering. 'You are led to wonder at times', writes Joseph Warren Beach, 'whether he had ever consciously *learned* the technical refinements of his art, whether perhaps the formal perfection of *The Native* or of *Tess* might not be a mere happy accident.'[2]

The obvious rejoinder to this is that Hardy, in his own explanation, was attempting less, and so achieved less.[3] The ambition was not there in the first place. On the other hand, these works were written under virtually the same conditions as the 'Novels of Character and Environment'—all of which, with the exception of *Under the Greenwood Tree*, were originally published in serial form—and there is nothing to suggest at any stage that Hardy made any distinction in his attitude towards his productions, although all his comments on the results are necessarily retrospective. We can only gather our impressions from occasional random notes, in which he mentions (for instance) that the character of Paula in *A Laodicean* 'tantalized the writer by eluding his grasp for some time', or that, although it appears now merely as a 'slightly-built romance', he had had 'high aims' for *Two on a Tower*. It is, therefore, not so much a question of the height of Hardy's ambition in these novels as of whether or not this was fulfilled. We must assume that each of these works was initially designed to maintain, in its own way, a view of life as important to its author as that more successfully expressed in *Far from the Madding Crowd* or *The Return of the Native* or *Jude the Obscure*.

Many explanations for Hardy's so-called 'failures' have been offered. Donald Davidson, for example, claims that Hardy's best work is 'unconscious' to the extent that it is developed from non-literary, ballad-type narrative, and that the 'inferior' novels are quite simply those which do not fit into this thesis, but which can be seen as 'Hardy's attempt to be a fully modern—and literary—novelist'.[4] John Holloway sees them as being those works which fail to display completely 'what might be called Hardy's cosmology, his view of the world and of man's situation'—in other words, the conflict between the stabilizing natural world and the opposing forces of modernity.[5] Guerard speaks of the 'lapse of creative energy' and of the abandonment of difficult or stimulating ventures for lazy schematizing, while Beach, a much earlier critic, is driven despairingly to 'some hypothesis of the demands of the market, exhausted imagination, or impaired physical vigour'. Nevertheless, explanations such as these must form only a part of the answer. The comparative poverty of these particular works is not necessarily due to simple cause-and-effect. The 'Romances and Fantasies' and the 'Novels of Ingenuity' are not uniformly 'bad'; neither are the 'Novels of Character and Environment' uniformly 'good'. Even in Hardy's most successful work there is frequently a glimpse of potential which is greater than its fulfilment. Virginia Woolf, writing of the novels of E. M. Forster, puts her finger on the problem:

... if there is one gift more essential to a novelist than another it is the power of combination—the single vision. The success of the master-pieces seems to lie not so much in their freedom from faults—indeed we tolerate the grossest errors in them all—but in the immense persuasiveness of a mind which has completely mastered its perspective.[6]

By 1871, Hardy had been privately writing poetry for some time, but apart from *The Poor Man and the Lady*, which was never published, *Desperate Remedies* was his first serious attempt at the art of the novel. In many respects, this early work appears now as quite a remarkable experiment. Hardy's own initial pride in his effort is revealed by his reaction to its critical reception; among some good reviews he received one which was damning (the *Spectator*, 22 April 1871): 'The bitterness of that moment was never forgotten; at the time he wished that he were dead'.

Obviously, by reason of its naiveté and spontaneity, *Desperate Remedies* is likely to reveal a great deal about its author, and the work is, therefore, worthy of more than a cursory glance or a dismissing comment. One critic describes it, very aptly, as being 'one of the most interesting bad novels in the English language, bad with verve, bad with passion, bad (one might even say) with distinction'.[7] Its 'badness', however, is largely due to its refusal to break away from the model of the standard 'mystery story' popular at the time: this novel is not all Hardy, but tries, for the most part, to be Wilkie Collins. Its significance lies in those passages where Hardy's individual creativity can be seen, breaking rather awkwardly through the artificial veneer.

It is hard, in a novel of this kind, to separate the worthwhile from the trivial. One must accept the blatant melodrama (' "I give it all up for life—dear life!" he cried with a hoarse laugh. "A reckless man has a dozen lives—see how I'll baffle you all yet!" ') (Ch. xx, ii), the hideous pathos (' "My Cytherea! My stolen pet lamb!" ') (Ch. xiii, iv) and the incredible twists of plot. These, after all, were what the public expected from such a novel; the title already suggests that the tale is to be extreme. Harder to accept or to explain are the uneven patches, the strange admixture of Gothic and prosaic, the heightened rhetoric which collapses suddenly into ludicrous bathos. Despite its numerous faults, though, the novel does succeed in holding the reader's attention, and not merely because he is anxious to see what kind of *dénouement* the twisted threads are leading to. It is an exciting, irritating, intriguing tale, one to which Hardy's comment that the reader must, if he is to be entertained, believe 'slavishly' in whatever incredible events the author chooses to show him, can well be applied. Yet if *Desperate Remedies* is treated not completely as an aberration, but rather as an experimental novel in which the author, as he himself admits, is 'feeling his way to a method' (1889 preface), some important points begin to emerge, and we can see in embryo some of the most important techniques used in the later novels.

This is essentially a work which must be read in the same spirit as it was read by its contemporary audience; present-day critics tend to occupy themselves with Freudian slips which Hardy himself presumably failed to notice or deem important. (Interestingly, critics of the time found a major bone of contention in the fact that Hardy dared to suggest that a lady of Miss Aldclyffe's status could possibly be the mother of an illegitimate child. In the preface to a later edition (February 1896), Hardy humorously notes that certain characteristics which provoked most discussion in my latest story [*i.e., Jude the Obscure*] were present in this my first—published in 1871, when there was no French name for them).

The formula used in the book is that of involving ordinary, credible characters in quite extraordinary events. The events in *Desperate Remedies*, however, drastically outweigh even our nominal concern with the fates of the characters; they become in our minds mere figures, distinguished only in so far as they are good or bad, dark or fair. With these rather stereotyped characters Hardy sets up a plot so complicated that no single novel can adequately contain it. The problem for the author in sorting out the crowded action results finally in long explanations, conversations postulating pros and cons and even in direct tabulating of possibilities, while some semblance of order is attempted by the regulation of a strict time-scheme. Each chapter and division of chapter has an allotted time and is subdivided into exact dates and precise hours (the action might take place, for example, under the heading 'From Five to Eight O'Clock p.m.'). The strictest attention to detail is observable throughout, and the intense documentary realism is obviously intended to give a semblance of credibility to the strangest of events. Often the mechanics of the plot are simply ludicrous; we might be forgiven for refusing to believe that Manston's buttons, hands and watch-chain could make so clear an imprint on a convenient piece of mud that they give a vital clue to his whereabouts. Sometimes, though, the strangeness is of the time; presumably Ann Seaway's magnificently incongruous act of pouring a glassful of wine into her bosom would not have seemed so humorous to Hardy's original readers. It is fruitless, however, to attempt too much justification on the grounds of contemporary acceptability, and the plot must be seen eventually as an ingenious effort, with the author straining his imagination and intellect for the sake of padding out a fairly simple framework. As a result, we tend to lose sight of various characters and events for pages at a time. The role played by Miss Aldclyffe, for example, is highly concentrated at the beginning, but progressively diminishes in importance. Although her connection with Manston is continually hinted at, it seems at the end to be rather an irrelevant invention and makes little difference to the final *dénouement*; the intervening incidents overshadow the

man is direct and immediate ('He *looked* and *smelt* like Autumn's very brother', Ch. xxviii) and the idea of his being part of the natural world is reinforced continually throughout the book. In the descriptions I have quoted, however, there is no reinforcement, nothing of the intrinsic meaning of the later description, where every detail forms part of the pattern. Perhaps there is even a slight self-consciousness on Hardy's part; he presents this picture of ordinary life passively (the apple-pips *were to be seen*). Similarly, if one looks at the seemingly detailed description of the cider-pressing, one finds that the details are in fact vague and non-pictorial. In effect Hardy only gives his impression of a busy and crowded scene by putting it all into a busy and crowded sentence. The interest in 'local colour' is there, but it is not employed artistically; nevertheless, the impressionistic technique is much the same as that which Hardy later employed so effectively. Necessarily, throughout *Desperate Remedies* the detail is circumstantial, expressly developed to add colour and verisimilitude to a particular scene, as befits a novel where credibility must be assured for its success. Often it seems that Hardy takes every scene separately, measures its proportions and takes note, with mathematical exactness, of every bump and hollow, every stick and stone. Sometimes this gives us an acute and delicately drawn picture, as in one of the most impressive of the early scenes, that in which Cytherea's father falls to his death. Emotion is most powerfully conveyed by this method of detailed impersonal presentation. The exact size and position of the church tower are shown through the eyes of one so far away that the men working on the spire are distinguishable only by the colour of their clothes; four are in white and one is 'in the ordinary dark suit of a gentlemen'. The distance and brightness of the scene are emphasized by being seen 'like an illuminated miniature, framed in by the dark margin of the window' through which Cytherea is looking. The men are shown as completely removed from and unconscious of the living world: 'They appeared little larger than pigeons, and made their tiny movements with a soft, spirit-like silentness' (Ch. i, iii). Hardy's portrayal of this first accident, the fuse which sets off the subsequent train of events, is brilliantly and effectively understated. In a novel where blood and passion are seemingly of prime importance, Ambrose Graye's death is deliberately contrasted in its unearthly detachment. The unremarkable, impersonal visual image of death gives greater weight to the repercussions which must follow. By seeing, with the author, through the eyes of the characters involved, we can sense their feelings more sharply than we could if we were directly *told*. The picture suggests the event, and remains in our minds; in the same way, Hardy tells us, Cytherea for ever afterwards associates 'mental agony' with the scene, represented in essence for her by an image of 'sunlight streaming in shaft-like lines' (Ch. i, iii).

Hardy's thesis, that 'Emotions will attach themselves to scenes that are simultaneous . . . as chemical waters will crystallize on twigs and wires' (Ch. i, iii) is nowhere more clearly illustrated than in one of the scenes of Manston's courtship of Cytherea. The ruins, the metallic sky and the swampy vegetation all convey the tastelessness of the episode, and although the bizarre touch of the imaginary shrieking mandrakes seems rather too contrived, the very silence and stagnation suggest, far more positively than this falsely melodramatic touch, the dullness and passivity of the girl's mind. The picture of the setting sun, inexorable as it is, is highly symbolic, and the exquisite fascination of the quietness, the

purple haze, against which a swarm of wailing gnats shone forth luminously, rising upward and floating away like sparks of fire (Ch. xii, vi)[8]

is noteworthy for its echoing of a mental state, in which the fireflies, free and exotic, floating away, suggest the almost hypnotizing fascination of the man for the woman, a fascination which is inconsequentially part of her apathy towards him. As R. C. Carpenter points out, Hardy uses clustered images to convey a state of mind, providing 'a vital objective correlative which communicates more powerfully and accurately to the reader's thoughts and feelings than could any amount of discursive philosophizing'.[9] Referring first to the famous garden scene in *Tess of the d'Urbervilles* (Ch. xix) Carpenter goes on to remark on the similarity between this and the episode I have just discussed. His conclusion, though, is that the latter scene, in comparison, is 'too crude, too obvious and discursive'. Nevertheless, 'such scenes as this strike a different note, present us with a grimmer dissonance than characterizes the usual nineteenth century melodrama'.

Hardy's effects here are not simply visual or decorative. They are, I think, more closely and subtly akin to those he uses in *Tess of the d'Urbervilles* than Carpenter suggests. In *Desperate Remedies* the overpowering physical and mental effect of their surroundings creates in Cytherea, as in Tess, a sort of trance, ('. . . she felt as one in a boat without oars, drifting with closed eyes down a river') (Ch. xii, vi), one in which the mere presence of the man exerts an unconscious magnetism. ('Their clothes touched', says Hardy, forcing us to remember his description of the first meeting between Manston and Cytherea, when she feels strangely electrified by him through the simple contact of their garments.) Here, as in *Tess of the d'Urbervilles*, a hypnotic sexuality is implied by remote suggestion, the building up of meaningful effects. Both women are almost unconscious of what they are doing, and the heavy, vaguely repugnant nature of their environments is described, in both cases, in terms of exotic luxuriance. To Tess the overgrown sticky garden is a sort of fertile Paradise; Cytherea, on a rather lower scale, is lulled by the curiously attractive oppressiveness of the place into a state of unwitting acceptance. As Tess is part of the garden, surrounded and absorbed by it, so too Cytherea, in the flat, passive humidity of her surroundings, feels 'a sense of bare equality with, and no superiority to, a single entity under the sky' (Ch. xii, vi).

This method of implication rather than statement contrasts noticeably in *Desperate Remedies* with the more stereotyped emotional symbolism of the type epitomized in the popular paintings of the day. In the scene immediately following Cytherea's wedding to Manston she gazes at her erstwhile lover, Edward Springrove, from the opposite side of an impassable frozen river; the symbolic handclasp as they just reach each other, despite the treacherous barrier, predicts too obviously the probable course of action. Hardy is determined, however, to lift this episode out of the ordinary, and this blatant picture is preceded by the dreamlike concept of the lovers each independently gazing at the inverted image of the other, reflected in the water, while their real selves are hidden from view by a huge ice-covered tree. And after the pathetic touching of hands comes an ironically unemotional comment:

The river flowed on as quietly and obtusely as ever, and the minnows gathered again in their favorite spot, as if they had never been disturbed. (Ch. xiii, iv)

On the one hand this is part of the rather conventional little picture, a sentimental gesture towards the apparent futility of this love; on the other, it predicts Hardy's concern with the ironic ambivalence of unconscious natural processes, the self-contained and disregarding other world.

All through the novel we find this conflict of the imaginative and the stereotyped, the dream-world and the real world with all its inconsequential detail. Unfortunately, the rift between the two is excessive and the story and the characters fail on both levels; they are at the same time too ordinary and too unreal. Cytherea has flashes of independent spirit but she cannot escape the confines of the golden-haired heroine in whose image she is painted; Manston is only a mediocre hedonist and a pseudo arch-villain; Miss Aldclyffe, suffering worst of all, dwindles from a Vittoria-type figure to a pathetic old lady with a past, even though Hardy does try to lift her death-scene by the addition of a ghost. In this novel he is not completely at ease with either the realistic or the melodramatic approach, whereas in the works of his greatest artistry the balance is almost complete and we have a real world made, if possible, more real by the addition of a fantastic element.

The melodrama in *Desperate Remedies* is enthusiastic, if somewhat erratic. The Edward Springrove who leans 'almost hanging' on the Aldclyffe monument ('knights damp and green with age ... and above them a huge classic monument ... heavily sculptured in cadaverous marble') is described with relish by Hardy in the manner of Edgar Allen Poe or Harrison Ainsworth:

The sight was a sad one—sad beyond all description. His eyes were wild, their orbits leaden. His face was of a sickly paleness, his hair dry and disordered, his lips parted as if he could get no breath. His figure was spectre-thin. His actions seemed beyond his own control. (Ch. xiii, iii)

The picture is one of Gothic intensity, the background and circumstances carefully planned to give utmost impact. Edward is not Edward ('or his spirit'), but a portrait of a forsaken lover playing his part, a lover in the Romantic tradition, who possesses not eyes but orbs. His appearance is a startling one, more so in that (with Hardy's favourite technique) he is illuminated suddenly by the radiance of the candles streaming through the just-opened church door. It is a fascinating vignette of a particular tradition and the language perfectly conveys the type of effect which Hardy intends. The description of Edward Springrove, for instance, is given in short, breathless sentences—the drama of the moment cannot be overshadowed by sonorous rhetoric, which is appropriately saved for the musty charnel-house atmosphere framing the picture. Yet from such exalted, artificial heights Hardy plunges immediately into a scene of honest reality, which, in contrast, is only ludicrous anti-climax. The bride sees her haggard lover:

. . . there broke from her in a low plaintive scream the words, 'He's dying—dying! O God, save us!' She began to sink down, and would have fallen had not Manston caught her. The chief bridesmaid applied her vinaigrette.

'What did she say?' inquired Manston.

Owen took advantage of the hindrance to step back to where the apparition had been seen. He was enraged with Springrove for what he considered an unwarrantable intrusion. (Ch. xiii, iii)

The two styles and attitudes are mutually exclusive. In *Desperate Remedies* the ghoulish and the melodramatic are used as embellishment only. Perhaps the chief reason for their incongruity is their non-functional character—at least the gargoyle in *Far from the*

Madding Crowd accomplishes a useful purpose; in *Desperate Remedies* the mandrake's is only an imagined shriek.

Occasionally, though, we do find an almost perfect blend of the real and the strange. Most often this is achieved by describing reality through the eyes and imagination of one of the characters, so that we have the illusion of truth through emotional immediacy. Essentially this is an impressionistic style; thus the description of Cytherea's first view of Miss Aldclyffe is initially a striking non-description. Her position is first suggested to Cytherea by a glowing line of light beneath the closed door. Then, after a suitable pause for expectation and the beginning of another segment, the door is opened and the scene revealed:

> The direct blaze of the afternoon sun, partly refracted through the crimson curtains of the window, and heightened by reflections from the crimson flock paper which covered the walls, and a carpet on the floor of the same tint, shone with a burning glow round the form of the lady . . . The stranger appeared to the maiden's eyes—fresh from the blue gloom, and assisted by an imagination fresh from nature—like a tall black figure standing in the midst of fire. (Ch. iv, ii)

The typical observation of the young woman (the colour and texture of the furnishings) is transmuted with a finely theatrical touch into an imaginative vision of a supernatural, almost hellish place with Miss Aldclyffe as a striking sort of demon. Our total impression of the latter character is at least partially coloured by this one picture, which expresses more than all her posturings and stereotyped phrases. Aeneas Manston's first appearance corresponds in impressiveness and stagey contrivance; he is standing on a flight of steps and a storm is brewing. He appears

> partly from the relief the position gave to his figure, and partly from fact, to be of towering height. He was dark in outline, and was looking at the sky, with his hands behind him. (Ch. viii, iv)

In the descriptions of both 'sinister' characters, all the effects are explained in practical, everyday terms; the atmosphere only *seems* to be supernatural. Hardy sticks closely to his maxim that all strangeness must be believable. To Cytherea, as to us, it is an imaginative response based on reality.

(ii)

It can be seen, in this earliest novel, that Hardy is most convincing when his story, regardless of its improbability, is made to seem *imaginatively* true. By the same token, the weaknesses of *A Laodicean*, as a further instance, lie almost solely in Hardy's inability—for various reasons, not least of which was his serious illness at the time of composition—to maintain a consistent imaginative viewpoint. The gap between the recognizably real and the patently fictitious is too often and too painfully apparent. This is not to say that the actual story-line of *A Laodicean* is any more strikingly 'impossible' than that of, say, *The Return of the Native* or *The Mayor of Casterbridge*. There is notably, in the former novel, a minimal use of direct symbolism or calculated theatrical effect; its subtitle, 'A Story of Today', adequately proclaims Hardy's relatively sober intentions. Yet there is no doubt that we are more disposed to accept as credible (for example) his picture of Henchard selling his wife, or Eustacia's weirdly brilliant masquerade in mummer's costume, than the far more mundane description of William Dare blackmailing Abner Power in a church vestry. The difference between our attitude towards Henchard or Eustacia and our attitude towards the ambiguous Dare is simply the difference in Hardy's method of presentation. Although the plot of *A Laodicean* is ultimately un-convincing, the weakness of the novel as a whole does not lie primarily in its obvious factitiousness. John Holloway has wisely observed that: 'Literature often narrates (or dramatizes) the wildest improbabilities; and failure seems almost never to reside in an improbability *per se*, but in some defect of presentation, some crudity or casualness in writing, which makes the improbable unconvincing, but would make the probable unconvincing too'.[10]

A Laodicean might perhaps best be described in Hardy's own words as being a 'mechanical and ordinary' production 'concern-

F

ing ordinary society life and habits' (*Life*, p. 149). Its basic theme—
the tension between modern progressiveness and a decadent
Romanticism—is firmly bound into the contemporary world as
Hardy knew it and as he felt himself obliged accurately to describe
it. Herein lies the fundamental problem; and it is a problem also
shared, in different degrees, by *Desperate Remedies, The Hand of
Ethelberta, Two on a Tower* and *The Well-Beloved.* There is little
doubt that Hardy was uncomfortable in depicting the foibles of a
well-defined stratum of society to a reading public eager for a
familiar and faithfully rendered portrait of such a way of life.
We know that, at the time of writing *The Hand of Ethelberta*, he
felt it was his 'duty' as a popular novelist 'to carry on his life
not as an emotion but as a scientific game' (*Life*, p. 104), and that
in order to do this he had perforce to study fashionable life so that
he might record it in detail. It was, by reason of its unadaptability
to Hardy's characteristic artistic method, a medium which he
patently disliked. Later, in 'The Profitable Reading of Fiction', he
wrote:

With regard to what may be termed the minor key of action and
speech—the unemotional, every-day doings of men—social refinement
operates upon character in a way which is oftener than not prejudicial
to vigorous portraiture, by making the exteriors of men their screen
rather than their index, as with untutored mankind. Contrasts are
disguised by the crust of conventionality, picturesqueness obliterated,
and a subjective system of description necessitated for the differentiation
of character. (*PRF*, p. 124)

A Laodicean shows, perhaps more clearly than any other of Hardy's
novels, the contrast between his objective, analytic style and his
evidently painstaking attempts to record subjectively, in the
intangibles of conventional thought and conversation, the minutiae of 'ordinary' contradictory personalities. For the length of the
first book, at least, Hardy maintains a coolly detached point of
view which is perfectly congruent with the light-hearted polemic
of his subject-matter. The basic contrast between reason and the
imagination is neatly embodied in motifs of religion (Dissenter

versus Paedobaptist), history (Puritan versus Cavalier) and human achievement (scientific versus artistic), and the struggle between the opposing sides is centred with pleasing appositeness in the capricious mind of the 'Laodicean' Paula Power.

Paula's appearance, her characteristic way of life, the architectural details of her castle home (pure Gothic touched incongruously with the modern addition of a telegraph wire) and the habitual inconsistencies of her mental attitude (practical enlightenment mingled with a *prédilection d'artiste* towards the ancient de Stancy family, who once owned the aristocratic pile in which she now lives), are all faithfully represented. The pace is leisurely, the observation sparked with some wryness, largely at the expense of feminine caprice as it appears to the logical and single-minded George Somerset, whom Paula has engaged as an architect. There are one or two mildly exciting incidents: Somerset falls into the darkened well of a stairless turret and is rescued by a dour footman; both he and Paula narrowly escape being run down by a passing railway train; Somerset suspects the existence of foul play regarding his sketches for the restoration of Stancy Castle; Paula throws a garden party. Generally, though, the action is subordinated to the matter-of-fact recording of scenes and situations.

Hardy's concentration on a method of detached and impartial observation results, in this first book, in a prosaic but delicately drawn picture of conventional manners shaped around the developing relationship between the scientific, romantically inclined Paula and the romantic, scientifically inclined Somerset. As in *Desperate Remedies*, his presentation of specific emotion is not based on a directly subjective analysis, but is shown dispassionately as being an imaginative intensification of external conditions. The polite relationship between Paula and Somerset is brought sharply into focus when Somerset, after an awkward conversation with his goddess on the respective merits of noble or resourceful ancestry, goes dutifully to examine the railway tunnel built by her engineer father. The sudden awesome nearness of the giant man-made cavern, which seemed from a distance to be nothing more than 'a little blue-black spot like a mouse-hole', is made to appear to the young architect as part of another world:

> Down Somerset plunged through the long grass, bushes, late summer flowers, moths, and caterpillars ... The tunnel that had seemed so small from the surface was a vast archway when he reached its mouth, which emitted, as a contrast to the sultry heat on the slopes of the cutting, a cool breeze, that had travelled a mile underground from the other end. Far away in the darkness of this silent subterranean corridor he could see that other end as a mere speck of light. (Bk 1, Ch. xii)

In contrast, the all-important Paula seems from her position at the top of the cutting to be tiny and almost irrelevant; her carriage is 'so small to the eye that it might have been made for a perform-ance by canaries'. However, with the sudden passing of a train through the tunnel and Somerset's inexplicable disappearance, the distant lady descends in a fright to see what has become of her architect. With the latter's assurance that everything is all right, the two turn to go back.

> They were crossing the railway to ascend by the opposite path, Somerset keeping his eye on the interior of the tunnel for safety, when suddenly arose a noise and shriek from the contrary direction behind the trees ... the probability of a train from the opposite quarter had been forgotten. It rushed past them, causing Paula's dress, hair, and ribbons to flutter violently, and blowing up the fallen leaves in a shower over their shoulders.
> Neither spoke, and they went up several steps, holding each other by the hand, till, becoming conscious of the fact, she withdrew hers ... (Bk 1, Ch. xii)

The sudden reversal of perspectives and expectations leads to an immediate imaginative transformation of accepted truths. The conventional and everyday is reduced to inconsequential smallness, both pictorially and emotively, as the overpowering unexpected-ness of instinctive feeling is effectively translated into simple physical terms. There is a similar prophetic use of the startling and other-worldly in Hardy's luminous portrayal of Somerset's first avowal of love to Paula at the latter's garden party. The couple have momentarily left the throng of guests and the dancing, and are seated by themselves in a little summerhouse, when a storm bursts, completely separating them from the others:

The side of the tent from which they had emerged still remained open, the rain streaming down between their eyes and the lighted interior of the marquee like a tissue of glass threads, the brilliant forms of the dancers passing and repassing behind the watery screen, as if they were people in an enchanted submarine palace. (Bk I, Ch. xv)

Once again, Hardy's sudden removal of his characters from the realms of predictable normality provides an imaginative mental reconstruction of their emotional state. To Somerset and Paula reality appears dreamlike, and their own situation, by its very remoteness, is doubly intensified—until Paula, with a rather strained air of practicality, breaks into the spell (' "I am so glad that my aunt had the tent lined . . ." ').

The tantalizing presence of such exquisitely realized minor episodes in the first part of this erratic novel points the more clearly to the reasons for its subsequent failure. Hardy himself explains the problem in a general note:

Among the qualities which appertain to representations of life, construed, though not distorted, by the light of the imagination— qualities which are seldom shared by views about life, however pro- found—is that of self-proof or obviousness. A representation is less susceptible of error than a disquisition; the teaching, depending as it does upon intuitive conviction, and not upon logical reasoning, is not likely to lend itself to sophistry. (*PRF*, p. 114)

The collapse of *A Laodicean* is ample illustration of the truth of such a statement in its application to Hardy's own work. For the most part, the tentative love-story of the first book, culminating in the delicately poised equivocation of the scene in the summer- house, is made up of a series of visual observations interpreted to us through the perception of the architect George Somerset. Our view of Paula is largely an impression as seen through his eyes, developing from sheer romantic fancy ('. . . so imaginative was his passion that he hardly knew a single feature of her countenance well enough to remember it in her absence') (Bk I, Ch. xi), to a concentrated awareness:

... he could not criticize or weigh her conduct; the warmth of her presence still encircled him. He recalled her face as it had looked out at him from under the white silk puffing of her black hat, and the speaking power of her eyes at the moment of danger. The breadth of that clear-complexioned forehead—almost concealed by the masses of brown hair bundled up around it—signified that if her disposition were oblique and insincere enough for trifling ... she had the intellect to do it cruelly well. (Bk I, Ch. xii)

Despite his use of what is ostensibly a subjectively orientated viewpoint, Hardy's approach is essentially one of objective representation, couched in simple, precise language. However, with the partial abandonment of the eminently normal Somerset as a useful frame of reference, and the subsequent reliance on various 'unlikely beings' to facilitate the contrivance of an exciting serial narrative, there is a radical change in perspective. From then on there is an increasingly discursive style of writing, necessitated by the sudden movement away from what is basically a truthful, if circumscribed, portrait of a changing society.

As in all Hardy's novels, the story-line of *A Laodicean* is dependent largely on a pattern of chance, coincidence and deception, where the probable is sacrificed willingly for an insistence that in life anything is possible. In this novel, though, there is little to justify our acceptance of the unexpected. True, there are at first implications of mystery and drama. Paula's castle, with its grim dungeons, crypts and arrow-slits, and its multitudinous paintings of the de Stancy ancestors (portraits casually mentioned as being executed by 'those who usually appear in such places; Holbein, Jansen, and Vandyck; Sir Peter, Sir Godfrey, Sir Joshua, and Sir Thomas') is adequately supplied with all the Gothic trimmings of romance and intrigue, but all is too clearly established by such specific detail as being 'historically true' in a world where beautiful or antique objects are merely the indications of material wealth. There is scarcely any background of fantasy or mystery, overt or suggested, in the transcription of the conflicting forces inherent in a particular way of life; the whole is geared towards a believable manifestation of reality. Accordingly, the careless insertion of the multi-lingual fanatic William Dare and the pock-marked Abner Power into the restrained and civilized world of the hero and heroine has a rather odd effect. Both Dare and Power are explicitly introduced as creatures of mystery and uncertain provenance, neither of them being possessed of those qualities which Hardy designates as 'English'. Dare is characterized by his unusual physiognomy (his hair is fringed 'in the fashion some-times affected by the other sex'), his indeterminate age, and his seemingly sinister cosmopolitan background (' "I have lived" ', he says, ' "mostly in India, Malta, Gibraltar, the Ionian Islands, and Canada" '). In accordance with Hardy's tendency to depict rather than to explain the intricacies of personality, there is a rather naive assumption that such incredible characters should *look* incredible, this being their outward brand of abnormality. So, too, Abner Power, that 'breathing refrigerator' who is likewise sworn to cooling the relationship between Paula and Somerset, is shown to us as a weird being, a stranger of terrible but intriguing appearance:

His visage, which was of the colour of light porphyry, had little of its original surface left; it was a face which had been the plaything of strange fires or pestilences, that had moulded to whatever shape they chose his originally supple skin, and left it pitted, puckered, and seamed like a dried watercourse. (Bk III, Ch. ix)

Nevertheless, holding fast to his theory that all characters should be believable, Hardy quickly moderates his presentation of these bewildering harbingers of evil by neatly assimilating their strangeness into the background of normality. The unctuous Dare is soon established as being Captain de Stancy's bastard son, while the foreign death's-head, appearances notwithstanding, is accepted unquestioningly into the household at Stancy Castle, where he speedily exerts an astonishing influence, being, we discover, simply the lovely Paula's long-lost uncle. With the human associa-tions of these strategic characters thus unswervingly established,

Hardy is able logically to point out psychological reasons for the apparent unnaturalness of their actions. We are carefully shown, for example, that it is Dare's illegitimacy which makes him so peculiar, and which explains his unscrupulous scheming on his father's behalf. ' "I have acted according to my illumination" ', he remarks to Captain de Stancy. ' "What can you expect of a man born to dishonour?" ' (Bk v, Ch. v). Dare's unsubtle efforts to interest his disinherited father in the new owner of Stancy Castle are in the same way facilitated by the fact that the strangely diffident Captain is suffering from a severe repression induced by his own vow—made in deference to the boy's dead and unwed mother—' "to forswear the society, and if possible the sight, of women young and attractive" '. The ravishing spectacle of Paula Power doing gymnastic exercises in a 'pink flannel costume' has, however, a remarkable effect on the Captain's starved brain. This startling vision is the involuntary cause of what Dare describes as ' "a purely chemical process" '; the result is the total restoration of sexual instinct and a mad ardour on the part of the fascinated victim to win the hand of the sprightly heiress. De Stancy hereafter abolishes all his former resolves. ' "A man again after eighteen years" ', he murmurs, tipping out all his bottles of mineral water and toasting the fair object of his passion in a glass of ruby red wine (Bk III, Ch. i).

Paula's Laodicean indecision, her inability to choose whether she wishes to base her life on a theory of progressive modernism or on a romantic conception of ancient glories, is thus trammelled adroitly into a simple choice between two lovers. Henceforward, Hardy's basic theme serves only the slightest of functions, as its conflicting elements are incorporated almost solely into the working out of the plot. With this direct reversal of technique, Hardy's concern is no longer with the transcription of the 'intuitively true', but rather to establish an incontrovertible reasonableness. The artistic inadequacy of *A Laodicean* lies not so much in his projection of an obviously questionable reality, as in his determined refusal to allow any margin for poetic disbelief. Thus, Paula's fortuitous interest in a seventeenth-century portrait which is later shown to resemble significantly her would-be suitor, de Stancy, is self-consciously justified as being 'a coincidence common enough in fact, though scarcely credited in chronicles'; and the gallant Captain's doggedness in pushing the resemblance as far as possible (to the extent of dressing in the ancestral armour, reciting copious verse, and pretending to fall on his sword in imitation of the portrait's ill-fated original) is described with dryly unromantic exactness:

He set down the candles, and asking the girls to withdraw for a moment, was inside the upper part of the suit of armour in incredibly quick time. Going then and placing himself in front of a low-hanging painting near the original, so as to be enclosed by the frame while covering the figure, arranging the sword as in the one above, and setting the light that it might fall in the right direction, he recalled them; when he put the question, 'Is the resemblance strong?' (Bk iii, Ch. ii)

De Stancy's enhancement in Paula's eyes by the imaginative detail of his family likeness is potentially an effective and revealing illustration of both characters, but it is pushed to pantomimic absurdity by Hardy's laborious emphasis on accuracy. There is a similar bathos in the earlier revelation of William Dare's sinister potentialities. When Somerset's rival architect, James Havill, attempts to uncover the mystery of the tattoo on the 'man-boy' Dare's breast, the latter calmly retaliates by pointing a revolver at the unfortunate man's head. Havill finally breaks down, crying, ' "Do put away that thing! It is too ghastly to produce in a respectable bedroom. Why do you carry it?" ', to which the imperturbable Dare replies, with the sort of unanswerable conviction which predominates throughout the novel, ' "Cosmopolites always do" ' (Bk ii, Ch. iii).

In the absence of a setting specifically depicted as being conducive to imaginative fantasy, Hardy is constrained to develop his improbabilities of plot from the relatively uncompromising elements of his painstakingly constructed 'real' world, a contemporary setting of dinner-parties and Continental journeys, of steam-trains and modern Non-Conformist chapels. Hence, to the end of maintaining a reasonable congruity, the twisting of the real is ingeniously based around such things as may be explained 'scientifically' within their immediate context: a concocted telegram, the insertion of a false announcement in a newspaper, or an artful trick photograph which represents the sober George Somerset to his beloved Paula as having 'the distorted features and wild attitude of a man advanced in intoxication' (Bk v, Ch. iv). Yet somehow it is all too easily explicable, too crude; the mystery is gone, and there is something of the side-show about it all. Hardy's diligent attempts to reduce his more improbable situations to believable proportions often result in an unintentionally humorous incongruity. We feel more entertained than edified, for instance, when the local photographer displays his samples of misrepresentative portraiture to little Charlotte de Stancy:

'... There's one,' he said, throwing out a portrait card from a drawer. 'That represents the German Emperor in a violent passion: this one shows the Prime Minister out of his mind; this the Pope of Rome the worse for liquor.' (Bk v, Ch. xiii)

In *A Laodicean*, Hardy's use of the startling or the grotesque seems to have no other artistic purpose than of revealing to us the astonishing depths of man's gullibility. His strenuous involvement with proving the bare probabilities of his story leads inevitably to a superabundance of meditative theorizing, incidental padding, authorial explanations and asides. Events unwind in a framework which has essentially little to do with the mental conflict of the characters; action and emotion alike are replaced by an extensive and often verbose method of reporting in which the likelihood or the unlikelihood of events are secondary considerations, and all the characters seem to converse in accents indistinguishable from Hardy's own.

In contrast, the relative effectiveness of quite obviously 'contrived' incidents in the 'Novels of Character and Environment' is in most cases achieved through the detachment of the author, and the direct emotional credibility of the characters involved. Take, for example, the scene of Bathsheba's confrontation with Troy over Fanny Robin's coffin in *Far from the Madding Crowd*. The episode gains its enormous impact, despite the blatancy of its melodrama, largely because the improbable ghoulishness of the situation is translated into terms of Bathsheba's own poignant, intensely *living* sense of personal outrage: ' "*You will, Frank, kiss me too!*" ' (Ch. xliii). Or, as proof that implausibility need not imply artistic failure, consider the tact with which Hardy represents the death of the insubstantial Alec d'Urberville merely by a stark, symbolic blot of blood, which is at once perfectly in harmony with its subject and with the rich network of imagery which unifies all the disparate elements of the tale. By the use of such a simple summarizing device, Hardy avoids the inevitable bathos which would result if this imaginative tissue of lies were to be dragged into the daylight. The crises and revelations of *A Laodicean* have perhaps the virtue of being explicable in factual terms (whoever heard of blood dripping *right through* a ceiling?) but they are infinitely less convincing by their very matter-of-factness. Dare's flamboyant reminder to his father of the circumstances of his birth is, in its odd mixture of the prosaic and the sensational, incongruously comic:

He threw open his shirt-front, and revealed tattooed on his breast the letters DE STANCY; the same marks which Havill had seen in the bedroom by the light of the moon.
The captain rather winced at the sight. 'Well, well,' he said hastily, 'that's enough . . .' (Bk II, Ch. v)

Often, in the more obviously fabricated incidents, it seems that Hardy deliberately avoids the problem of portraying a genuine human instinct, and substitutes, more appropriately (as he did, too, in *The Hand of Ethelberta*), a sly, rationalizing humour. ' "You feel the room close, Mr Power?" ', inquires the solicitous Dare, pausing in his flowing blackmail speech. ' "No," ' replies the other, with ghastly politeness. ' "I suffer from attacks of perspiration whenever I sit in a consecrated edifice—that's all. Pray go on" ' (Bk v, Ch. xi). The same method, less crudely used, can be observed in the last book of the novel, where Paula's pursuit of her elusive lover through several countries is treated with a delightful sense of the absurd and a corresponding freshening of life amongst the main protagonists. Humorous or not, however, the humanization of the artificial has its limits, and Captain de Stancy's resigned plea to his evil offspring: ' "Promise me that you will be a better boy!" ' (Bk v, Ch. v), in no way increases the latter's credibility for us.

With the introduction into *A Laodicean* of an obviously contrived makeshift plot and obviously contrived *personae*, the presence and function of the author undergo a noticeable change. He becomes less concerned with the imaginative transformation of the real, and is forced, by reason of his new stance, to make the artificial and extraordinary appear, however unconvincingly, to be at least a reasonable facsimile of the truth. Suddenly there is no consistent point of reference, no single all-enveloping perspective; instead, Hardy's ability to transcribe the unseen by reference to the seen, his skill at evoking thought and emotion by translating them into terms of the material world as it is uniquely observed by him, is distorted into an ingenious exercise in false logic. In his portrayal of 'ordinary' human beings—such as George Somerset— Hardy's delineation of character is achieved largely through showing scenes and events as they appear *to them*—in other words, by maintaining a series of individual perspectives. When he attempts to do the same thing with characters who are empty and unbelievable in themselves, the system breaks down irretrievably, and there is an awkward necessity for authorial intrusion, a method which in *A Laodicean* extends dismally to the narration of most of the story, with a few exceptional incidents. The vivid representative dramatization of his characters' lives in relation to the basic theme of the novel tends to dwindle into dryly discursive analysis, often thinly disguised as being the mental or verbal observation of the characters themselves. Even at moments of crisis, the implications and possible developments of events are diligently expatiated on by Hardy himself, in a ponderous style quite at variance with the dictates of a fast-moving tale of intrigue. The increased emphasis on *telling* rather than on *showing* results in an enforced dependence on style as a method of characterization. Yet, if they are to be judged on the 'subjective system' of their description, the transcription of their immediate thoughts and speech, then Dare, Havill, Abner Power and a host of supernumeraries might be said not to exist at all; they relate significantly to nothing more than their roles in the story, and each of them (with the exception of Dare, who appropriately returns, ghost-like, to set his ancestral home on fire) is made conveniently to disappear when his immediate usefulness has come to an end.

It is clear, from readings of both *Desperate Remedies* and *A Laodicean*, that Hardy's peculiarly visual means of expression can function successfully only when the overtly fictitious is shown to be firmly established within the limits of human mental or physical experience. His concern, always, is with the specific vision rather than with the minute workings of the mind, but in all his work, from *Desperate Remedies* to *Jude the Obscure*, there are drab spots where the conviction of the imagination falters and the author must openly intercede to explain, cover up or direct the plot into new channels. One of Hardy's recent critics has said of him that 'he goes away from reality to try to return to it by a long detour';[11] the essential point, however, is that the reality must be there in the first place—the detour may be long, but it must develop naturally from what *is*, and it must be based on imaginative rather than on logical truth. The partial failure of the weaker novels is, I think, largely owing to the fact that in each of them Hardy has tried to force a story from the barest of logical possibilities. Whatever the original idea, the result in each case is a fictitious mental fabrication, a complicated welding together of stray ends. Plot and characterization lean unsteadily on each other, and have no larger real or imaginative background from which they take their natural derivation. The 'Novels of Character and Environment', as their name suggests, take their 'truth' from the substantial and all-embracing Wessex countryside, the essential credibility of which gives some solidity to even the flimsiest of romantic falsehoods. The advance in artistry of these novels is chiefly in Hardy's method of using the variable and contrary real

Under the Greenwood Tree
and The Trumpet-Major

Deserting the more conventional, and far less agreeable, field of imaginative creation . . . the author has produced a series of rural pictures full of life and genuine colouring, and drawn with a distinct minuteness . . .

Horace Moule, in *The Saturday Review*, 28 September 1872

(i)

Hardy's art is represented at its simplest level in *Under the Greenwood Tree* and *The Trumpet-Major*—works which are frequently dismissed as being distinctly minor achievements in his canon. His first wife doubtless summed up many a critic's opinion of their worth in her rather inane exclamation about *The Trumpet-Major*: 'Ah, yes! That's one of the pretty ones.'[1] Joseph Warren Beach, in his brief analyses of half a century ago, calls *Under the Greenwood Tree* 'a charming study',[2] and *The Trumpet-Major* 'a light and pleasing confection . . . —a graceful diversion and unbending of genius—not altogether unworthy of the hand that could do so much more serious work'.[3] Some twenty years later, Q. D. Leavis, representing the so-called 'New Critics', remarks scornfully of the earlier novel that '[its] facetious tone . . . and its being made entirely out of Hardy's comic-relief material without anything to be relieved, anything (that is) which comes from the deeper and more vital sources of his experiences and interests, must strike any critical reader',[4] while Lord David Cecil, writing at the same time, proclaims it unequivocally to be 'one of Hardy's most faultless works'.[5]

Eight years separate the publication dates of these two novels, but nevertheless they have much in common. Both are stories of light, often humorous romance, barely touched by extravagances of coincidence and melodrama, seldom straying beyond the bounds of probability or into the realms of passion and tragedy. Curiously, though, both exhibit a consistency of stylistic polish and pleasing imagery, with few incongruous lapses. Their tone is familiar, warm, deceptively simple. I say 'deceptively' because I feel that their *artistic* merit is at least comparable with that of those novels in which Hardy's 'view of life' is more explicitly and forcefully illustrated. These shorter and more frivolous tales are mere sketches in comparison, but show in their very delicacy and lightness some of the qualities of vision which are often so drastically misinterpreted in the more ambitious works. John F. Danby goes so far as to say of *Under the Greenwood Tree* that it is 'not less deep and not less transcendent' than *Jude the Obscure*, even though it was not designed as a profound work.[6] Hardy himself later regretted that he had not tackled his subject in more depth, writing in the Preface to the 1912 'Wessex' Edition that

In rereading the narrative after a long interval there occurs the inevitable reflection that the realities out of which it was spun were material for another kind of study of this little group of church musicians than is found in the chapters here penned so lightly, even so farcically and flippantly at times.

Nevertheless, despite their avowedly limited aims, both novels are unique in that they reveal, in almost unadulterated form, Hardy's basic technique of implication through simple pictorial devices. They are simply portraits of an age or of a society, whose 'point' is made almost solely by subtle widening and narrowing of perspective, and by the corresponding variations of the author's attitude as he presents his material in different lights—sympathetic, ironical, pathetic or purely objective. Their artistic importance lies, above all, in the consistency of Hardy's rôle as a sympathetic onlooker, and in the unity which this careful detachment imparts to his calculatedly omniscient vision.

Although both *Under the Greenwood Tree* and *The Trumpet-*

Major are ostensibly (though in a limited sense) novels of 'manners', the observation of individual characters is less important than the presentation of a larger tapestry of society, shown in the developing framework of history and tradition. Against this background each separate life is inevitably portrayed as rather comic or pathetic in its transient importance, though at the same time it is given artistic magnitude as a vital part of the continuing pattern of life. Superficially, at least, these so-called 'minor' novels present an intensely real portrait of life, sharply detailed with a conscientious reliance on sensory and visual images, the precise verbal reproduction of light, sound, and colour. In retrospect, however, the 'reality' of both works is seen to be tinged with a flavour of extreme artifice, and the colour and detail become secondary to the framework surrounding it. Largely, this is due to the fact that in *Under the Greenwood Tree* and *The Trumpet-Major* there is scarcely any middle distance. Physical appearance and action 'stand for' and encompass the subtleties of thought and emotion, which then become part of the larger pattern of the story, relating to the universal rather than to the particular. The individual character is firmly related to his background, and is chiefly functional in helping to create the atmosphere of the total living society, from which he cannot be separated.

For this reason, we cannot enter creatively into the lives of the characters; rather, Hardy shows them to us as if they are on a stage. In the later novels, this method occasionally acts as a serious barrier to the portrayal of character in any depth; here, though, it is a calculated advantage and the invisible screen between audience and play becomes one of Hardy's most successful 'effects'. In *The Trumpet-Major*, especially, it is an historical distancing, so that the final impression is of a whole world, recreated in miniature but, as in a theatre, rather brighter than life. It is almost as if, through Hardy's eyes, we see the characters and their actions through the wrong end of a telescope. We are continually aware of the all-pervading authorial intrusion because of the consciously created sense of time in which the novels live, and we must always recognize the fact that for all their deceptive brilliance these small

G

societies are ephemeral—infinitesimal fragments in the larger pattern of history and tradition.

It is because of this that *The Trumpet-Major* has, on reflection, a misty, slightly melancholy aura. In spite of its apparent lively progression of happenings, we are reminded always that it is over and done, a step back into history. Similarly, in *Under the Greenwood Tree*, the immediacy of festivities and gatherings and warm fires is frequently only a backcloth for stories of the past, of men now dead, of family traits still recognizable, of old sayings and reminiscences. These are essentially pictures in time; *Under the Greenwood Tree* looks backwards and is mellowed by silent knowledge of what has gone before and what must inevitably follow, while *The Trumpet-Major* gains a certain nostalgia from our realization that at the time of telling even now the characters are already dust. A gentle yet massive irony pervades every aspect of the apparent living reality. Our anticipation is conditioned by our fore-knowledge.

It is in order to achieve this effect that Hardy makes extensive use in both novels of techniques which objectify and distance his subjects, so that the ironic framework is preserved. In *Under the Greenwood Tree*, his method is avowedly pictorial. As the subtitle, 'A Rural Painting of the Dutch School' suggests, it attempts to portray life in the mellow, homely and detailed fashion of the Dutch Masters; always serene, always domestic, unexaggerated and natural. It is a stylized realism, concentrating only on one aspect and excluding all that is not relevant. The story unwinds serenely within its own created world, in which every detail is part of the whole, and in which the only contrasts are of the new and the old. Nevertheless, the particular scene is less memorable than the entire work. There is none of that effective crystallizing of meaning into separate vividly etched symbolic pictures: the whole novel is a painting of one thing, reflected in all its various details. The vignettes of the tale are nearly always specific descriptions of places or of activities—nutting, sewing, bee-keeping, dancing, playing in the 'quire', but the essence of each scene is conveyed more by word and gesture than by precise line and detail. The bulk of the novel is in expository style and the progress of the plot comes to us mainly in the words of the characters themselves. Hardy's most obvious pictorial techniques are those which tend to throw the characters in relief, to isolate them from their moving background and to place them in a perspective not of their own time. Suddenly made static against the flux of seasons and generations, they are shown as at once important and negligible, as individuals and as representatives of all men. Thus we see Dick Dewy first as a black figure silhouetted like cardboard against the sky and yet bound inextricably to the earth; then the members of the quire are referred to as 'advancing against the sky in flat outlines, which suggested some processional design on Greek or Etruscan pottery' (Pt I, Ch. i). Fancy Day is seen by the quire as something akin to a spiritual vision, framed as she is by the window architrave and 'unconsciously illuminating her countenance to a vivid brightness by a candle she held in her left hand, close to her face'. She appears unreal: ' "If she'd been rale wexwork she couldn't ha' been comelier," said Michael Mail' (Pt I, Ch. v). The same effect of fixing and distancing is seen in Hardy's description of Mr Penny as 'a framed portrait of a shoemaker by some modern Moroni':

He sat facing the road, with a boot on his knees and the awl in his hand, only looking up for a moment as he stretched out his arms and bent forward at the pull, when his spectacles flashed in the passer's face with a shine of flat whiteness, and then returned again to the boot as usual. Rows of lasts, small and large, stout and slender, covered the wall which formed the background, in the extreme shadow of which a kind of dummy was seen sitting, in the shape of an apprentice with a string tied round his hair (probably to keep it out of his eyes). (Pt II, Ch. ii)

Generally, Hardy's descriptions of his characters tend to be purely surface ones, with a Rembrandt-like interest in texture and peculiarities. Mr Shiner, for instance, is permanently depicted for us as 'a character principally composed of a crimson stare, vigorous breath, and a watch-chain, with a mouth hanging on a dark smile but never smiling' (Pt I, Ch. vii). Mrs Day is briefly outlined as having 'an ordinary woman's face, iron-grey hair, hardly any hips, and a great deal of cleanliness in a broad white apron-string as it appeared upon the waist of her dark stuff dress' (Pt II, Ch. vi).

Wholeness of portraiture is conspicuously absent. These are people destined to be remembered by their most obvious features: the rest dissolves into a mist. By showing them as they are remembered, Hardy paints them as if for all time, carefully relating them to the past and the present, casting an imaginative depth of time around them and at the same time suggesting their impermanence on the face of the earth. The very form of the novel, divided into seasonal episodes, shows the rhythm of natural processes, the cycle of birth, fruition and death, against which the lives of men take on only a transient significance. Dick's wooing of Fancy, the beginning, slackening and growth of their love, are reflected in the natural pattern of living things, as ephemeral and as permanent as the blossoming and withering of plants. The importance of their romance to them is not nearly as vital to us; we never become fully involved, but see them with Hardy's ironic fore-knowledge. Dick, in the blindness of his idyllic happiness, cannot possibly realize that his life will to some extent follow the same old pattern:

Dick wondered how it was that when people were married they could be so blind to romance; and was quite certain that if he ever took to wife that dear impossible Fancy, he and she would never be so dreadfully practical and undemonstrative of the Passion as his mother and father were. The most extraordinary thing was that all the fathers and mothers he knew were just as undemonstrative as his own. (Pt I, Ch. viii)

Everywhere the present moment is contrasted, if somewhat facetiously, with the past and the future. The clear and memorable impressions of faces and actions must take their proper places within this enveloping frame of reference.

In both novels, it is the muted background of rustic characters which gives solidarity and coherence to the lighter and more clearly etched individuals whose fortunes create the moving plot.

In *Under the Greenwood Tree* the quire and the Dewy family, represented as they are by three generations in whose time ways of life have changed little, epitomize the stability of accepted traditions. Against this prevailing norm are set the main characters in the romantic sequence—Dick, Fancy Day, Shiner and Parson Maybold. In the setting up of this pattern, Hardy makes subtle use of pictorial technique, subordinating the mass of the quire and bringing out the more important characters in sharp relief, each in order of importance. Dick is first singled out for us at the beginning of the book, then later the quire, visiting in turn the residences of Fancy, Shiner and Maybold, presages the course of the action in which each character will figure. Fancy, as befits her role as heroine, is attractively illuminated; Shiner, relatively unimportant, appears first as an angry voice and then as a voiceless shape, and the neutral vicar is identifiable only by his refined accents.

Of these, the only character who develops in the very slightest degree is Fancy herself, but her development is shown by Hardy to be not very profound. Although ultimately she does marry Dick Dewy, her final act in the story is to resolve never to reveal to him her previous decision to marry Maybold. Her evasiveness, typified by her flirtations and indecisions throughout the novel, remains her chief quality, and Dick is, we feel, to remain pleasantly deceived all his life. Yet, in spite of this, Fancy is the one 'moving' character in the gallery of portraits. Against the solid, warm, half-toned villagers, with their slow and redundant speech and their stable philosophies of life, she appears as continually vacillating, shadowy, chameleon, described throughout in quick impressionist touches. Even her name, 'Fancy', implies a butterfly brittleness; we see her as a fluttering combination of flowers, curls and feathers, indistinct and indefinite. At the crux of the story, the scene in which she plays the new organ in the church while the old quire looks on, Hardy exaggerates this rather artificial quality. Dick, in his sombre funeral suit, sees her as a 'divinity', floating down the school steps 'in the form of a nebulous collection of colours inclining to blue', but Hardy places our sympathies entirely with the quire, now scattered round the church 'with humbled hearts'. In the light of their disbanded solidarity Fancy's performance is shown to us as having something of the unnatural accomplishment of a circus pony:

... they stood and watched the curls of hair trailing down the back of the successful rival, and the waving of her feather as she swayed her head ... But, whether from prejudice or unbiassed judgement, the venerable body of musicians could not help thinking that the simpler notes they had been wont to bring forth were more in keeping with the simplicity of their old church than the crowded chords and interludes it was her pleasure to produce. (Pt IV, Ch. v)

Although on the surface the world of Mellstock appears in many respects idyllic, it is touched throughout with deepening shadows of the strange and mysterious, the deviation from the norm, the suggestion that not all is as it appears, and that the life of man hovers precariously between the realizable and the inexplicable. In *Under the Greenwood Tree* this effect is all the stronger because the work does not stray from its one level. Its centre and controlling force is the life of the village, which in turn is governed by the cycle of the seasons. The slightly grimmer side of the pastoral is itself a part of the same sequence. The movement of time, for instance, is not stressed by Hardy as the tragedy of the inevitable, but is fitted into the normal, matter-of-fact scheme of things. Death is not more significant or tragical than life, and is accepted in the same way as the tranter reacts to Maybold's suggestion that the quire be disbanded: ' "Well then, Mr Mayble, since death's to be, we'll die like men any day you name (excusing my common way)" ' (Pt II, Ch. iv). Even in the smallest details, the process of death and survival is a mystery, unalterable and inexplicable, but necessary:

'The proper way to take honey, so that the bees be neither starved nor murdered, is a puzzling matter,' said the keeper steadily.

'I should like never to take it from them,' said Fancy.

'But 'tis the money,' said Enoch musingly. 'For without money man is a shadder!' (Pt IV, Ch. ii)

Strangely at variance with this acceptance of the major forces of destiny is the villagers' suspicion of 'differentness'. The characters of the witch, Elizabeth Endorfield, and of Fancy's father, Geoffrey Day, provide the touch of fantasy and incongruity beloved by Hardy. The former, with her red cloak and pointed chin, is shrewder and more intelligent than the rest of the rustic population and shares with keeper Day a quality which their contemporaries describe as 'deep'. The Days' house, with its duplication of every article it contains and the almost human clocks continually at war with one another, is described initially as a sort of fairy cottage:

A curl of wood-smoke came from the chimney and drooped over the roof like a blue feather in a lady's hat; and the sun shone obliquely upon the patch of grass in front, which reflected its brightness through the open doorway and up the staircase opposite, lighting up each riser with a shiny green radiance and leaving the top of each step in shade. (Pt II, Ch. vi)

The attractive and mysterious qualities of its inhabitants are reflected by the novel way in which even the house looks at things:

The window was set with thickly-leaded diamond glazing, formed, especially in the lower panes, of knotty glass of various shades of green. Nothing was better known to Fancy than the extravagant manner in which these circular knots or eyes distorted everything seen through them from the outside—lifting hats from heads, shoulders from bodies; scattering the spokes of cart-wheels, and bending the straight fir-trunks into semi-circles. (Pt II, Ch. vi)

Geoffrey Day himself, a man whose reputation is such that even his silence is taken as being full of wisdom, is appropriately grotesque in appearance: 'His nose had been thrown backwards by a blow in a poaching fray, so that when the sun was low and shining in his face people could see far into his head' (Pt II, Ch. vi).

At the end of the tale it seems that perhaps Fancy, or at least the unthinking youthfulness she epitomizes, has triumphed in more ways than one. Spring, the time of her wedding with Dick, is a little more than a seasonal renewal of warmth and rebirth. It is a time when

country people go to bed among nearly naked trees . . . and awake next morning among green ones; when the landscape appears embarrassed with the sudden weight and brilliancy of its leaves; when the night-jar comes and strikes up for the summer his tune of one note; when the apple trees have bloomed, and the roads and orchard-grass become spotted with fallen petals; when the faces of the delicate flowers are darkened and their heads weighed down by the throng of honey-bees, which increase their humming till humming is too mild a term for the all-pervading sound; and when cuckoos, blackbirds and sparrows, that have hitherto been merry and respectful neighbours, become noisy and persistent inmates. (Pt v, Ch. i)

Time has passed with a vengeance, and the new season is perhaps rather more brilliant and new and noisy than the older inhabitants had expected. The change of seasons is present not only in the appearance of the trees and the noise of the birds, but also in the lives of the people. Suddenly everything is sharper, clearer, louder, as the old makes way for the new. Hardy's final group-scene is of the older villagers sitting around the trunk of the tree in a space 'allotted rather grudgingly by the young ones, who were greedy of pirouetting room', reciting 'stories of great impressiveness' (Pt v, Ch. ii).

Although the substance of the work is slight, Hardy has treated his commonplace subject with sympathy and subtlety. The result is a faithful representation of everyday life, which, despite its apparent simplicity, is irradiated with a sense of the mystery to be found in the smallest things.

(ii)

The Trumpet-Major differs from *Under the Greenwood Tree* in its far greater emphasis on plot and action, and in its deliberate re-construction of an historical period. True to its chronicle form, it consists of a series of bright, highly coloured tableaux interwoven with a story which is entertaining and briskly told. To this end, the prime features of the novel are its vigour and energy, and the smoothness of Hardy's transferences from picture to action, from reminiscence to immediacy.

The depth of the work lies almost certainly, again, in its

orientation towards the past and the future; the fortunes of the individual characters are unimportant compared with the greater theme of the mass destiny of man. Separately, the characters are stereotyped enough not to warrant intensive examination. The struggle of three men for one woman repeats in a more complicated fashion the plot of *Under the Greenwood Tree* and the combination of the good brother, the flighty brother, the blustering coward and the pretty, rather vapid heroine is a common enough phenomenon in the tradition of light romantic novelettes.

Perhaps because of his comparative uninvolvement with the development of his characters and because of his intense interest in making the period come alive, Hardy is, as Douglas Brown has said, 'more than usually absorbed and delighted by the mere invention and relation of this tale'.[7] His selection of material is emotional rather than objective; in his 1895 preface to the novel he remarks that 'the lingering remains' of the predicted invasion 'brought to my imagination in early childhood the state of affairs at the date of the war more vividly than volumes of history could have done'. Huge events have a nightmare, half-unrealized quality which is almost unimportant beside the continuing cycle of generations of living. The more realizable and lasting things of life, those things man has touched or created, reflect his presence more surely than his thoughts or his actions. In his descriptions of the small world of Overcombe, Hardy combines exact historical detail with an amused observation of reality. His portrayal of the Mill, for example, carries with it a mixture of the elegiac and facetious, as the miller and his employee are shown immobilized in history, still and ghostly additions to the architecture of their home, which endures long after they are gone:

Overcombe Mill presented at one end the appearance of a hard-worked house slipping into the river, and at the other end of an idle, genteel place, half-cloaked with creepers at this time of the year, and having no visible connexion with flour. It had hips instead of gables, giving it a roundshouldered look, four chimneys with no smoke coming out of them, two zig-zag cracks in the wall, several open windows, with a looking glass here and there inside, showing its warped back to the passer-by; snowy dimity curtains waving in the draught; two mill doors, one above the other, the upper enabling a person to step out upon nothing at a height of ten feet from the ground; a gaping arch vomiting the river, and a lean, long-nosed fellow looking out from the mill doorway, who was the hired grinder, except when a bulging fifteen-stone man occupied the same place, namely, the miller himself. (Ch. ii)

In the picture as it appears in time, the Mill and its owner have changed characteristics; the Mill itself is humanized and living, and for comic and historic purposes the miller is only a decorative superstructure. The feeling of immediate and continuing existence is, however, a calculated deception, and we know instinctively that this is merely the static picture of a memory. The impression is nowhere explicit; in the very vividness and humour of the picture lies its deeper implication.

Sometimes, however, Hardy deliberately intrudes into his tale with a reminder that the historical perspective is ever-present. In the middle of the story he suddenly 'freezes' an action, a scene or a gesture, indicating by this reference to remembered detail that the circumstances or the person have long since vanished. Here such a switch in perspective brings an unexpected wistfulness to the gaiety of the miller's 'little entertainment':

The present writer, to whom this party has been described times out of number by members of the Loveday family and other aged people now passed away, can never enter the old living-room . . . without beholding the genial scene through the mists of the seventy or eighty years that intervene between then and now. First and brightest to the eye are the dozen candles, scattered about regardless of expense, and kept well snuffed by the miller, who walks around the room at intervals of five minutes, snuffers in hand, and nips each wick with great precision, and with something of an executioner's grim look upon his face as he closes the snuffers upon the neck of the candle. Next to the candle-light show the red and blue coats and white breeches of the soldiers—nearly twenty of them in all besides the ponderous Derriman—the head of the latter, and, indeed, the heads of all who are standing up, being in dangerous proximity to the black beams of the ceiling. There is not one among them who would attach any meaning to 'Vittoria', or gather from the syllables 'Waterloo' the remotest idea of his own glory or death. Next appears the correct and innocent Anne, little thinking what things Time has in store for her at no great distance off. (Ch. v)

From the present tense, the irony of which is that it immediately places the scene in the past, Hardy slips back into the historic time of the action with the direct speech of Derriman, whose approach Anne has been fearing in the picture, and from this the action progresses as if it had not been interrupted. The tone fluctuates throughout this passage from gay to reflective, from flippant to sombre, as we move from Hardy's objectifying distance back into the minds and actions of the stilled characters, and then back into dramatic reality. The details of practical living (the candles are numerous 'regardless of expense') add to the poignancy of our knowledge, and yet Hardy is saved from sentimentality by his basic humour of approach—as in his picture of the miller grimly snuffing the candles, taking on the responsibility of one who is creating time rather than being caught in its flood.

To the characters themselves, material things matter more than abstract possibilities. The soldiers live for the day, little thinking of what might happen to them, and the villagers, content to use 'hurdle-sticks and cabbage-stumps' in place of rifles for their military drill, are more concerned by the fact that the choir might be starting without them than that Boney might be marching down at that very minute.

The predominantly domestic atmosphere is established at the very beginning, with the slightly tongue-in-cheek description of Anne, on a fine summer morning, working at her window, and gazing idly out of the open casement. The first intimation that something larger than life is about to enter this quiet sunshiny world is given with appropriate inconsequence: 'her attention was attracted by the sudden rising and running away of the sheep squatted on the down' (Ch. i). The coming of the soldiers has little or nothing to do with war and death and unpleasantness. They appear like creatures of another world: 'The burnished chains, buckles and plates of their trappings shone like little looking-glasses, and the blue, red and white about them was unsubdued by weather or wear'. It is with the gentlest ridicule that Hardy, describing the spectacle as it appears in Anne's eyes, remarks that the troopers 'rode proudly on, as if nothing less than crowns and empires ever concerned their magnificent minds'. His treatment of them is deliberately ponderous; he shows them as splendid puppets, important uniforms, who perform their mechanical actions 'obviously according to some preconcerted scheme'. It is a clever mingling of his omniscient view with her romantic and uninformed ideas. To Anne, watching from the window, the oncoming of the cavalry is mysterious and wonderful as she sees more and more of them, enveloped in a cloud of dust, 'their arms and accoutrements reflecting the sun through the haze in faint flashes, stars and streaks of light'. Her reaction as she calls to her mother, ' "Here's such a fine sight! What does it mean?" ' is Hardy's first indication that in life the real meaning is frequently secondary to the glory and splendour of the moment. 'Life', to the credulous and unambitious villagers, is a bright moving spectacle, something they may stare and wonder at, and perhaps imagine themselves taking part in. It is a brilliant pageant enacted before their eyes, a kind of dream-world in which the actors are larger than life. Later in the story, the king and queen, en route for Budmouth, appear, are analysed, cheered and marvelled at, and disappear, more imagined than appreciated. Widow Garland, struggling to get the smallest glimpse of the royal party, is satisfied with a smattering of unimportant detail which, enlivened by the imagination and an aura of something more than human, surpasses genuine knowledge:

After the review came a sham fight, during which action the crowd dispersed . . . enabling Widow Garland to get still clearer glimpses of the King, and his handsome charger, and the head of the Queen, and the elbows and shoulders of the princesses in the carriages, and fractional parts of General Garth and the Duke of Cumberland; which sights gave her much gratification. She tugged at her daughter at every opportunity, exclaiming, 'Now you can see his feather!' 'There's her hat!' 'There's her Majesty's India muslin shawl!' in a minor form of ecstasy . . . (Ch. xii)

When Anne herself accidentally meets the king, he appears little more than a kindly pantomime figure, though scarcely different in appearance from anyone else. Even the main characters in the novel are seen by the anonymous 'crowd' as possessing the romantic qualities indicated by the manner of their dress:

Anne went back towards the pavement with her trumpet-major, whom all the girls envied her, so fine-looking a soldier was he . . . his artistic taste in preferring a horse and uniform to a dirty, rumbling flour-mill was admired by all. She, too, had a very nice appearance in her best clothes as she walked along—the sarcenet hat, muslin shawl and tight-sleeved gown being of the newest Overcombe fashion, that was only about a year old in the adjoining town, and in London three or four. (Ch. xiii)

At no stage does Hardy hint at greater awareness on the part of his characters; their sublime ignorance and concentration on the obvious and present emotion is entirely a part of their light, almost two-dimensional aspect. These are ordinary people, caught up in extraordinary events; their partial knowledge of what is going on, coupled with their superstitious awe of the spectres suddenly surrounding them, are minor shadows on the bright surface of their immediate thoughts and actions. Nobody suffers, nobody dies; they exist in time and space. In *The Trumpet-Major* death is a mass event, but is glossed over entirely or reported as a distant phenomenon. Uncle Benjy's death is in effect the death of a dead man; he has no reality as a living character. Hardy stresses the ludicrous tragi-comedy of his passing by having him appear as if alive, the husk of his body, 'dry and fleshless as that of a dead heron found on a moor in January', being found propped upright on a fence (Ch. xl). John's death is but a walking out into the night, literally, a walking out of the novel—an appropriate close to a 'set-piece' where drama and tragedy exist in reported speech and food, comfort and romance are, at least on the surface, the only things that matter.

Both *Under the Greenwood Tree* and *The Trumpet-Major* show only one side of the world, unashamedly limited and often contrived but, I think, frequently more credible than the multi-faceted vision which Hardy more often chooses to represent. In each he shows his vision of life on one self-contained level, hinting only occasionally at the deeper realities. The world of Mellstock, quiet and homely, where the least ripple of change has proportionally a far greater effect, contrasts and compares with the historically placed world of Overcombe and Budmouth, where the largest and most drastic changes have in retrospect a dreamlike quality, and, in their immediacy, a flavour at once comic and unreal.

IV

Far from the Madding Crowd

... we cannot for our lives understand how any person of ordinary penetration, much more a skilled critic, could ever have supposed it to be written by George Eliot. The author of *Romola* and *The Mill on the Floss* is a great artist, too much of an artist sometimes. The author of *Far from the Madding Crowd* is a dauber in comparison, but if a dauber at all, a dauber who throws on the colours, and arranges the figures, and manages the composition with a vast deal of reckless skill.

Review in *The Observer*, 3 January 1875

(i)

Far from the Madding Crowd sees a distinct development in Hardy's artistic vision. Its quiet pastoral background is scarcely distinguishable from that of *Under the Greenwood Tree*, yet it has all the 'absurdities, improprieties, ... incongruities and suddenly sensational incidents'[1] of its other predecessors, *Desperate Remedies* and *A Pair of Blue Eyes*. What is most interesting in the book is the manner in which Hardy combined the two styles, and the effect which each produces. For the first time, the distinction between romance and reality ceases to be an artistic flaw in the unity of the novel, and the formula which counters the mundane with the incredible, the beautiful with the grotesque, is extended into its very theme.

In *Far from the Madding Crowd*, by his use of strange contrasts and ambiguities, the author constantly reiterates his artistic conception of the dual nature of the world, and the irony of man's interpretation of it. His treatment of his theme is, however, in itself ambiguous. Oddly enough, in those scenes which superficially suggest a highly coloured and dramatic treatment, the style is for the most part restrained and subdued, while the apparently simple pastoral scenes often contain a hint of the weird or malignant. In the famous description of the storm (Chs xxxvi and xxxvii), for example, he combines a faithful and perceptive vision of natural processes with an exaggerated and fanciful treatment. In many ways, as I shall show later, this episode is the crux of the novel, demonstrating finally the contrasts between the solid Gabriel Oak and the other two chief male characters, Troy and Boldwood, who both represent, as Roy Morrell suggests, different 'aspects of romantic unreality'.[2] In addition, it can be seen as epitomizing Hardy's art in this novel, showing as it does the lengths to which realism and melodrama can progress until they become mutually dependent and mutually illuminating. Yet the success of this *tour de force* is not simply fortuitous; it is part of the painstaking development and presentation of scene and action which is established at the very beginning of the novel, and which is maintained, with only a few lapses, until the end.

As a part of this skill, it is in *Far from the Madding Crowd* that we first see effectively developed Hardy's tendency to summarize theme or action by presenting a series of isolated, almost static episodes at various points of the narrative. Irving Howe speaks of these passages as 'miniature dramas . . . which in a page or two illuminate whole stretches of experience': 'what strikes the ear and eye, first and last, is the colour of the depicted scenes, the sheer narrative energy, the way intention becomes absorbed into action. Some of the best, and best-known, sections of *Far from the Madding Crowd* are quite detachable as set-pieces: flights of bravura, spectacular and self-contained'.[3] The effect of these scenes, however, is not only in their vivid and unusual quality; more importantly, they incorporate the elements of the realistic natural background which supports the action and gives credibility to the most melodramatic of events.

It is also noticeable that in this later novel the main characters undergo a far greater artistic development than the pale, unspectacular heroes and heroines we find in *Desperate Remedies* and *A Pair of Blue Eyes*. In these works, it is painfully obvious that Hardy intends the unassuming credibility of his *dramatis personae* to act as a solid foil for the theatrical improbabilities of plot; as a result, the villainous characters and the exaggeratedly comic rustics, though stagey and sometimes ridiculous, carry undue weight in the total structure of the work. In these stories, the events revolve around the characters, whose own distinguishing traits and personalities remain more or less incidental. In *Far from the Madding Crowd*, on the other hand, the characters represent in themselves the qualities which Hardy is exploiting thematically. Their thoughts and actions and emotions fit into and help create the pattern of the whole, and are not simply excrescences tacked on to give an effect of psychological verisimilitude.

Nevertheless, it is essential to Hardy's method that he seldom renders character by direct means, by thought, dialogue or sympathetic interpretation. Most often he develops his background, consistently co-ordinating it with the action itself to show, by inference, the mental state of his protagonists. These are characters who *are* what they see and do; scarcely ever does Hardy rationalize their motives or reactions in any depth. So it is that many of the sharpest scenes in the book are not simply pictorial or dramatic effects; they serve a double purpose, portraying conflicting emotions and ambiguous feelings more surely than any direct exposition could do. Hardy suggests indirectly and by implication, using, as his metaphorical equivalents to emotion, effects of light and colour, sound and sensation. Each character represents, to a certain extent, a different facet of human perception and understanding, and each is developed according to the kind of consciousness which he or she exhibits. In this there is, inevitably, something of a tendency towards 'staginess', as the contrasting personalities are largely created for us by their setting and the props or symbols by which we identify them. Sometimes this is done by Hardy with appropriate crudity, as in the case of Sergeant Troy, sometimes with ever-increasing discernment, as with Bathsheba, whose environment and circumstances are continually explored and developed imaginatively to show us, at the end of the novel, a very different woman from the vain and unsophisticated girl described for us in the first chapter. It is in his portrayal of Bathsheba that we see most clearly how far Hardy has extended his technique of

H

suggestion⟩since he first experimented with it in *Desperate Remedies*.

Our first glimpse of Bathsheba carefully prepares us for a thorough appreciation of her character and predicts many of the subsequent scenes in which vital moments of her life, reflected through her own consciousness, are to be depicted. Our awareness of her as an individual is closely allied with her own awareness of herself, and her progression from naive complacency to deepening self-recognition is traced for us in a series of connected yet distinctly differentiated pictures, in which the description of natural background illuminates our reaction towards its human subject. In all these pictures, Hardy's use of colour and of sensually evocative words is of prime importance. Through the author's imagination the natural world is made almost the equivalent of Bathsheba's mental world, the expression of her own perception and emotional reactions.

The first scene, shown to us through the eyes of Gabriel Oak, is exquisitely redolent of freshness and brightness, of a romantic but rather unreal domestic tranquillity. She is seen riding on 'an ornamental spring wagon', laden with household goods, which stops directly in front of him:

> The girl on the summit of the load sat motionless, surrounded by tables and chairs with their legs upwards, backed by an oak settle, and ornamented in front by pots of geraniums, myrtles and cactuses, together with a caged canary—all probably from the windows of the house just vacated. There was also a cat in a willow basket, from the partly-opened lid of which she gazed with half-closed eyes, and affectionately surveyed the small birds around. (Ch. i)

The pleasing oddness of the scene is reinforced by its bright contrasts of colour; Bathsheba is expressly shown as part of the natural background but as alien to it as spring in the middle of winter.

> It was a fine morning, and the sun lighted up to a scarlet glow the crimson jacket she wore, and painted a soft lustre upon her bright face and dark hair. The myrtles, geraniums and cactuses packed around her

were fresh and green, and at such a leafless season they invested the whole concern of horses, wagon, furniture and girl with a peculiar vernal charm. (Ch. i)

Similarly her impulsive act of smiling at her own reflection in a looking-glass has nothing of artificiality or coquettish vanity about it; it is simply a gesture of admiration, given a certain novelty (which, as Hardy says, 'it did not intrinsically possess') by being enacted out of doors. 'The picture was a delicate one. Woman's prescriptive infirmity had stalked into the sunlight, which had clothed it in the freshness of an originality.' Hardy is careful always to relate the imaginative to the actual, and neatly twists this scene, with a slightly self-conscious denial of authorial omniscience, to a prophecy of Bathsheba's fortunes:

She simply observed herself as a fair product of Nature in the feminine kind, her thoughts seeming to glide into far-off though likely dramas in which men would play a part—vistas of probable triumphs—the smiles being of a phase suggesting that hearts were imagined as lost and won. Still, this was but conjecture, and the whole series of actions was so idly put forth as to make it rash to assert that intention had any part in them at all. (Ch. i)

The episode of her meeting—or, more appropriately, tangling—with Troy at once blends and contrasts with the oddly fairy-tale quality of this first picture; it is the inevitable corollary to Hardy's suggestion that her romantic fancies will be fulfilled in one way or another. Again, although the setting is homely and tranquil (she is going the rounds of her farm at night, checking on the animals in the stables, being snuffled and nibbled at by horses and cows), the scene for her encounter with the evil genius of flattery and deception is characteristically set apart from this peaceful, prosaic background. It is a path through a plantation of firs, whose foliage creates a wall so dense that it excludes all light. Hardy gives it the imaginative construction of a fantastic palace, whose elements approximate those made by man:

a vast, low, naturally formed hall, the plumy ceiling of which was supported by slender pillars of living wood, the floor being covered with a soft dun carpet of dead spikelets and mildewed cones, with a tuft of grass-blades here and there. (Ch. xxiv)

Troy's appearance, too, has something of a visionary quality, an unreal and almost theatrical brilliance in contrast with his unseen presence, which is made tangible to Bathsheba only by her falling against 'warm clothes and buttons':

A hand seized the lantern, the door was opened, the rays burst out from their prison, and Bathsheba beheld her position with astonishment.

The man to whom she was hooked was brilliant in brass and scarlet. He was a soldier. His sudden appearance was to darkness what the sound of a trumpet is to silence. Gloom, the *genius loci* at all times hitherto, was now totally overthrown, less by the lantern-light than by what the lantern lighted. The contrast of this revelation with her anticipations of some sinister figure in sombre garb was so great that it had upon her the effect of a fairy transformation. (Ch. xxiv)

The understated ambiguities of the dark and mouldering reality and the startling brilliance of the vision are immediately blended into the grotesquely foreboding aspect of their enforced conjunction:

. . . the lantern standing on the ground betwixt them threw the gleam from its open side among the fir-tree needles and the blades of long damp grass with the effect of a large glow-worm. It radiated upwards into their faces, and sent over half the plantation gigantic shadows of both man and woman, each dusky shape becoming distorted and mangled upon the tree-trunks till it wasted to nothing. (Ch. xxiv)

The mingling of the actual scene with Bathsheba's dazzled and unconscious perception of it becomes in Hardy's own vision a symbolic prediction which achieves much of its force through the limitation and imaginative use of the setting.

Similar in its self-enclosed unity and in its premonitory and reflective use of the bright colours surrounding Bathsheba's dreamlike romance with Troy, is the chapter titled 'The Hollow amid the Ferns', in which is recounted the heavily symbolic 'sword-exercise'. The setting is shown to us, at this crucial stage of their relationship, in specifically sensuous terms.

The hill opposite Bathsheba's dwelling extended, a mile off, into an uncultivated tract of land, dotted at this season with tall thickets of brake fern, plump and diaphanous from recent rapid growth, and radiant in hues of clear and untainted green.

At eight o'clock this midsummer evening, whilst the bristling ball of gold in the west still swept the tips of the ferns with its long, luxuriant rays, a soft brushing-by of garments might have been heard among them, and Bathsheba appeared in their midst, their soft, feathery arms caressing her up to her shoulders. (Ch. xxviii)

Troy, seen in the distance, is 'a dim spot of artificial red'—clearly contrasted against the natural freshness and beauty of the ferns. Once again, Hardy makes of the natural setting a contrived stage for the action. This time it is, fittingly enough, a sort of arena where the soldier can display his skill:

The pit was a saucer-shaped concave, naturally formed, with a top diameter of about thirty feet, and shallow enough to allow the sunshine to reach their heads. Standing in the centre, the sky overhead was met by a circular horizon of fern: this grew nearly to the bottom of the slope and then abruptly ceased. The middle within the belt of verdure was floored with a thick flossy carpet of moss and grass intermingled, so yielding that the foot was half-buried within it. (Ch. xxviii)

In contrast with this luxurious softness the microcosmic universe created by Troy is dangerous, brilliant and mesmeric. Troy himself is hard and metallic, 'as quick as electricity': only the sword, touched by sunlight, is 'like a living thing' and is described always as a natural phenomenon, being likened to a rainbow, a firmament of light, a sky-full of meteors. It takes up the whole sky: its 'luminous streams' are an '*aurora militaris*', while Troy himself is scarcely noticeable. Hardy continually emphasizes his unreal, magical quality in Bathsheba's eyes. When he finally leaves her, his scarlet form vanishes 'like a brand quickly waved'.

The subtle combination of the real and the fantastic, the soft and voluptuous natural world and the artificial trance-like vision of Troy's strange power, creates a specifically emotional atmosphere in which the two states of dazzled bewilderment and acquiescence are mingled in Bathsheba's own mind. The romance she has anticipated is at once part of her natural environment and completely alien to it. Its essence is of an insubstantial dream—an effect which is largely due to the fact that Troy himself is never clearly delineated for us. He is present only as a voice, a uniform, a splash of bright colour, and for the rest Hardy merely describes him metaphorically or in terms of vague and rather sinister splendour. Within the concept of the book he is at once a romantic dream-character and a fairly innocuous melodramatic villain. Scarcely ever is he seen or described in realistic terms.

The shattering of Bathsheba's illusions about Troy is portrayed in terms which are explicitly synonymous with those of her fascination by him. After the final humiliation, Hardy shows her as reverting instinctively to the action of a wounded animal. Fleeing the house, she reaches a thicket of withering ferns, where 'she could think of nothing better to do with her palpitating self than to go in . . . and hide' (Ch. xliv). Here she spends the night and, awakening 'with a freshened existence and a cooler brain', she finds that the deceptions and fantasies of her life with Troy dissolve into the fresh realities of the ordinary everyday world. Slowly she is made aware of the 'interesting proceedings' of daily life going on: the sounds of the birds, the song of the ploughboy, the stamping and flouncing of her own team of horses drinking at a nearby pond. 'Day was just dawning, and beside its cool air and colours her heated actions and resolves of the past night stood out in lurid contrast.' The hectic and unreal colours of her romance with Troy are shown here only as withered red and yellow leaves: she shakes them from her dress and they flutter away, as Hardy pointedly notes, ' "like ghosts from an enchanter fleeing" '. Everywhere the contrast with the previous fresh and dazzling fantasy is made implicit; the beautiful ferns are now yellowed, and Bathsheba can see in the daylight that below them the ground slopes down to 'a species of swamp':

A morning mist hung over it now—a fulsome yet magnificent silvery veil, full of light from the sun, yet semi-opaque—the hedge behind it being in some measure hidden by its hazy luminousness. Up the sides of this depression grew sheaves of the common rush, and here and there a peculiar species of flag, the blades of which glistened in the emerging sun, like scythes. But the general aspect of the swamp was malignant. From its moist and poisonous coat seemed to be exhaled the essences of evil things in the earth, and in the waters under the earth. The fungi grew in all manner of positions from rotting leaves and tree-stumps, some exhibiting to her listless gaze their clammy tops, others their oozing gills. Some were marked with great splotches, red as arterial blood, others were saffron yellow, and others tall and attenuated, with stems like macaroni. Some were leathery and of richest browns. The hollow seemed a nursery of pestilences small and great, in the immediate neighbourhood of comfort and health, and Bathsheba arose with a tremor at the thought of having passed the night on the brink of so dismal a place. (Ch. xliv)

There is still the hint of mysterious imagined beauty, but now it is only a mist, an ironical veiling of the truth. Again, Hardy's treatment of his subject is ambiguous; despite the noxiousness of the swamp and the fungi, he points their almost repulsive attractiveness. His words are deliberately tactile, creating a sensuous network of sound imagery: 'arterial splotches', 'saffron', 'macaroni', 'richest browns'. The silvery mist, 'fulsome yet magnificent', lit with the sun, and the sharp leaves of the flag which glisten like scythes, recall for us the dazzling mesmeric mist of Troy's sword, flashing and bristling with light in the earlier episode. *the morning after Troy's disappearance*

Bathsheba's awakening illustrates symbolically her conscious and unconscious reactions to what has gone before. Clear perception, in which she at last recognizes separate existences other than her own (in a splendid touch, Hardy shows how she hears the birds not in a confused medley of song, but each with his own individual note) is still countered in her mind with a feeling of *language* hypnotic fascination, metaphorically represented by the enticingly rich and repulsive swamp. In many ways, this scene corresponds with and develops from that of *Desperate Remedies* in which Cytherea feels an unaccountable and almost repugnant attraction towards Manston; there is the same use of ambiguity and 'atmospheric' imagery to suggest conflicting emotions.

It is of course possible to over-interpret Hardy's use of these particular scenes to point the progress of Bathsheba's infatuation and subsequent disillusionment with Troy. They do not form a comprehensive symbolic pattern, and there are many other episodes which might be considered equally important in relation to this part of the story. Yet it seems to me that each of the scenes I have described 'stands out' from the rest of the narrative; each is isolated from the progression of the action by the more intensive use of image, metaphor and colour, and each shows in some sense a rearrangement of natural elements to fit a preconceived emotional state. In each case, Hardy creates a specifically self-enclosed imaginative world which is, however, only an intensification of the ordinary. Within this context even the smallest details can legitimately have a deeper meaning.

In connection with this we can see, for example, that the use of colour and the imagery of flowers and foliage make a fairly consistent pattern throughout the novel, especially relating to the triangle of Bathsheba, Troy and Fanny Robin. Sometimes their significance is ironically juxtaposed against that of the major scenes I have mentioned; for instance, in the light of Hardy's early association of Bathsheba with freshness and greenness, the portrayal of the debauchery in the barn during the storm takes on an added meaning. Amidst the tangle of drunken bodies, Gabriel sees that 'the candles suspended among the evergreens had burnt down to their sockets, and in some cases the leaves tied around them were scorched'. In the middle of the scene, demon-like, 'shone red and distinct the figure of Sergeant Troy, leaning back in a chair' (Ch. xxxvi). The celebration of the Harvest Supper and the Wedding Feast together has an ominous significance in that, to Troy, neither is of the slightest account. In another instance there is the ironical victory of Fanny Robin who, after her death, proves herself capable of holding Troy's affections as Bathsheba never could. In a grim reminder of Bathsheba's journey to her aunt's home, we are shown Fanny's coffin on a bright spring-cart, completely surrounded with flowers and greenery which parody in their freshness the out-of-season potted plants that signified the innocence and beauty of the young Bathsheba. The comparison is implicit, and is further heightened by Troy's futile planting of flowers on Fanny's grave—flowers which Bathsheba replants after the gargoyle has washed them away. ⌐

(ii)

Far from the Madding Crowd was the first novel in which Hardy made use of the word 'Wessex' to identify the geographical setting for his tales. His original intention was that it should give unity to 'the horizons and landscapes of a partly real, partly dream-country', and when he found that the title was becoming 'more and more popular as a practical provincial definition', he warned against this tendency in his 1895 preface to the novel:

... I ask all good and idealistic readers to forget this, and to refuse steadfastly to believe that there are any inhabitants of a Victorian Wessex outside these volumes in which their lives and conversations are detailed.

It is expressly an invented world, not a product of photographic reproduction, and within this world even the obviously realistic detail frequently has a function which is almost supernatural. The unusualness of the events is more than prepared for by the fantasy which Hardy finds in even the smallest things. Thus, in the chapter which deals with the sheep-shearing, a simple description of field-flowers reveals unexpected grotesqueries:

It was the first day of June, and the sheep-shearing season culminated, the landscape, even to the leanest pasture, being all health and colour. Every green was young, every pore was open, and every stalk was swollen with racing currents of juice ... Flossy catkins of the later kinds, fern-sprouts like bishops' croziers, the square-headed moschatel, the odd cuckoo-pint—like an apoplectic saint in a niche of malachite— snow-white ladies'-smocks, the tooth-wort, approximating to human flesh, the enchanter's nightshade, and the black-petalled doleful-bells, were among the quainter objects of the vegetable world in and about Weatherbury at this teeming time ... (Ch. xxii)

Christian and pagan imagery blend in a kind of medieval pageant, as the ordinary unspectacular products of the earth are shown as magical and mysterious, with a strange beauty compounded of ugliness and sorcery. Spring and gaiety is heralded by age and black magic. The relish with which Hardy describes his odd specimens does not necessarily suggest that his intention was overtly symbolic. Rather, the frequent hints of fantasy and oddity make a continual extra dimension enriching the realistic background to the story, and by so doing prepare our acceptance of the macabre and grotesque effects which are directly symbolic.

The differing threads forming the substance of the background are so finely interwoven that sometimes it is difficult to tell whether or not Hardy's imagery is deliberate or simply fortuitous. For example, when he describes the appearance of the newly married Troy at Bathsheba's bedroom window, the picture is an odd combination of simplicity and ingenuity. The birdsong is 'confused', the 'wan blue of the heaven', the yellow lights and 'attenuated' shadows all intimate a rather tardy joy on the part of the outside world, while the creeping plants around the window are 'bowed with rows of heavy water-drops, which had upon objects behind them the effects of minute lenses of high magnifying power' (Ch. xxxv). The use of the romantic pathetic fallacy (nature's disillusionment with this unnatural marriage) contrasts markedly with Hardy's peculiarly original use of the weeping raindrops; suddenly the normal images are fixed and intensified, and the oddity of the close observation heightens the diffused effect of the general impression. The freshness of early morning is shown emotionally as a time of undeveloped ripeness and weakened effects, but in the final image, somehow, the whole created atmosphere is incongruously crystallized and intensified— perhaps because the point is made with complete detachment. The honeymoon from its inception is marked with portents and signs of sickliness, yet the tokens which Hardy mentions are not blatantly symbolic, and the total effect is undoubtedly intended merely as an imaginative comment on the action.

The same technique, extended and exaggerated, is used for the

episode in which the gargoyle ruins Troy's floral tribute to his
dead mistress. The gargoyle, in effect, embodies in itself all the
paradoxes which man can invent: although it is carved of stone,
its action is described as that of a living creature, and it combines
various characteristics of human, animal and mythological beast,
the whole 'fashioned as if covered with a wrinkled hide':

It was too human to be called like a dragon, too impish to be like a man,
too animal to be like a fiend, and not enough like a bird to be called a
griffin. (Ch. xlvi)

Hardy's use of this symbol appears strained and improbable only
when it is taken out of the context of the story; within the tale,
which itself deals with the tensions and ambiguities of the real and
the imagined, it becomes a simple statement of the mysterious,
unpredictable truth above the common vision of man. Its perennial laughter, voiceless in dry weather and in wet heard 'with a
gurgling and snorting sound', is an unceasing mockery of the
artificial state of mankind in which the real truth is seldom
noticed. Thus Troy's attitude towards Fanny's death (which was
treated in a rational fashion by the practical rustic characters) is
shown to us as an ironically sentimentalized anomaly. His
representative action of placing values where they do not exist
extends even to his attaching of special 'meanings' to the flowers
themselves; for instance, he places lilies and forget-me-nots over
her heart, in a bitter parody of his real legacy to her. In comparison,
the basic and elemental starkness of Fanny's death and burial
corresponds with the gargoyle's direct, uncompromising comment on convention and artificiality, and the whole chapter in
which the episode is isolated represents not so much the futility of
Troy's gesture as the wrongness of his attitudes. Within the framework of life and death, intention and repercussion, and the
distortion of the natural to fit preconceived false ideals, the values
embodied by the gargoyle have a grotesquely appropriate significance.

Throughout *Far from the Madding Crowd*, Hardy's technique is
to describe ordinary things in such a way that they have a peculiar

imaginative depth of feeling. His use of metaphor and simile is frequently macabre, sometimes over-ingeniously so (for example, there is his description of the Casterbridge Union House, the 'grim character' of which 'showed through it, as the shape of a body is visible under a winding sheet') (Ch. xl). This being his predilection, one might expect an over-dramatic treatment of plot in the novel, but, strangely enough, the scenes in which action predominates tend towards understatement. Often they are merely a cursory gathering of threads. The mystery of Troy's supposed drowning and his subsequent reappearance is sketchily explained, and the description of his rôle as Dick Turpin in a travelling side-show is less interesting than the exotic picture Hardy gives us of the multi-coloured sheep ascending the downs. His second performance in front of Bathsheba is, in comparison with the first dazzling display, a tawdry and rather pathetic affair. It is imbued with a sense of the ridiculous rather than of dramatic irony, and the comic aspect is increased by the presence of the childishly uncomprehending rustics who believe it is all 'true'—as Bathsheba believed Troy was 'true' not so long before.

It is so, too, with Troy's death. We are adequately prepared for his intended entrance at Boldwood's Christmas party, but any hint of melodrama is considerably discounted by the overt realism with which the action is presented. The whole is shown matter-of-factly, and with almost none of the Gothic sensationalism which marked similar exciting moments in *Desperate Remedies*. The moment of Bathsheba's recognition of her husband is prepared for very slowly, by skilful use of the dramatic contrast between knowledge and ignorance. We have already been told of Troy's intentions, and our awareness is soon intensified with the discovery by some of the rustic characters that he is loitering on Boldwood's property. His startling and ghostly appearance at the window is made entirely credible by the subsequent sober comments of these ordinary men:

The light from the pane was now perceived to be shining not upon the ivied wall as usual, but upon some object close to the glass. It was a human face.

. . . The men, after recognizing Troy's features, withdrew across the orchard as quietly as they had come. The air was big with Bathsheba's fortunes tonight; every word everywhere concerned her. When they were quite out of earshot all by one instinct paused.

'It gave me quite a turn—his face,' said Tall, breathing.

'And so it did me,' said Samway. 'What's to be done?'

'I don't see that 'tis any business of ours,' Smallbury murmured dubiously.

'But it is! 'Tis a thing which is everybody's business,' said Samway. 'We know very well that master's on a wrong tack, and that she's quite in the dark, and we should let 'em know at once. Laban, you know her best—you'd better go and ask to speak to her.' (Ch. liii)

The quiet suspense is further built up by setting the solemn debating in the darkness against the bright, unconcerned activity inside the house:

Laban then went to the door. When he opened it the hum of bustle rolled out as a wave upon a still strand— . . . and was deadened to a murmur as he closed it again. Each man waited intently, and looked around at the dark treetops gently rocking against the sky and occasionally shivering in a slight wind, as if he took interest in the scene, which neither did. (Ch. liii)

The suspense is conveyed through understatement, in Hardy's calm presentation of the facts, without any extra heightening or embellishment.⌉

Troy's prediction that he will be received like 'a sort of Alonzo the Brave' has already prepared us for some kind of Gothic fantasy:

('. . . when I go in the guests will sit in silence and fear, and all laughter and pleasure will be hushed, and the lights in the chamber burn blue, and the worms—Ugh, horrible!—Ring for some more brandy, Pennyways, I felt an awful shudder just then!') (Ch. lii, vii)

Yet this is almost the only concession Hardy makes to the popular romance tradition⌊ Troy's actual entrance is anticlimactic in its inconspicuousness. Bathsheba thinks at first that he is the coachman come to fetch her; Boldwood welcomes him in; some of the guests notice and recognize him, some do not. Bathsheba's first state of shock passes unnoticed until Troy, like the conventional villain he has impersonated throughout the novel, begins to laugh 'a mechanical laugh'; then, simply, Hardy says, 'Boldwood recognized him now'.

Still, realism predominates over sensationalism. Bathsheba does not scream or faint in an attractive heap; her shock is described in terms of detached observation:

She had sunk down on the lowest stair; and there she sat, her mouth blue and dry, and her dark eyes fixed vacantly upon him, as if she wondered whether it were not all a terrible illusion. (Ch. liii)

Hardy is no more than a reporter: he merely describes emotions and actions as they appear, inventorially. The gun shot is

. . . a sudden deafening report that echoed through the room and stupefied them all. The oak partition shook with the concussion, and the place was filled with grey smoke.

In bewilderment they turned their eyes to Boldwood. At his back, as he stood before the fireplace, was a gun-rack, as is usual in farmhouses, constructed to hold two guns. (Ch. liii)

It is a clever reconstruction of scene; the keen eye of the reporter, parenthetically commenting on farm customs, contrasts dramatically with the stupefaction and confusion of the onlookers. There is no room for emotion. Even Troy's death is described scientifically and economically:

. . . the charge of shot did not spread in the least, but passed like a bullet into his body. He uttered a long guttural sigh—there was a contraction—an extension—then his muscles relaxed, and he lay still. (Ch. liii)

As a factual description of dying, this resembles very closely Hardy's later account of the death of the pig in *Jude the Obscure*. There is the same precision of observation, the same concentration on physical actuality. The words follow, in their quick jerky phrasing, the very actions of dying. Compared with this, Boldwood's reaction (his 'gnashing despair' and 'swollen veins', and the 'frenzied look' that gleamed in his eye) is rather unconvincing. Nevertheless, Hardy's theatrical touches do not really mar the episode because they are continually countered by quick reversions to apparent normality. The general atmosphere is made credible by the stress laid on the reactions of the outsiders to the drama. Blankness and bewilderment are the main emotions portrayed, and the whole takes place in slow-motion, as though shock has crystallized even action. It marks a considerable progress from the final scenes of *Desperate Remedies*. In effect Hardy has completely reversed his melodramatic technique. Instead of intensifying the bizarre and extraordinary, he shows us, through the attitudes and reactions of the other, uninvolved characters, that the incredible is real.

(iii)

The scenes depicting the storm are without doubt the most important in the book, and for this reason I have left them till last. Not only do they illustrate, in combination, almost all the techniques Hardy uses in *Far from the Madding Crowd*, but they also form a major centre of the action and bring together a great many of the images and effects which make a detailed pattern throughout the novel. Impression combines with exact observation; realism contrasts with exaggeration and metaphor; action and spectacle become indistinguishable from each other. The natural process of the storm, at its particular point in the narrative, blends with and highlights what has gone before and what is to come. Together with the sword-exercise and the episode of the gargoyle (all, inevitably, related to the artificial and spectacular figure of Troy, who is the 'deviation from the norm' in the novel), it sums up the total impression of what Hardy is trying to convey within the fabric of the story in a single concentrated image. More specifically, it helps to point the role of man in the scheme of things, integral with it (like Gabriel Oak) or removed from it by his own actions (like Troy).

In presenting dramatic action Hardy deliberately tones down

the elements of incredibility, inserting the comments and reactions of uninvolved characters to emphasize the enormity of actual events. In the episode of the storm, however, he uses artificial and frankly melodramatic imagery in order to highlight what is in its essence the portrayal of extreme realism. Again, the moment of greatest impact is built up to very slowly, just as Troy's arrival at Boldwood's party is long delayed and anticipated. John Holloway describes the storm as 'an extended and slow-changing complex of many natural processes', whose 'mere spectacle . . . is only hinted at through a chronicle of events which make it part of the natural order'.[4] The length and subtlety of its treatment not only stress the intensity and force of the actual moment of breaking, but also relate the storm's horror and magnificence to the smallest details of everyday living and to the lives of the insects and animals. The orchestration of effects begins at ground level, as we see through Oak's sympathetic vision first the toad, travelling humbly across the path to safety, then the slug and the spiders who creep indoors, and then the sheep, who huddle together around a furze-bush, forming in perspective a pattern 'not unlike a vandyked lace collar'. Interspersed with the quiet scenes of nature's warning are flashbacks to the actions of the unconcerned human beings. The drunken men in the barn, noisily sleeping and oblivious of the potential disaster brewing, give added emphasis to the still awareness and suspense of the outside world.

The transition from reality to fantasy is always accomplished by the skilful blending of both elements. Accordingly, from the ordinary terror of the land creatures, Hardy develops fanciful similes relating the processes of the atmosphere to the actions of huge nightmare beasts: the breeze becomes a hot breath 'from the parted lips of some dragon about to swallow the globe'; a huge cloud is 'a grim misshapen body' in the 'teeth of the wind'; the smaller clouds are likened to a terrified young brood 'gazed in upon by some monster' (Ch. xxxvi). Sometimes the storm's uncanny life is only hinted at in a vivid compressed metaphor; the first flash of lightning is described in one concise verb as a huge phosphorescent bird—'A light *flapped* over the scene' (my italics):

simultaneously the blinding speed, almost the sound, is conveyed in this one word, and a greater dread is implied by the transferring of a weird animal existence to this inanimate force. Then, immediately, we are returned to earth with the quiet vision of Bathsheba's bedroom window, the candle shining, and her shadow sweeping to and fro upon the blind. All the drama is otherworldly; the living creatures of the earth are now revealed only in flashes, frozen in attitudes of fear, like unreal drawings. Trees and bushes are 'distinct as in a line engraving'; heifers in a paddock are momentarily visible in the act of 'galloping about in the wildest and maddest confusion, flinging their heels and tails high into the air, their heads to earth'; a poplar is like 'an ink stroke on burnished tin' (Ch. xxxvii). Most amazing in this description is Hardy's control and economy, his selection of vivid random images to create a total picture. Myriad shades of meaning are compressed into single words; intensity is conveyed by sudden changes from brilliant weird light to smothering darkness. The skies become a battlefield in which vast manoeuvres are planned, as the lightning gleams 'like a mailed army'. Yet in the context of this concentrated and understated preparation, the actual breaking of the storm has none of the melodramatic exaggeration which the passage, taken alone, might signify. To Oak and Bathsheba, working on the hay-ricks, the first huge flash

was almost too novel for its inexpressibly dangerous nature to be at once recognized, and they could only comprehend the magnificence of its beauty. It sprang from east, west, north, south, and was a perfect dance of death. The forms of skeletons appeared in the air, shaped with blue fire for bones—dancing, leaping, striding, racing around, and mingling altogether in unparalleled confusion. With these were intertwined undulating snakes of green, and behind these was a broad mass of lesser light. Simultaneously came from every part of the tumbling sky what may be called a shout; since, though no shout ever came near it, it was more of the nature of a shout than of anything else earthly. In the meantime one of the grisly forms had alighted upon the point of Gabriel's rod, to run invisibly down it, down the chain, and into the earth. (Ch. xxxvii)

I

Here, as so often in Hardy's descriptions, it is the *effect* which first strikes us. In comparison with what has gone before, the style is almost clumsy, too polysyllabic (as in 'inexpressibly dangerous', 'unparalleled confusion'), consciously rationalizing ('... what may be called a shout'). Taken in its context, it is the imagery alone which is striking, and this gains most of its force by its contiguity with the infinitesimal human beings on whom the imaginative effect is being made. The success of Hardy's most extreme effects is almost entirely in his relation of them to human scale: '... love, life, everything human, seemed small and trifling in such close juxtaposition with an infuriated universe'.

It has been hypothesized[5] that Hardy's inspiration for the storm scene was derived from a similar description in Harrison Ainsworth's *Rookwood*, that most melodramatic of Gothic novels. If this is so (and the inclusion of the staging of Turpin's ride into *Far from the Madding Crowd* might be extra proof of the influence), then the mastery of Hardy's extended version becomes even more apparent. Like Ainsworth, Hardy lists the anxious movements of animals, instinctively aware of the coming danger, and he too likens the first rumbles of thunder to the rattle of artillery. Ainsworth's description, however, is a great deal shorter and relies largely for effect on conscious archaisms (cattle are 'kine', rooks have 'pinion') and on poetical images ('night rushed onwards like a sable steed ... in ten minutes it was dunnest night ...').[6] Melodramatic effects are here deliberately used to enhance the scene and the whole has a contrived air, even though the conception is basically less extravagant than Hardy's.

Hardy, on the other hand, extends and simplifies the background of the scene and contracts his nightmare images into sharp separate pictures, only hinting at the unreal terror on the face of actuality by isolated words and phrases. The effect of reality is gained by the use of sudden oppositions—the inclusion of harsh, onomatopoeic words in a string of soft sounds, the quick contrasting of ordinary actions and everyday thoughts with the vast awesomeness of the universe. The random thoughts of Gabriel Oak as he notes 'how strangely the red feather of her hat shone in this light' give way precipitately to the crash and blaze of white heat as a tree is sliced in half by lightning, and a 'new one among those terrible voices mingled with the last crash of those preceding' (Ch. xxvii). At one moment the soft crunching sounds of the spar gads seem loud in the uncanny silence and blackness; at the next the whole earth is shaken with bursts of light and demoniacal sound. In the total impression the credible and the supernatural are practically inseparable, because even the most startling concepts are built up from the minutest observation of reality. The metaphorical descriptions of the storm develop from these prosaic, natural representations to an imaginative transference of reality, and from there to the grotesque and ghoulish images in the dream-world of the sky.

The importance of these scenes does not lie only in the skill with which Hardy implies the connection between the universal and the particular. The dramatic intensity of the storm also starkly illustrates the principles guiding the lives and actions of the main protagonists, especially in their relationships with Bathsheba; thus Troy remains selfishly unaware and unconcerned, Oak struggles calmly against the odds and ultimately succeeds, while Boldwood just lets it rain. All through the novel Hardy traces a pattern of imagery which highlights these differences, especially the disparity between Oak and Troy, which is epitomized in the warring of the sky and the earth, man against lightning. In many ways, Hardy's portrayal of the storm at its breaking recalls the meteoric brilliance of Troy's sword-play earlier in the story. The lightning of his thrusts and the scarcely realized fear of their striking parody in miniature the fiendish shouts and yells of the humanized electricity in the sky, while Bathsheba's dazed state of unawareness as he surrounds her with the 'circling gleams' of a 'firmament of light' parallels her bewildered acceptance of the nightmare elemental war in the later scene. The impressionistic description of Troy vibrating like a 'twanged harpstring' is continued in the simile of the skies, filled with an incessant light, 'frequent repetition melting into complete continuity, as an unbroken sound results from the successive strokes on a gong' (Ch. xxxvii). In both scenes the effect is one of hypnotic excitement, in which speed, sound and colour, together with rapid alternations from real to unreal, create an impression of continual movement and extreme emotional tension.

Early in the novel, Hardy suggests a continuity between the mundane and the spectacular. Before the introduction of Troy there are subtle premonitions of conflict, and even the preparations for shearing-time hint at something more than earthly:

All the surrounding cottages were more or less scenes of the same operation; the scurr of whetting spread into the sky from all parts of the village as from an armoury previous to a campaign. Peace and war kiss each other at their hours of preparation—sickles, scythes, shears and pruning hooks, ranking with swords, bayonets and lances, in their common necessity for point and edge. (Ch. xx)

Oak, we are told, stands at the grindstone 'somewhat as Eros is represented when in the act of sharpening his arrows'. His dexterity in piercing the gas-swollen sheep parallels Troy's skill and accuracy with his sword in the trivial acts of spitting caterpillars and cutting off locks of hair. The picture of the shearers, too, reflects in miniature the picture of Troy surrounding Bathsheba with flashes of sword-light:

. . . the shearers knelt, the sun slanting in upon their bleached shirts, tanned arms and the polished shears they flourished, causing these to bristle with a thousand rays . . . Beneath them a captive sheep lay panting, quickening its pants as misgiving merged in terror, till it quivered like the hot landscape outside. (Ch. xxii)

In each case Hardy shows how the earthly responds to the meta-physical; how human and animal alike are controlled by the power of something they do not understand. Yet, always, the mystery is itself part of the real and is transformed only by imagination or ignorance. Troy's air of martial splendour is only a fleeting vision and palls beneath the terrifying battle of the storm, but in a sense he shares with it an identical uncanny force—even though Gabriel Oak's bond with the soil is a more durable strength.

The blending of imagery—real and unreal, rural and artificial, earth and sky—creates a structural and thematic pattern within the novel. The implied similarities and contrasts between the individual characters and the universe are completely absorbed into the action of the narrative. The metaphors range in depth as well as breadth and contain much of the ambiguity and irony of the connecting story, which Henry James dismisses as being 'very short and simple', and 'distended to its rather formidable dimensions by the infusion of a large amount of conversational and descriptive padding . . .'[7] The 'padding', and its combinations and ramifications, are worked out with consummate skill, even to the personalities themselves. Bathsheba herself contains elements linking her to all sides of the story; she is intrinsically rural, likened to summer skies and fresh flowers, panting like a robin, blushing like a sunset; again, she is romantic and vain, coquettish and artificial, believing in dreams and impossible fantasies. Frequently unaware of the reality surrounding her, she is yet able to battle with the vagaries of nature and ultimately to understand the workings of her own mind. Like a chameleon, she is seen in totally different ways by the three men who want her: to Oak she is part of the natural world he loves and understands; to Troy, she is a challenging enemy; to Boldwood, who epitomizes the reversal of rationality, she is an exaggerated and impossible dream.

Far from the Madding Crowd is the first of Hardy's novels to show a distinct pattern of imagery relating to the theme, and the first to show consistently the extended relationship between the mental and physical states, between the worlds of absolute reality and imagined truth. For the first time, too, the action of the novel is directly related to its artistic structure and to its theme, instead of being simply a mechanical contrivance producing incredibility and suspense in equal quantities. One might say, perhaps, that the pattern of the whole is a little too neat; Troy is too precisely the opposite of Gabriel Oak, and each character tends to become a set of metaphorical equivalents rather than a distinct and developing individual. To a large extent this is an inevitable result of Hardy's dramatic visualization of key scenes, and, taken within the range

The Return of the Native

It is not that the story is ill-conceived—on the contrary, there are the elements of a good novel in it; but there is just that fault which would appear in the pictures of a person who has a keen eye for the picturesque without having learnt to draw.

The Athenaeum, 23 November 1878

If any single novel may be taken as the key to Hardy's mind and art it is probably *The Return of the Native* . . .

Walter Allen, *The English Novel*, p. 235

For nearly all his critics, Egdon Heath remains the enduring symbol of Hardy's philosophy of art and life. Walter Allen remarks that

The heath is not just so much scenic background to the action, it is all-pervasive; without it, the novel would be unimaginable, for the heath provides it with the especial dimension in which it has its being. The heath holds the action of the novel and its characters as though in the hollow of the hand. . . . Its function in the novel is to describe, as carefully and thoroughly as Hardy can, the real circumstances in which man lives.[1]

As humanity is part of the heath, so too Egdon is frequently shown as a gigantic living creature. Its humanization is a 'grotes-querie', a metaphorical necessity to place this rambling and diffuse area in a closer relationship with those who live on it. The contrast is more important than the similarity. The heath is every-thing man is not, as well as what he is; its powerful impact within the novel is less in its personification than in its epitomizing of opposites which exist in infinite time. It is by this symbolizing of his limited universe that Hardy has managed to give an impression of complete life within a narrow compass.

The heath, in its essence, embodies the aesthetic principle which binds structure and theme together in the novel. Harsh and sombre, 'singularly mysterious in its swarthy monotony', it is still beautiful, embodying in its wild grandeur all the elements necessary to 'emotional development and a full recognition of the coil of things' (Bk I, Ch. i). In his presentation of this 'real' and circumscribed landscape as universal and timeless, Hardy again reverts to his specialized 'rhetoric of painting', a method which Edwin Muir approximately describes in his discussion of the laws governing the vision of the artist:

What gives the painter his particulars for a picture is the world of space: trees, rocks, houses, people, landscapes, lights, shadows, anything that the eye can see. What makes his vision of those things absolute is the moment of supreme concentration in which time is annihilated, and in that annihilation is made unconditional. It is as if in ignoring time, he renders it present untouched, unparticularized, and therefore universal. If he had made the universal his subject-matter, and essayed it directly, he would only have been able to achieve a parable concerning it; for it cannot be stated concretely; it can only be there when the particular is evoked. The background of eternity or of infinity, then, or of something suggesting one of these, is necessary to give the particular form, whether plastic or musical, its universality, and make it absolute.[2]

In *The Return of the Native*, Egdon Heath is the 'absolute' encompassing all other elements of the novel. Everything ultimately relates to this nodal point. The structural excellence of the whole work lies in the planning of the immense contrasts within it, contrasts which range from varying artistic 'tones' to antitheses in character and ways of life. Startling imaginative effects are contrasted with mundane reality throughout, yet the essential balance of credibility within the novel is maintained because the action never moves from its central setting: the heath *is* the world, so far as the novel is concerned, and has within it, sharply focussed and defined, all the antinomies and idiosyncrasies of the real, larger world.

The world surrounding the heath is present only in thoughts and dreams (Eustacia's dream of Paris, for example, or Diggory

Venn's description of Budmouth), and as such it is calculatedly shown by Hardy as having a peculiarly artificial tinsel quality. On the one hand it is a gay, meaningless place; on the other it has a strange, mysterious remoteness, exemplified in Venn's wonderment as he observes the migratory birds which have settled temporarily on the slopes of Mistover Knap:

Here in front of him was a wild mallard—just arrived from the home of the north wind. The creature brought within him an amplitude of Northern knowledge. Glacial catastrophes, snow-storm episodes, glittering auroral effects, Polaris in the zenith, Franklin underfoot—the category of his commonplaces was wonderful. But the bird, like many other philosophers, seemed as he looked at the reddleman to think that a present moment of comfortable reality was worth a decade of memories. (Bk i, Ch. x)

Like Eustacia's grandfather, the old sea-captain, and Clym, who has lived in Paris, they accept gratefully the solidarity of the heath, beside which the glamour of foreign places seems remote and cold, almost sinister.

Egdon Heath, then, is the presiding reality:

The great inviolate place had an ancient permanence which the sea cannot claim. Who can say of a particular sea that it is old? Distilled by the sun, kneaded by the moon, it is renewed in a year, in a day, or in an hour. The sea changed, the fields changed, the rivers, the villages and the people changed, yet Egdon remained. (Bk i, Ch. i)

It surrounds and incorporates all types and degrees of actuality; the independent world of insects and animals; the world of human conventional everyday living; the world of dream and fantasy, of superstition and witchcraft, of nightmare mysteries and childish credulity. On these three levels, contrasting and yet related, the story of *The Return of the Native* is enacted. Artistically and thematically, the novel illustrates Hardy's impression of the conflicts between truth and deception, reality and imagination, and the surrounding higher mystery of life itself. The reactions of human beings to their environment and to each other merge imperceptibly into implied theories of truth and art, the tension between the real and the ideal. Hardy might have written specifically of the characters he created in this novel, as he wrote in his diary, that

... people are somnambulists—that the material is not the real—only the visible, the real being invisible optically. That it is because we are in a somnambulistic hallucination that we think the real to be what we see as real. (*Life*, p. 186)

Darkness and light, blindness (real and metaphorical), deceptions, dreams and illusions form an ever-changing pattern throughout the tale. The characters exist in different imagined worlds and different states of awareness. Eustacia and Clym embody in themselves the prime antitheses of the novel, even though, ironically, they are married (representing, in fact, the two sides of the one truth which they cannot realize), while Diggory Venn and Mrs Yeobright, who have greater conventional awareness, provide some kind of 'norm' against which their actions and ideals are judged.

The overall impression of the novel, its tone and colouring and the style in which it is written, evoke subtly the emotions and contrasts within it. Hardy makes extensive use of the emotional overtones of colour, or the lack of it; similarly, he selects or blurs the detail as it is relevant or irrelevant to his picture. By his altering of perspective and lighting, he can show the different visions of life mingling or in ironic tension with each other, so that the unexpected and dreamlike contrast vividly with the real and probable. Egdon itself, as 'a place perfectly accordant with man's nature' (Bk I, Ch. i), encompasses all the phases of reality which correspond with the emotional viewpoints of the main characters. In its perennial native state it demonstrates the varying colours of man's imaginative interpretation of the world: not only black and white, but all the colours in between. At night it is completely obscured without gradation, yet in the daytime its swarthiness is seen to be alive with creeping things—snakes, beetles and butterflies, and with wild-flowers and bushes of furze. Hardy shows its enveloping night transformed into vividly detailed life, full of sound and movement; even the puddles are homes for infinitesimal wriggling creatures. Yet, with the technique which he later used in *The Woodlanders*, Hardy shows that between the oblivion of night and the clear openness of day there is a twilight world of dreams and superstitions, romantic fantasies and misguided passions. It is a world of imagination based on reality, a world which, placed against the dark background of Egdon, is high-lighted with greater distinctness. The opening chapters of the novel, for example, show ordinary people celebrating Bonfire night:

. . . the permanent moral expression of each face it was impossible to discover, for as the nimble flames towered, nodded and swooped through the surrounding air, the blots of shade and flakes of light upon the countenances of the group changed shape and position endlessly. All was unstable; quivering as leaves, evanescent as lightning. Shadowy eye-sockets, deep as those of a death's head, suddenly turned into pits of lustre; a lantern-jaw was cavernous, then it was shining; wrinkles were emphasized to ravines, or obliterated entirely by a changed ray. Nostrils were dark wells; sinews in old necks were gilt mouldings; things with no particular polish on them were glazed; bright objects, such as the tip of a furze-hook one of the men carried, were as glass; eyeballs glowed like little lanterns. Those whom Nature had depicted as merely quaint became grotesque, the grotesque became preternatural; for all was in extremity. (Bk I, Ch. iii)

It is more than merely a fine description; in essence it predicts the pattern of the novel. Nothing is as it seems. Changed circumstances, fluctuating emotions, or the light of the imagination can all transform the apparently stable truth into something un-recognizable, distorting it or illuminating it in a new way. The mind can discover the hidden detail behind the obvious, but it can also be tricked into believing that the artificial is real.

In 1876 Hardy wrote, 'I sometimes look upon all things in Nature as pensive mutes' (*Life*, p. 114). In *The Return of the Native* the heath is in effect a witness of human existence, but it also helps to shape its progress and destiny. At the same time, it provides a constant stable force against which these fluctuating lives can be shown in their true perspective: the transient suddenness of light and bright colour appearing against this sombre background directly highlights the distinction. Many important scenes in *The Return of the Native* stand out in this way. We remember vividly the ritual bonfires by which Eustacia summons Wildeve; her startling appearance in mummer's garb; Diggory Venn's strange red figure and the weird glow-worm-lit gambling scene with Wildeve; the intense glaring heat as Mrs Yeobright goes on her journey to her son's cottage; the long flames eating into Eustacia's wax effigy.

Our different views of the heath are essential to a complete picture of this dramatically isolated world. It has no single aspect, but is many things at once, changing its character and colour according to the perspective and imagination of each spectator. To Eustacia it is dark, bleak and empty, a place which frustrates her and which she ignores as far as possible; to Clym it is a friend, a creature of his own hue. In describing Eustacia's vision, Hardy concentrates on abstracts and generalities, on atmosphere and contrast rather than on detail. Her view is expansive and un-selective, coloured always by her own emotions: she says to the reddleman, ' "There is a sort of beauty in the scenery, I know; but it is a jail to me" ' (Bk I, Ch. x). The natural world is hidden to her, but to the purblind Clym the real beauty of life is rooted in his microscopic vision of the small animals and insects surrounding him as he works. In direct contrast with Eustacia, his emotions and identity are subordinated to the most basic and elemental things. He becomes completely absorbed by the heath, 'a brown spot in the midst of an expanse of olive-green gorse, and nothing more' (Bk IV, Ch. ii). In writing of him, Hardy employs a simple, straightforward style, accurate and unemotional, to show how, in Clym's perspective of this independent world, there is a strange beauty usually unseen or disregarded by man:

In and out of the fern-dells snakes glided in their most brilliant blue and yellow guise, it being the season immediately following the shedding of their old skins . . . Litters of young rabbits came out from their forms to sun themselves upon hillocks, the hot beams blazing through the delicate tissue of each thin-fleshed ear, and firing it to a blood-red transparency, in which the veins could be seen. None of them feared him. (Bk IV, Ch. ii)

Compared with this, Eustacia's world-view is entirely subjective and impressionistic. Normality, as in this description of her dance with Wildeve, ceases to exist.

The grass under their feet became trodden away, and the hard, beaten surface of the sod, when viewed aslant towards the moonlight, shone like a polished table. The air became quite still; the flag above the waggon which held the musicians clung to the pole, and the players appeared only in outline against the sky; except when the circular mouths of the trombone, ophicleide, and French horn gleamed out like huge eyes from the shade of their figures. The pretty dresses of the maids lost their subtler day colours and showed more or less of a misty white. Eustacia floated round and round on Wildeve's arm, her face rapt and statuesque; her soul had passed away from and forgotten her features, which were left empty and quiescent, as they always are when feeling goes beyond their register . . .
. . . She had entered the dance from the troubled hours of her late life as one might enter a brilliant chamber after a night walk in a wood. (Bk IV, Ch. iii)

The difference is not only in the style—here drifting, mesmeric and poetic—but especially in Hardy's selection of detail. In the latter passage his concern is with effect; accuracy gives way to metaphor and impression. The perception is that of a dream or of a static painting, where only the most obvious things matter, and the rest is a mist. It is worth contrasting this scene with the realistic depiction of the lively dancing at the Yeobrights' festivities, when 'the brushing of skirts and elbows, sometimes the bumping of shoulders, could be heard against the very panels' (Bk II, Ch. v). For Eustacia the same movements are transposed into those of a euphoric trance, unmarred by everyday vulgarities. Sound and motion are conveyed only by visual means, so that the feeling of unreality is heightened.

Similarly, in the book entitled 'The Closed Door', we see how Mrs Yeobright's emotional state is revealed almost entirely by the use of visual detail. Tied to the mundane level of human knowledge and error, she is yet half-conscious of the other, happier worlds of complete delusion or complete ignorance. Even the seemingly prosaic is imbued for her with a dreamlike significance. As she arrives at the door of Clym's cottage, the smallest details are made to assume, in the somnolent, shimmering atmosphere, a tremendous importance:

There lay the cat asleep on the bare gravel of the path, as if beds, rugs and carpets were unendurable. The leaves of the hollyhocks hung like half-closed umbrellas, the sap almost simmered in the stems, and foliage with a smooth surface glared like metallic mirrors. A small apple tree, of the sort called Ratheripe, grew just inside the gate, the only one which throve in the garden, by reason of the lightness of the soil; and among the fallen apples on the ground beneath were wasps rolling drunk with the juice, or creeping about the little caves in each fruit which they had eaten out before stupefied by its sweetness. By the door lay Clym's furze-hook and the last handful of faggot-bonds she had seen him gather; they had plainly been thrown down there as he entered the house. (Bk IV, Ch. v)

In this deliberate, unhurried description, Hardy perfectly translates the physical details of what the woman sees into her mental state; the heat and her weariness and confusion contrast vividly with the eager, nervous clarity of her perception. Needless random thoughts (the condition of the soil, the variety of apple tree), alert perception (the drunken wasps) and logical reasoning all combine to give a surface impression of extreme emotional tension. By slowing down the action, as in his description of Eustacia dancing with Wildeve, Hardy also isolates such scenes and gives them a special artistic prominence. There is a sort of violent unreality, a reversal of the norm, in this apparently ordinary prospect. Grotesquely, the foliage of the trees appears like metal and insects are greedy and drunken, for in this nightmare world of sudden lucidity nature parodies man and man-made things. The sun is not an ordinary natural force but appears to her, on her journey home, as a deliberate foe, 'a merciless incendiary, brand in hand, waiting to consume her' (Bk IV, Ch. vi). Finally she becomes 'as one in a mesmeric sleep'; the atmosphere is so still that only 'the intermittent husky notes of the male grasshoppers from every tuft of furze' show that the independent insect world is still 'busy in all the fulness of life'. The tiny actions of these insignificant creatures assume in perspective an importance and normality far removed from the human state of mental anguish and delusion:

In front of her a colony of ants had established a thoroughfare across the way, where they toiled, a never-ending and heavy-laden throng. To look down upon them was like observing a city street from the top of a tower.

The complete freedom and unconcern of the natural world is epitomized by Hardy's almost visionary description of the heron:

... as he flew the edges and lining of his wings, his thighs, and his breast were so caught by the bright sunbeams that he appeared as if formed of burnished silver. Up in the zenith where he was seemed a free and happy place, away from all contact with the earthly ball to which she was pinioned; and she wished that she could arise uncrushed from its surface and fly as he flew then. (Bk IV, Ch. vi)

The three levels of being here intermingle and yet are in ironic tension with each other. The ideal state, a fantasy of freedom, is completely unattainable, and so too is the eternal unchanging state of the insects. The human mind can comprehend both the higher and the lower levels, but is forced to keep its own state of imperfect, emotion-ruled vision. It cannot live in a glittering Paradise or accept a mindless existence of routine toil, but is in a sense the victim of both worlds, always striving to distinguish the reality from the shadow.

As the differing emotional perspectives of each character are reflected consistently in Hardy's artistic presentation of them, so, too, the varying facets of the total vision are partly conveyed to us by significant modulations of style. This pattern is established throughout the novel in his illusive and ambiguous method of depicting the all-enveloping background to the story: the opposites epitomized by the 'universe' of Egdon Heath are inherent even in the language with which he portrays it. M. A. Goldberg has observed that in Hardy's descriptive technique, the poetic vision with its simple phrasing is frequently countered with 'stiff, wooden, harsh phraseology', 'the dull diction of reports',[3] and that natural or romanticized images are juxtaposed with scientific Latin terminology. Goldberg claims that by this method Hardy is establishing a dialectical tension between 'the point present and the ever-present flow of time', to which is related a similar tension between the scientific and the poetic points of view. Examples abound in *The Return of the Native*. See with what care, for instance, Hardy describes the thin elusive voice of the heath:

It was a worn whisper, dry and papery, and it brushed so distinctly across the ear that, by the accustomed, the material minutiae in which it originated would be realized as by touch. It was the united products of infinitesimal vegetable causes, and these were neither stems, leaves, fruit, blades, prickles, lichen nor moss.

They were the mummied heath-bells of the past summer, originally tender and purple, now washed colourless by Michaelmas rains, and dried to dead skins by October suns. So low was an individual sound from these that a combination of hundreds only just emerged from silence, and the myriads of the whole declivity reached the woman's ear but as a shrivelled and intermittent recitative. (Bk I, Ch. vi)

The third sentence, containing the simple emotional description, is barred on both sides by an objective scientific explanation, intellectual and rather ponderous. The contrast between the *impression* and the *actual* is established; factual statement forms a solid base for the vague and unearthly.

In the same way, Hardy depicts Clym's surroundings at a spot where he has arranged to meet Eustacia, just before their wedding:

He was in a nest of vivid green. The ferny vegetation round him, though so abundant, was quite uniform: it was a grove of machine-made foliage, a world of green triangles with saw-edges, and not a single flower. The air was warm with a vaporous warmth, and the stillness was unbroken. Lizards, grasshoppers, and ants were the only living things to be beheld. The scene seemed to belong to the ancient world of the carboniferous period, when the forms of plants were few, and of the fern kind; when there was neither bud nor blossom, nothing but a monotonous extent of leafage, amid which no bird sang. (Bk III, Ch. v)

On one level, the still monotony of the scene, coupled with its bizarre beauty and heavy, sensuous atmosphere, effectively echoes Clym's mingled feelings of oppression and excitement, the memory of his mother's reaction to Eustacia and his own fascinated love for her. The unity and suggestiveness of such a setting in relation to its human subject can well be compared with the similar description of Bathsheba awaiting Troy in *Far from the Madding Crowd* (Ch. xxviii). In this later scene, however, the implications ramify enormously. As in the picture of Henry Knight face to face with the fossilized trilobite on 'the Cliff without a Name' in *A Pair of Blue Eyes*, or that of Gabriel Oak's tiny hut on the hill beneath the wheeling stars, the presence of man with his immediate vision is only the focal point from which the larger perspective extends. Here, in his imaginative reconstruction of Clym's environment, Hardy's combination of styles balances the 'romantic' conception of nature (bud and blossom) with the scientific truth, showing the strangeness and mystery of what *is* by implying its even more mysterious evolution from the weird elemental beauty of prehistoric times. The ephemeral present moment evoked by immediacy of sensation (the warmth of the air, the brilliant colours and clear shapes, the living insects) is implicitly surrounded by infinities of history. Man's emotional, conventional conception of his own little world is continually examined and questioned. Thus, on Egdon, the dimensions of time and imagination crystallize together as Hardy, by a mingling of the actual and the poetic, manages to convey an impression of simultaneous vision.

Throughout *The Return of the Native*, Hardy's concern is not so much with action as with description. At all possible stages of the plot, events are portrayed as tableaux rather than as continuing actions. The ironic contrasts in the novel derive primarily from the artistic comparison of attitudes and perspectives and for this reason there is far greater emphasis on presentation, 'effect' and 'atmosphere' than hitherto in Hardy's work. Every detail is

K

orientated towards the total impression and every scene is carefully arranged and detailed so that all the elements relate 'to one another and to a whole preconceived scheme, as in a painting'. In fact, says Lloyd Fernando, after this work 'the painter is never again so predominant over the novelist, there is never again the same devotion to style for its own sake'.[4]

At its most extreme form, this preoccupation is apparent in Hardy's presentation of his characters. For example, it is essential to his purpose that Eustacia, the dreamer, be seen as artificial and larger-than-life, both for ironic and artistic reasons. His characterization of her is built up in numerous different ways; he shows her first as a minute, featureless figure, then as a kind of witch, then, poetically, in the guise of a mythological goddess. Only intermittently and infrequently do we see her as a psychologically credible living woman. Our chief impression of her comes from the famed portrait (Bk I, ch. vii) which Fernando describes as like an idealized Rossetti painting, sensuous and immobile. 'Like the Pre-Raphaelites, Hardy relie[s] heavily on emotion to inspire imagination'; like them, he strives for 'quintessential effect'. Of the painters, Fernando remarks that 'This tendency brought a decisive exoticism into their portraits, making their subjects attractively self-sufficient, no doubt—but in their own dim resonant worlds, not in actual life'.[5] Similarly, Eustacia appears (at least superficially) to be, as a 'real' character, a complete failure. She is ridiculously romanticized, too obviously conceived, as Forster would say, 'from a great height'. In reading Hardy's description of her, one is initially tempted to agree with the critic of *The Athenaeum* quoted above that the author is indeed simply indulging his eye for the picturesque, with rather flamboyant results. When the picture of Eustacia is taken in its context, however, and seen in its relationship to the novel as a whole, the importance of Hardy's 'artificial' method becomes more apparent.

The two distinctive prose styles, each evoking a different mood, reach their highest points of contrast in the portraits of Clym and Eustacia. Thematically, both are in a sense 'misfits'. Eustacia is an unwilling prisoner on the heath, longing for a life of gaiety and grandeur and passion, while Clym is an idealist living in a rural world which is not yet ripe for him. Initially, Hardy shows their similarity by introducing them in almost identical ways. Although the description of Clym occurs in the novel some time after that of Eustacia, it is worthwhile to compare the opening sentences of each passage.

Eustacia Vye was the raw material of a divinity. On Olympus she would have done well with a little preparation. She had the passions and instincts which make a model goddess, that is, those which make not quite a model woman. Had it been possible for the earth and mankind to be entirely in her grasp for a while, had she handled the distaff, the spindle, and the shears at her own free will, few in the world would have noticed the change of government . . .

She was in person full-limbed and somewhat heavy; without ruddiness, as without pallor; and soft to the touch as a cloud. To see her hair was to fancy that a whole winter did not contain darkness enough to form its shadow: it closed over her forehead like nightfall extinguishing the western glow. (Bk I, Ch. vii)

In Clym Yeobright's face could be dimly seen the typical countenance of the future. Should there be a classic period to art hereafter, its Pheidias may produce such faces. The view of life as a thing to be put up with, replacing that zest for existence which was so intense in early civilizations, must ultimately enter so thoroughly into the constitution of the advanced races that its facial expression will become accepted as a new artistic departure. People already feel that a man who lives without disturbing a curve of feature, or setting a mark of mental concern anywhere upon himself, is too far removed from modern perceptiveness to be a modern type. Physically beautiful men—the glory of the race when it was young—are almost an anachronism now; and we may wonder whether, at some time or another, physically beautiful women may not be an anachronism likewise . . .

The lineaments which will get embodied in ideals based upon this new recognition will probably be akin to those of Yeobright. The observer's eye was arrested, not by his face as a picture, but by his face as a page; not by what it was, but by what it recorded. His features were attractive in the light of symbols, as sounds intrinsically common become attractive in language, and as shapes intrinsically simple become interesting in writing. (Bk III, Ch. i)

It is clear, I think, that Hardy intends us to find in the latter description an immediate comparison with the earlier sketch of Eustacia. Both characters are described in a detached and objective fashion and the tone of the writing is academic, allusive, a little pedantic. Obviously there are many implied contrasts (Eustacia resembles the goddesses of antiquity, while Clym epitomizes 'modern man') and later the contrasts are made even more explicit ('Take all the varying hates felt by Eustacia Vye towards the heath, and translate them into loves, and you have the heart of Clym') (Bk III, Ch. i). Similarly, there are worlds of implication, here and later, in the use of classical images and references.[6]

Yet more important, and in fact central to the whole theme of the novel, is the method and extent of visualization Hardy employs in his presentation. It is vital that Eustacia's presence should be primarily evoked by her outward beauty, that her image should, in John Paterson's words, inspire 'allusions to the history and legend and literature of an exotic antiquity'. True to her appearance, she *is* the quintessence of romantic unreality, while Clym, whose presence is arresting 'not by his face as a picture, but by his face as a page; not by what it was, but by what it recorded', represents a different ideal, one of philosophic rationalism. The essential attributes of feeling and imagination inspired by the character of Eustacia are illustrated by Hardy in his treatment of her as a being compounded of vast and vague sensuality:

Her presence brought memories of such things as Bourbon roses, rubies and tropical midnights; her moods recalled lotus-eaters and the march in 'Athalie'; her motions, the ebb and flow of the sea; her voice, the viola. In a dim light, and with a slight rearrangement of her hair, her general figure might have stood for that of either of the higher female deities. (Bk I, Ch. vii)

Her emotions, too, are unspecific and limitless: 'To be loved to madness—such was her great desire ... And she seemed to long for the abstraction called passionate love more than for any particular lover' (Bk I, Ch. vii). Her reproach to life is directed against those forces greater than human—Destiny, Fate, Chance.

She imagines herself a heroic character, and cannot understand that her greatest failure is her inability to accept the realities of life. Thus she cannot ultimately give herself to Wildeve because

'He's not *great* enough for me to give myself to—he does not suffice for my desire! . . . If he had been a Saul or a Buonaparte—ah! . . . How I have tried and tried to be a splendid woman, and how destiny has been against me! . . . I do not deserve my lot! . . . O, the cruelty of putting me into this ill-conceived world! I was capable of much, but I have been injured and blighted and crushed by things beyond my control! . . .' (Bk v, Ch. vii)

Her conceptions of reality are, like her portrait, dim and romanticized—('Seeing nothing of human life now, she imagined all the more of what she had seen') (Bk i, Ch. vii)—and her attitudes are consequently erroneously based on the great and glorious figures and episodes of the past. Ironically, it is only in her coffin that her 'stateliness of look' can at last find 'an artistically happy background' (Bk v, Ch. ix).

   Yet her stature is by no means consistently larger-than-life; in comparison with the other characters she must seem, to a certain extent, artificial, pretentious, and rather pathetic. Hardy's attitude towards his own contrived presentation of her is indicated by his occasional lapsing into an almost cynical bathos:

Viewed sideways, the closing-line of her lips formed, with almost geometric precision, the curve so well known in the arts of design as the cima-recta, or ogee. The sight of such a flexible bend as that on grim Egdon was quite an apparition. It was felt at once that that mouth did not come over from Sleswig with a band of Saxon pirates whose lips met like the two halves of a muffin. (Bk i, Ch. vii)

The over-consciously 'artistic' (written obviously with tongue in cheek) is countered by an equally conscious ridicule. In this way, Eustacia's dignity and imperiousness are shown as being noble but, at the same time, faintly ludicrous: 'The only way to look queenly without realms or hearts to queen it over is to look as if you had lost them; and Eustacia did that to a triumph' (Bk iii, Ch. i). She is thus at once 'real' and 'unreal'. We must see her as she sees

herself, and also with Hardy's ironic vision. Often, Hardy himself
seems to confuse the two perspectives, dragging the monumental
down to human scale with rather embarrassing results:

> She placed her hand to her forehead and breathed heavily; and then
> her rich, romantic lips parted under that homely impulse—a yawn.
> (Bk I, Ch. xi)

The intended irony is too clumsy and becomes unintentionally
ridiculous.

At all times our chief sympathy with Eustacia is gained, not by
seeing her as gloriously inhuman, but as pathetically human, an
escapist living in a dream-world, herself the heroine of every
dream. Living in the middle of the heath, with its undeviating
sombreness, she imagines a greater reality:

> There was no middle distance in her perspective: romantic recollections
> of sunny afternoons on an esplanade, with military bands, officers and
> gallants around, stood like gilded letters upon the dark tablet of
> surrounding Egdon. Every bizarre effect that could result from the
> random intertwining of watering-place glitter with the grand solemnity
> of the heath, was to be found in her. (Bk I, Ch. vii)

The dream and the prosaic truth mingle in her marriage to Clym.
To her, at first, he is even more romantic than Wildeve, himself
compounded of elements both gaudy and attractive. She is more
than half in love with him before she has even met him, having
'recognized' him in a dream which has

> . . . as many ramifications as the Cretan labyrinth, as many fluctuations
> as the Northern Lights, as much colour as a parterre in June, and [is] as
> crowded with figures as a coronation. (Bk II, Ch. iii)

Gradually, evolving from the crowded scenes comes

> . . . a less extravagant episode, in which the heath dimly appeared
> behind the general brilliancy of the action. She was dancing to wondrous
> music, and her partner was the man in silver armour who had ac-
> companied her through the previous fantastic changes, the visor of his
> helmet being closed. The mazes of the dance were ecstatic. Soft

whispering came into her ear from under the radiant helmet, and she felt like a woman in Paradise. Suddenly these two wheeled out from the maze of dancers, dived into one of the pools of the heath, and came out somewhere beneath into an iridescent hollow, arched with rainbows. 'It must be here', said the voice by her side, and blushingly looking up she saw him removing his casque to kiss her. At that moment there was a cracking noise, and his figure fell into fragments like a pack of cards. (Bk II, Ch. iii)

The delusion of this vivid fantasy is sharply brought out by the progression of real events; almost every detail, every image is ironically reversed. The heath, dim and unimportant in her dream, is the overwhelming barrier to their married happiness in reality; it is she herself who is to wear the costume of a knight in order to meet Clym; it is in a dance that her re-enchantment with Wildeve begins, and in the dark pool of Shadwater Weir they both meet their death.

Eustacia's clutching at illusion rather than truth is significantly paralleled by Clym's rational dismissal of a dream which is in fact premonitory. Awakening soon after his mother has irretrievably left the cottage, he says,

'I have had such a tremendous dream, too: one I shall never forget . . .

It was about my mother. I dreamt that I took you to her house to make up differences, and when we got there we couldn't get in, though she kept on crying to us for help. However, dreams are dreams. What o'clock is it, Eustacia?' (Bk IV, Ch. vii)

Like Eustacia, he is deluded by appearances; he marries her, believing that she is something she is not, and then mistakenly attempts to fit her into a mould which she has already rejected. Eustacia deceives others, unwittingly, as much as she herself is deceived. Throughout the novel she is presented, more or less, as a chameleon. The heath-dwellers' belief that she is a witch is not simply a fortuitous bit of local colour. Hardy continually emphasizes her mysterious characteristics, her strange pseudo-occult powers and her supernatural beauty. She is constantly associated with darkness and fire, and the first appearance of

Wildeve in answer to her bonfire is deliberately described to us as the conjuring of a vision:

... the contour of a man became dimly visible against the low-reaching sky over the valley, beyond the outer margin of the pool. He came round it and leapt upon the bank beside her ... She let her joyous eyes rest upon him without speaking, as upon some wondrous thing she had created out of chaos. (Bk I, Ch. vi)

Her calculated meeting with Clym has, too, more than a tinge of the supernatural. Dressed up to escape detection, she appears to Charley in a sudden transformation—

... she struck the light, revealing herself to be changed in sex, brilliant in colours, and armed from top to toe. (Bk II, Ch. iv)

Even her identity is fraught with ambiguities. She is not a 'native'. Mrs Yeobright objects to her mysterious background: ' "A Corfu bandmaster's daughter! What has her life been? Her surname even is not her true one" ' (Bk III, Ch. v). Even Clym says afterwards that she has 'bewitched' him and implies that she has evil powers (" ... you have held my happiness in the hollow of your hand, and like a devil you have dashed it down!" ') (Bk V, Ch. iii). Throughout the novel Hardy symbolizes the delusion of his love for her. They meet first in darkness, and later during an eclipse of the moon, and it is Clym's literal loss of sight which becomes one of the primary causes of their estrangement.

Even when describing her in terms of natural phenomena, Hardy stresses the changeableness of Eustacia's essential being: she is

like the tiger beetle, which, when observed in dull situations, seems to be of the quietest neutral colour, but under a full illumination blazes with dazzling splendour. (Bk I, Ch. x)

Just before her death, as she wanders past the firelight coming from the malevolent Susan Nunsuch's cottage, she appears

for an instant as distinct as a figure in a phantasmagoria—a creature of light surrounded by an area of darkness: the moment passed, and she was absorbed in night again. (Bk V, Ch. vii)

The preternatural atmosphere surrounding Eustacia is reflected too in Hardy's descriptions of Diggory Venn, the reddleman. The lack of comprehension which leads the peasants to believe that Eustacia is a witch also places Venn in a world above the everyday. He too is supremely isolated, rejected by the community and a focus of superstitious fancies. Hardy makes it clear that he is completely at home on the heath, and that only his strange colour prevents him from being 'as agreeable a specimen of rustic man-hood as one would often see' (Bk I, Ch. ix). On the surface, though, he is to the eye of the imagination a fearful spectacle, and Hardy makes the most of this for artistic purposes. The accumula-tion of local legend about him is superficially more real and important than the truth. Even to the rational-minded he appears as 'blood-coloured', 'dull and lurid like a flame in sunlight' (Bk I, Ch. ix; Bk II, Ch. vii); to an impressionable child, regardless of rationality, he is a devil, more fearful even than gypsies:

... he lifted the lantern to his face, and the light shone into the whites of his eyes and upon his ivory teeth, which, in contrast with the red surrounding, lent him a startling aspect enough to the gaze of a juvenile. The boy knew too well for his peace of mind upon whose lair he had lighted. (Bk I, Ch. viii)

The heath-dwellers' irrational judgement of the unknown by its external features is exemplified even in the smallest details of everyday life; Christian Cantle, relating the story of Eustacia's being pricked with a stocking-needle by Susan Nunsuch, who believes the girl to be a witch, shows how completely they confuse fact and fiction:

'What a scream that girl gied, poor thing! There were the pa'son in his surplice holding up his hand and saying, "Sit down, my good people, sit down!" But the deuce a bit would they sit down. O, and what d'ye think I found out, Mrs. Yeobright? The pa'son wears a suit of clothes under his surplice!—I could see his black sleeve when he held up his arm.' (Bk III, Ch. ii)

This childlike credulity and limited perception has its counterpart, more subtly and more drastically, in the pattern of reactions and relationships amongst the main characters of the novel. Each has a kind of mask behind which his true identity is hidden to the others, and the action of the story revolves around the themes of deception and revelation, fantasy and reality. Clym, the returned traveller, rejects the outside world which, to those who do not know it, appears so fascinating:

'Yes, Paris must be a taking place', said Humphrey. 'Grand shop-winders, trumpets, and drums; and here be we out of doors in all winds and weathers—'

'But you mistake me', pleaded Clym. 'All this was very depressing.' (Bk III, Ch. i)

Yet his relationship with this world is as constantly misunderstood as are his high ideals for improving his own people and environment. His intellectual fantasies are as impossible as Eustacia's dreams of luxury and romance, and each mistakenly believes that the other can help make the vision reality. So, too, for the sake of external appearances, Thomasin marries Wildeve and rejects Diggory Venn. With this marriage, founded entirely on falsity and misunderstanding, is set off a train of events culminating in the quarrelling between Clym, Eustacia and Mrs Yeobright, each of whom refuses to see or believe any truth other than that which is immediately and obviously discernible.

The Return of the Native, then, is the first of Hardy's novels to explore thoroughly the artistic principles by which he wrote. More close-knit than most of his works (with the exceptions, perhaps, of *Under the Greenwood Tree* and *The Mayor of Caster-bridge*), completely self-enclosed in space and time (the story never strays from the heath, and the main part of the action takes place in the traditional year-and-a-day),[7] it fulfils almost perfectly Hardy's first criterion of worth, that 'a story should be an organism'. But it does more than this. By examining the antitheses and contradictions of life, it represents a fairly simple love-story as a tale illustrating high aesthetic problems. Its depth is achieved not only through the patterning and contrast of major symbols throughout the novel, but also through their intrinsic relationship with one thing—the heath—which *is* all these things, and which gives a solid factual base to the confused, dreamlike, evanescent human lives which exist on it. Yet for all that the tale appears static (one critic, with misguided irony, remarks that 'The one definite action in the novel is Wildeve's leap into the weir after Eustacia'),[8] it is continually moving, showing sides of life sometimes blurred and dim in detail, sometimes clear, vivid and sensuous: sometimes fantastic or mysterious, sometimes brilliantly 'real'. It is in the constancy with which it shows the uncertainty of reality and the relationships between art and life that *The Return of the Native* remains the apotheosis of Hardy's theories on the art of the novel.

The Mayor of Casterbridge

The Mayor of Casterbridge is, apart from his frivolously stylized earlier work, *The Hand of Ethelberta*, the first of Hardy's attempts to focus specifically on the moral and emotional situation of an individual protagonist, and, as in his two other 'portrait' novels, *Tess of the d'Urbervilles* and *Jude the Obscure*, the artistic form of the work and the progression of the story are based solidly on the pattern of circumstances illustrating 'one man's deeds and character'. The classic, balanced 'curve of destiny' method by which Hardy chose to depict the life and death of Michael Henchard has led many critics to dwell lengthily and reverently on the novel's relationship with what its author termed the 'epic, dramatic or narrative masterpieces of the past'. '*The Mayor of Casterbridge*', writes John Paterson, for instance, 'approximates, as perhaps no novel before or since has approximated, the experience of tragedy in its olden, in its Sophoclean or Shakespearean, sense'. Henchard, he says, is 'forced, like Oedipus and Faust and Lear, to rediscover in suffering and sorrow the actuality of the moral power he had so recklessly flouted'.[1] It is rather daunting, in the face of such grandiose claims, to find that Hardy's own trenchant comment on this supposedly incomparable work of art was merely that 'the plot ... was quite coherent and organic, in spite of its complication' (*Life*, p. 179).

While it is possible that Hardy, with his lasting interest in the Greek dramatists, conceived the character of Henchard and the structure of his story on classical lines, it is, I feel, more probable that his studies in Greek simply reinforced a natural tendency.

Hardy's basic theme in this work and his idiosyncratic use of plot are peculiarly demonstrative of his own ironic vision. 'Writers are conscious', he wrote in 1890, 'that the revised presentation of tragedy demands enrichment by further truths—in other words, original treatment.' For this reason, he himself advocated a

treatment which seeks to show Nature's unconsciousness not of essential laws, but of those laws framed merely as social expedients by humanity, without a basis in the heart of things; treatment which expresses the triumph of the crowd over the hero, of the commonplace majority over the exceptional few.[2]

In all his novels, to a greater or lesser extent, but especially in *The Mayor of Casterbridge*, *Tess of the d'Urbervilles* and *Jude the Obscure*, Hardy shows his main characters as being caught between and compromised by these conflicting values—those inherent in Nature, in the 'heart of things', and those which have been fabricated by man. D. H. Lawrence puts the matter with intuitive, if rather whimsical, accuracy:

These people of Wessex are always bursting suddenly out of bud and taking a wild flight into flower, always shooting suddenly out of a tight convention, a tight, hide-bound cabbage state into something quite madly personal. . . . They are people each with a real, vital, potential self, . . . and this self suddenly bursts the shell of manner and convention and commonplace opinion, and acts independently, absurdly, without mental knowledge or acquiescence.

And from such an outburst the tragedy usually develops. For there does exist, after all, the great self-preservation scheme, and in it we must all live.[3]

The Mayor of Casterbridge is unique among Hardy's novels in that it makes extensive use of an urban community setting to show the relationship of an 'exceptional' individual both to his immediate social environment and to the fixed and undeviating principles set down by the mass of humanity. In the earlier 'Novels of Character and Environment' the common people, usually rustics, almost invariably serve in the comparatively passive rôle of a chorus, a solid and credulous background to the action, or to provide comic relief. It was not until *The Return of the Native* that Hardy showed, in the character of Susan Nunsuch with her primitive fear and hatred of Eustacia, the directly opposing view of an inflexible section of humanity, suspicious of and hostile to a way of life which it does not comprehend. In *The Mayor of Casterbridge*, the active representatives of the 'commonplace majority', Joshua Jopp and the furmity-woman, bring into prominence the whole body of vociferous and down-to-earth citizens of Casterbridge as a foil for the depiction of individual lives. One has only to note how freely and frequently the narrative is carried on by the gossip of the local residents and how consistently the town or the townsfolk help directly to shape the action of the story, to realize that the survival of the main protagonists depends to a very large extent on their 'acceptance' by this limited and circumscribed social environment. From the very beginning, when he sells his wife at the Weydon-Priors fairground before a crowd of spectators, to the end, when he stipulates in his Will ' "that no man remember me" ', Henchard's history is acted out always against the existence of an uncompromising established human order. Always he must be seen both subjectively, as an individual, and objectively, as a mere fractional part of the great undifferentiated mass of humanity. Our conception of Henchard is essentially a combination of these views, and the contrasts inherent in Hardy's artistic presentation of his titular character also provide the bases for the working out of his underlying theme.

Hardy deliberately accentuates the isolation from the norm of all the main characters by portraying them initially (like Eustacia) as 'foreigners'. None of them was born or bred in Casterbridge: neither Henchard himself, nor Susan, Elizabeth-Jane, Farfrae, Lucetta, nor even the furmity-woman. Donald Farfrae is indeed so much a foreigner to the local people that Solomon Longways describes him as a gentleman ' "that's travelled a'most from the North Pole" ' (Ch. viii). Because they differ both in origin and social standing, these characters are targets for the discussions and speculations of the permanent town-dwellers, for whom life carries on as a continual round of work, gossip and convivial gatherings, unchanged by time.

The striking unity of *The Mayor of Casterbridge* is less the result of its carefully symmetrical structure than it is of Hardy's consistent and imaginative balancing of opposites in his seemingly unwieldy mass of material. Despite the complexity of the story and the regular points of suspense and climax which betray its serial origin, the novel succeeds primarily because the events in it are firmly embedded in and related to a background which is itself an intricate material reconstruction of the story's theme. Hardy's technique here is basically identical to that he used in *The Return of the Native*, but it functions on a rather different level. Whereas Egdon, though humanized itself, ultimately dwarfs the transient human lives which reflect its mystery, Casterbridge is the specific embodiment of its inhabitants, reflecting in its ancient brick and stone all the ambiguities of man's condition. This essential contradictoriness is subtly reflected in Hardy's depiction of a town which is in appearance 'as compact as a box of dominoes' but in character as diverse and unpredictable as the lives of the people existing within its boundaries. From a distant appraisal, Hardy tells us, it seems that country and town meet 'at a mathematical line', but a closer acquaintance gradually reveals a quaintly ambivalent mixture of urban and rural, with the latter encroaching upon and modifying the former: birds and butterflies fly straight down the high street, and thistledown and leaves choke the drains and creep into the houses 'with a hesitating scratch on the floor, like the skirts of timid visitors' (Ch. ix). The urban shops are paradoxically full of objects necessary for a farming existence; the old and crumbling stonework of the church is implanted 'with little tufts of stone-crop and grass almost as far up as the very battlements' (Ch. iv); and even the ancient warlike fortifications surrounding the town are now mellowed to a gentler usefulness and have been planted with trees to form a promenade. Yet even this placid, thriving town is later shown to conceal an uglier, sinister side in the presence of 'Mixen Lane', an area of swamp and disease and thievery which Hardy describes as the 'mildewed leaf in the sturdy and flourishing Casterbridge plant' (Ch. xxxvi). Here, too, everything is a contradiction of what it outwardly appears to be. The only 'church' is the inn called 'Peter's Finger', and far from indicating industry and cleanliness the white apron worn by so many of the local women is known in the area as the badge of the prostitute. In the main street of Casterbridge the houses with their open front doors are like tunnels through which one can see the mossy gardens at the back, glowing with flowers, but in Mixen Lane all is hidden and kept furtive. Although the front door of 'Peter's Finger' is kept shut and the step is cleanly sanded, this bland proclamation of respectability is only a blind for the real entrance, a much-worn slit at the side of the building into which the passing pedestrian might vanish in an instant, 'causing the gazer to blink like Ashton at the disappearance of Ravenswood' (Ch. xxxvi).

The close correlation between the town of Casterbridge and its inhabitants frequently approaches overt symbolism, but nowhere is this shown more markedly than in the description of Lucetta's house, 'High Place Hall', which parodies all the bewildering façades of its owner in epigrammatic succession:

It had . . . the characteristics of a country mansion—birds' nests in its chimneys, damp nooks where fungi grew, and irregularities of surface direct from Nature's trowel. At night the forms of passengers were patterned by the lamps in black shadows upon the pale walls.

At first glance it forms 'an example of dignity without great size . . . not altogether aristocratic, still less consequential', but maintaining, in its Palladian architecture ('a compilation rather than a design'), a 'reasonableness which made it impressive' (Ch. xxi). Surprisingly, however, as Elizabeth-Jane discovers, its back opens out into 'one of the little-used alleys of the town' which leads secretly to all the unsavoury haunts of Casterbridge—'the old play-house, the old bull-stake, the old cock-pit, the pool wherein nameless infants had been used to disappear'. This, and the grotesquely leering mask over the doorway suggest 'one thing above all others as appertaining to the mansion's past history—

intrigue' (Ch. xxi). Obviously, Hardy intended that this house, with its passable front and its sordidly secret back entrance, should be suggestive of Lucetta's own life with its discreetly veiled but dubious past. To Henchard, when he senses that he has a rival for her affections, the building even seems imaginatively to take on something of the character of its occupant: 'Her windows gleamed as if they did not want him; her curtains seemed to hang slily, as if they screened an ousting presence' (Ch. xxvi).

For both Lucetta and Henchard it is vital that the outward veneer of social respectability is maintained. In many respects their lives run parallel; Lucetta's anxiousness to redeem her guilt at having had what Hardy delicately refers to as an 'intimate relationship' with Henchard is a conscious echo of the latter's identical wish to atone for his unthinking crime against his wife Susan. By marrying Donald Farfrae instead of her former lover, Lucetta re-emphasizes the explosive potential contained in the transgression of socially accepted rules. Her terror of being betrayed by the jealous and bitter Henchard mounts in proportion to her love for Farfrae, just as, later, Henchard's desperate lie to Newson is indicative of the strength of his love for the girl who is not legally his, and of his longing to keep her for his own. So, too, Susan Henchard must initially conceal from her husband Elizabeth-Jane's true paternity, both for her own and for the girl's sake. And in each case the revelation of the conventionally unacceptable truth leads to the deterioration or loss of love, through anger or pride or death itself.

The themes of deception and concealment contained in the main story-line are reiterated in countless smaller ramifications of plot; in such things as secret marriages, mistaken identities, shady propositions and false promises, clandestine meetings and un-expected encounters. The pattern of deliberate secrecy and evasion which shrouds the actions of one character from another at vary-ing stages of the tale is subtly reinforced throughout the novel by Hardy's use of a consistent imagery of mistiness and obscurity, a pervasive dankness leading to decay. As in *Far from the Madding Crowd* and *The Return of the Native*, and later in *The Woodlanders*,

L

he exploits the artistic and dramatic possibilities of the contrast between light and darkness or between dream and reality, so, too, in *The Mayor of Casterbridge* he implies the human qualities of deceit and ignorance and ambiguity in the unhealthy creeping atmosphere which pollutes the town and causes crops to fail and wholesome wheat to sprout and grow mouldy. Physically, the unpredictableness of the weather is one of the predominant causes of Henchard's ruin; metaphorically, it symbolizes the inevitable consequences of his own actions. Bad wheat must make bad bread. It may be partially redeemed, as Henchard attempts to make good his own life, but, says Farfrae, ' "To fetch it back entirely is impossible; Nature won't stand so much as that . . ." ' (Ch. vii). The insidious connection between the atmospheric conditions and the corn-trade by which Henchard has made his fortune is neatly condensed into one image at the time of his remarriage to the pale woman whom the local boys call 'The Ghost'. On the morning of the wedding, we are told, the 'warm November rain . . . floated down like meal, and lay in a powdery form on the nap of hats and coats' (Ch. xiii). Despite its apparent soft innocence, such weather bodes ill in the eyes of the local people gathered outside the church:

The plain little brougham drove off in the mist, and the idlers dispersed. 'Well, we hardly know how to look at things in these times!' said Solomon. 'There was a man dropped down dead yesterday, not so very many miles from here; and what wi' that, and this moist weather, 'tis scarce worth one's while to begin any work o' consequence today.' (Ch. xiii)

Later, Henchard's proposed merrymaking for the populace is washed out by rain which, like his own ruin, begins to fall 'small and steady, commencing and increasing so insensibly that it was difficult to state exactly when dry weather ended or wet established itself', and which turns finally into 'a monotonous smiting of earth by heaven, in torrents to which no end could be prognosticated' (Ch. xvi). Farfrae, meanwhile, wins popularity by keeping his rival entertainment dry with the aid of a tent 'ingeniously constructed without poles or ropes'. Henchard's blind assumption of his own infallibility, and his inability to alter or postpone proceedings once they have begun, are made to look ridiculous by contrast with Farfrae's simple, intelligent planning. Similarly, when his secret consultation of the 'conjurer' weather-forecaster encourages him to buy and store huge quantities of grain in the hope of foul weather and a rise in prices, and when the first burst of sunshine prompts him impatiently to sell it off at a loss, Nature itself mocks his foolhardy capriciousness by turning on him at the last moment:

. . . no sooner had the sickles begun to play than the atmosphere suddenly felt as if cress would grow in it without other nourishment. It rubbed people's cheeks like damp flannel when they walked abroad. There was a gusty, high, warm wind; isolated raindrops starred the window-panes at remote distances: the sunlight would flap out like a quickly opened fan, throw the pattern of the window upon the floor of the room in a milky, colourless shine, and withdraw as suddenly as it had appeared. (Ch. xxvii)

The dark and sunless river-bound area of the town, where white frosts linger and which is 'the seed-field of all the aches, rheumatisms, and torturing cramps of the year' comes to have 'a lugubrious harmony' with Henchard's domestic situation (Ch. xix), while malevolence and subterfuge are epitomized by the low area of Mixen Lane, which Hardy describes as stretching out 'like a spit into the moist and misty lowland', and where 'business' is only carried on after nightfall. It is here, in this place of darkness and clammy breezes, that Lucetta's incriminating letters to Henchard are read and mocked, and her downfall plotted. The truth of her past history rapidly becomes common knowledge, spreading inexorably through Casterbridge 'like a miasmatic fog' (Ch. xxxvii).

The clash between Henchard and Farfrae which is the central action of the story is shown essentially as a conflict of their natures, a clash of the moody and unpredictable with the rational and consistent. Farfrae is clear-headed, resourceful and transparent, with the glow of poetry and romance about him; one whom even the plain townspeople view admiringly 'through a golden haze which the tone of his mind seemed to raise around him' (Ch. vii). Henchard is by comparison blundering and primitive, passionate and well-meaning, but lost in his own obscurity.

Character is Fate, said Novalis, and Farfrae's character was just the reverse of Henchard's, who might not inaptly be described as Faust has been described—as a vehement gloomy being who had quitted the ways of vulgar men without a light to guide him on a better way. (Ch. xvii)

The relationship of the two men is so twisted and thwarted by false pride and misunderstanding that finally each can see only evil and treachery in the other, so much so that when Lucetta's life is in danger, Farfrae coldly and distrustfully chooses to ignore Henchard's earnest entreaties to go to her, because he has been so often wronged by him.

   It is therefore with specific irony that Hardy uses the prevailing images of blurring and misting to underline metaphorically the lack of perception and the ultimate bafflement which exist between the rival men, and to point the defeat of the one by the other. The comparison between logic and emotion in terms of natural phenomena is emphasized at the beginning of their relationship. When Farfrae is first employed by Henchard, the former finds that the muddle-headed way in which the corn-merchant has kept his cash books has resulted in 'numerical fogs . . . so thick . . . as almost to baffle even the Scotchman's perspica-city' (Ch. xii). With Henchard's subsequent bankruptcy the image is extended to apply to the man himself, as he is seen, despite his towering physical presence, to have declined from his original bold and striking 'rouge-et-noir' appearance:

His countenance had somewhat changed from its flush of prosperity; the black hair and whiskers were the same as ever, but a film of ash was over the rest. (Ch. xxxi)

And when he is finally ousted by Farfrae, the reversal is shown significantly as the shrouding of one name by another. Elizabeth-

Jane, looking at the familiar gateway of her step-father's business premises, sees that

A smear of decisive lead-coloured paint had been laid on to obliterate Henchard's name, though its letters dimly loomed through like ships in a fog. Over these, in fresh white, spread the name of Farfrae. (Ch. xxxi)

With Hardy's concentration on one particular character in this novel, his use of specifically 'visual' techniques is rather more subjective than it is in *The Return of the Native* or *Far from the Madding Crowd*. More than Clym or Eustacia—who are presented essentially as being the halves of a perfect aesthetic whole—Henchard's character, as well as his thematic rôle, is determined by how he appears and what he does. His portrait is nowhere definitive, even though all the conflicting elements in his densely wrought personality are carefully built up from a series of images which work together to create the 'meaning' of his character within the framework of the novel. Henchard's life as a wealthy mayor of Casterbridge is continuously contrasted with the lingering image of his past; the way we see him is constantly shown to be at variance with what he really is.

The first two chapters of the novel are an admirable illustration of Hardy's artistic method as it works through these varying levels of perception, showing us first the simple picture, then the rational analysis of the external, and finally the action which demonstrates that analysis.

Our initial view of Henchard is largely based on a description of his appearance and his clothing, a carefully detailed but superficial view which gives us the briefest information about his occupation and personality, as seen by the 'casual observer':

The man was of fine figure, swarthy, and stern in aspect; and he showed in profile a facial angle so slightly inclined as to be almost perpendicular. He wore a short jacket of brown corduroy, newer than the remainder of his suit, which was a fustian waistcoat with white horn buttons, breeches of the same, tanned leggings, and a straw hat overlaid with black glazed canvas. At his back he carried by a looped strap a rush basket, from which protruded at one end the crutch of a hay-knife, a wimble for hay-bonds being also visible in the aperture. His measured, springless walk was the walk of the skilled countryman as distinct from the desultory shamble of the general labourer; while in the turn and plant of each foot there was, further, a dogged and cynical indifference personal to himself, showing its presence even in the regularly inter-changing fustian folds, now in the left leg, now in the right, as he paced along. (Ch. i)

Gradually, with the analytical detachment of the more perceptive observer, Hardy reveals to us the character beneath the surface as the immediately obvious qualities of indifference and stoicism are dissipated and transformed under the influence of rum-laced furmity:

At the end of the first basin the man had risen to serenity; at the second he was jovial; at the third, argumentative; at the fourth, the qualities signified by the shape of his face, the occasional clench of his mouth, and the fiery spark of his dark eye, began to tell in his conduct; he was overbearing—even brilliantly quarrelsome. (Ch. i)

The progressive assertion of Henchard's latent character, culmina-ting in his drunken proposal to sell his wife, takes place with the uncanny irrefutability of a nightmare. In the rising atmosphere of noise and jollity, such a gross intention is seen simply as part of the entertainment, until the cold separate sound of Newson's money chinking on to the table brings the whole scene abruptly back to actuality:

Up to this moment it could not positively have been asserted that the man, in spite of his tantalizing declaration, was really in earnest . . . But with the demand and response of real cash the jovial frivolity of the scene departed. A lurid colour seemed to fill the tent, and change the aspect of all therein. The mirth-wrinkles left the listeners' faces, and they waited with parting lips. (Ch. i)

After Henchard's deliberate completion of the contract, the crowd vanishes and the drunken man falls asleep on the table. In the morning, to his half-dazed and uncomprehending mind, the whole incident seems like a dream—until he sees, amongst other odds and ends, his wife's wedding-ring lying on the grass, and hears the rustling of the sailor's bank-notes in his own pocket. It is by these small, random, but intensely *real* details that Hardy accentuates the contrasting enormity of Henchard's deed and the conflicting elements of blind fanaticism and of a humbler awareness in his individual character.

Nevertheless, because this scene is isolated in time from the rest of the novel, the total effect for us is of a fantastic unreality, and the introduction immediately afterwards of Susan and Elizabeth-Jane, in circumstances precisely similar to those at the beginning of the book, reinforces our impression that nothing is changed, nothing in particular has happened. Susan's own life after she becomes Newson's 'wife' is 'told in two or three sentences' (Ch. iv), and Henchard's enormous rise in prosperity and importance during those same twenty years is not recorded at all. Our next view of him, some few pages later, shows him in the possession of 'an unexpected social standing' as denoted by 'an expanse of frilled shirt showing on his broad breast; jewelled studs, and a heavy gold chain' (Ch. v). Hardy deliberately telescopes the timespan between this and our first picture of the man, so that the revelation to Susan Henchard of her labourer husband as a wealthy and respected citizen is contrasted the more sharply with her memory of him. The effect is of an astonishing transformation: 'Time, the magician, had wrought much here'. At the same time, this immediate juxtaposition of the two vastly different pictures increases immeasurably the irony implicit in Henchard's confident arrogance, for we are shown later that the twenty years' concealment of his crime merely adds to the offence in the eyes of the people of Casterbridge. After the furmity-woman's denunciation of him at her trial, we are told that

The amends he had made in after life were lost sight of in the dramatic glare of the original act. Had the incident been well known of old and always, it might by this time have grown to be lightly regarded. . . . But the act having lain as dead and buried ever since, the interspace of years was unperceived; and the black spot of his youth wore the aspect of a recent crime. (Ch. xxxi)

All through the novel Hardy has interwoven the details of Henchard's past with those of his present life, in preparation for the moment when they finally come together and betray him. For this reason he maintains, at all levels of his protagonist's life, a neatly ambivalent pictorial imagery by which external appearance is shown as having, on the one hand, the simple and obvious connotation of social status and importance, and, on the other, as demonstrating a contrary moral or actual truth. Thus, the figure of Michael Henchard is shown to be based on the image he has chosen to present to his fellow-men—an image of wealth and confidence which will hide the man as he really is. The forceful solidarity of his basic self is corrupted and altered by the superficial trappings of respectability, but the original man, like the warlike foundations of Casterbridge itself, is still hidden beneath the new: 'There was temper under the thin bland surface—the temper which, artificially intensified, had banished a wife nearly a score of years before' (Ch. v).

The sharpness of detail with which Hardy depicts Henchard's outward appearance at all stages of his life is countered by a consistent use of natural metaphorical equivalents which point to the characteristics always discernible beneath the palpable surface. Through this continually altering perspective, we view him both as he is seen by his contemporaries and as he really is. When he resumes work as a labourer in Donald Farfrae's employ, for example, his decline in status is outwardly symbolized by his defiant shabbiness, shown significantly as the deterioration of an old image rather than the resumption of a new:

'I have worked as a journeyman before now, ha'n't I?' he would say in his defiant way; 'and why shouldn't I do it again?' But he looked a far different journeyman from the one he had been in his earlier days. Then he had worn clean, suitable clothes, light and cheerful in hue; leggings yellow as marigolds, corduroys immaculate as new flax, and a neckerchief like a flower-garden. Now he wore the remains of an old blue cloth suit of his gentlemanly times, a rusty silk hat, and a once black satin stock, soiled and shabby. (Ch. xxxii)

To Farfrae, observant only of appearances, this decrepit-looking man has none of the power he once had, and he is therefore incredulous of Elizabeth-Jane's warning that Henchard might wish to hurt him in some way. He has become now merely 'Henchard, a poor man in his employ', no longer in Farfrae's view 'the Henchard who had ruled him'. Yet, as Hardy prophetically observes, 'he was not only the same man, but that man with his sinister qualities, formerly latent, quickened into life by his buffetings' (Ch. xxxiv). Similarly, Hardy deliberately evokes the picture of Henchard's earlier appearance as a hay-trusser by his use of a harmonious elemental imagery of fresh flowers and plants; the obvious contrast between 'then' and 'now' points the more clearly to Henchard's incongruous alienation by temperament from the sophisticated life he has adopted, and in which he has no longer a part. Within the static, detailed studies of Henchard the citizen at all stages of his career, there is a great network of qualifying images which help to delineate the latent natural personality behind the façade. Henchard's instinctive being is on a par with winds and storms; his disappointments are 'felt like a damp atmosphere'; his 'strong, warm gaze' is 'like the sun beside the moon in comparison with Farfrae's modest look' (Ch. xxv). His eyes are described as always seeming to have 'a spark of red light in them', and his anger is likened to 'volcanic fires'. When he and Farfrae finally come together on equal terms and battle for supremacy, Hardy describes them as 'writhing like trees in a gale', and elsewhere Henchard's enormous physical power and corresponding strength of emotion are seen as the attributes of an untamed animal. He is 'tigerish' in his affections, but has a sense of finesse and diplomacy 'as wrong-headed as a buffalo's'. His own ultimate humiliation is ironically paralleled by the incident in which he manages to overpower a wild bull 'too savage to be driven' which has endangered the lives of Elizabeth-Jane and Lucetta:

He ran towards the leading-staff, seized it, and wrenched the animal's head as if he would snap it off . . . The premeditated human contrivance of the nose-ring was too cunning for impulsive brute force, and the creature flinched. (Ch. xxix)

The conscious similarity is further driven home by Elizabeth-Jane's fleeting sympathy for the humbled animal, as, after their rescue, she pauses for a moment to look at him, 'now rather to be pitied with his bleeding nose, having perhaps rather intended a practical joke than a murder'. Later, when Farfrae, in his role as mayor, forcefully turns the drunken Henchard away from making a spectacle of himself before the 'Illustrious Personage' then visiting Casterbridge, it seems to the degraded man that he is driven back as if he were 'a bull breaking fence'. In his final subjugation, he becomes 'a netted lion', the victim of conventional ideas and attitudes which he no longer cares to fight.

The contrast between natural life and the false order of the artificial values imposed on it by society is shown not only in the dual presentation of Henchard himself, but also in Hardy's method of depicting all the main characters in this novel. Weaving his story around the motifs of truth and concealment, he shows, through a fluctuating pattern of deception and intrigue, all the differing ways in which these characters are blinded to actuality whilst at the same time they contrive to maintain for themselves an ideal of integrity in the eyes of their fellow-men. Discussing with Lucetta her previous chequered history, Henchard himself observes that ' "it is not by what is, in this life, but by what appears, that you are judged" ' (Ch. xxv), and the old furmity-woman at whose trial he is to preside betrays his own past to the citizens of Casterbridge, not from reasons of personal spite, but simply because ' "It proves that he's no better than I, and has no right to sit there in judgment upon me" ' (Ch. xxviii).

It is essential to Hardy's method that his characters should exist on two levels; superficially and objectively, as they appear initially to one another, and subjectively, as they really are. For this reason, details of dress and appearance are made to function both as overt representations of character, and as a symbolic commentary on the novel's theme: Abel Whittle, without his breeches, is no longer a man, but simply an object of ridicule (Ch. xv). Thus, the newly rich Elizabeth-Jane, with her 'fieldmouse fear of the coulter of destiny despite fair promise', at first adopts a plain style of dress which is in keeping with her humble origin. Later, as an 'artistic indulgence', she takes to wearing pretty clothes and ribbons; and with such a change comes a corresponding alteration in personality, 'for as soon as Casterbridge thought her artful it thought her worth notice' (Ch. xv). The consciously artificial, one-dimensional aspect by which complex humanity presents itself to the outside world becomes the image by which others form their opinions; therefore, outward appearance is deliberately made to stand for the real person. When Elizabeth-Jane finds that Farfrae has suddenly begun to pay attention to her, she attempts to rationalize his interest by dressing in the same clothes she had worn on the evening she danced with him, and looking critically at herself in the mirror.

The picture glassed back was, in her opinion, precisely of such a kind as to inspire that fleeting regard, and no more—'just enough to make him silly, and not enough to keep him so,' she said luminously; and Elizabeth thought, in a much lower key, that by this time he had discovered how plain and homely was the informing spirit of that pretty outside. (Ch. xvii)

Typically, her own original attraction to the young Scotsman is purely visual:

. . . she looked at him quite coolly, and saw how his forehead shone where the light caught it, and how nicely his hair was cut, and the sort of velvet-pile or down that was on the skin at the back of his neck . . . (Ch. vii)

and her first meeting with Lucetta prompts an admiration which is again based quite simply on 'the artistic perfection of the lady's appearance', so that she returns home 'musing on what she had seen, as she might have mused on a rainbow or the Northern Lights, a rare butterfly or a cameo' (Ch. xx).

In all respects Lucetta is, as Henchard fondly remarks before she rejects him, 'an artful little woman'. Hardy emphasizes that the image she projects is a studied piece of contrivance, the adoption of a personality which is as spurious as the name behind which she disguises her real identity. Her chief fear is that she may be 'seen through', her masquerade pierced; her query, ' "How do I appear to people?" ' (Ch. xxiv) is a telling one. When preparing to plead with Henchard for the return of her inflammatory letters, she tries half-unconsciously to appeal to his tenderer susceptibilities by adopting the image of a haggard and much-wronged woman, impairing the 'natural presentation' of her 'pretty though slightly worn features' and selecting '—as much from want of spirit as design—her poorest, plainest, and longest discarded attire'. Her unintentional resemblance to his dead wife Susan so strongly revives in Henchard's soul the memory of that other ill-used woman that, says Hardy, he is 'unmanned' (Ch. xxxv).

Lucetta's careful 'creation' of her new fashionable identity has an ominous significance:

She called Elizabeth from her breakfast, and entering her friend's bedroom Elizabeth saw the gowns spread out on the bed, one of a deep cherry colour, the other lighter—a glove lying at the end of each sleeve, a bonnet at the top of each neck, and parasols across the gloves, Lucetta standing beside the suggested human figure in an attitude of contemplation.

'I wouldn't think so hard about it,' said Elizabeth . . .

'But settling upon new clothes is so trying,' said Lucetta. 'You are that person' (pointing to one of the arrangements), 'or you are *that* totally different person' (pointing to the other), 'for the whole of the coming spring: and one of the two, you don't know which, may turn out to be very objectionable.' (Ch. xxiv)

Her choosing of the red dress is surely symbolic, or was so to Hardy's original readers; and the tacit brand thus placed on her character lends a ritual inevitability to her ultimate degradation by the jeering dwellers of Mixen Lane. Although her fine airs have made her 'the observed and imitated of all the smaller tradesmen's womankind' (Ch. xxxiii), she appears to the embittered Jopp, to whom she once refused help, merely as a 'proud piece of silk and waxwork' who deserves to be toppled (Ch. xxxvi). Lucetta's meeting of the royal visitor with her husband as mayor marks the peak of her social triumph, but Nance Mockridge's censorious pronouncement, ' "I do like to see the trimming pulled off such Christmas candles" ' (Ch. xxxvii), is plainly indicative of what is to come. That same evening, Lucetta's flimsy vanity is parodied by the bawdy fantasy of the skimmity-ride which blazons noisily and 'with lurid distinctness' the scandal of her former relationship with Michael Henchard. The effigies of the two victims are so accurately dressed in the garb of the characters they represent that Lucetta cries, ' "She's me—she's me—even to the parasol—my green parasol!" ' (Ch. xxxix). To her fearful imagination, the crude distortion of her guilt made visible is more garishly and horribly real than the truth. So sudden and vivid is the revelation that it brings on a fatal epilepsy. The gruesome actuality of the nightmare vision as Hardy presents it is accentuated by the uncanny shadowiness of its perpetrators: when the police arrive to deal with the conspirators there is nothing to be seen. 'Effigies, donkey, lanterns, band, all had disappeared like the crew of Comus' (Ch. xxxix).

Lucetta is killed by the power of her own imagination, by the ribald exaggeration of an image of herself which she has kept carefully hidden, but which is more essentially 'she' than the other successful and sophisticated persona which she has so painstakingly tried to create. Ironically, though, when Henchard's imaginative contemplation of suicide by drowning is as if magically projected before his eyes as a material reality, the ghoulish apparition turns him in bewilderment from his original purpose.

In the circular current . . . the form was brought forward, till it passed under his eyes; and then he perceived with a sense of horror that it was *himself*. Not a man somewhat resembling him, but one in all respects his counterpart, his actual double, was floating as if dead in Ten Hatches Hole.

The sense of the supernatural was strong in this unhappy man, and he turned away as one might have done in the actual presence of an appalling miracle. (Ch. xli)

Yet what appears so vividly to be 'himself' is only, as Elizabeth-Jane afterwards shows him, a bundle of old clothes used in the skimmity-ride. For Lucetta and Henchard, the imaginative distortion of the truth can mean life or death, a destruction or a reawakening of the mind.

In depicting the convoluted lives of Henchard, Lucetta and Farfrae, Hardy frequently uses the character of Elizabeth-Jane as a detached observer through whom he can comment on their relationships and predict their fortunes. In the same way that he was to show Marty South in *The Woodlanders* as the one character in the midst of romantic chaos able to keep through her suffering an unswerving perspective, so, in *The Mayor of Casterbridge*, Hardy maintains, in the sober, diligent step-daughter of Michael Henchard, a quiet focal point 'from the crystalline sphere of a straight-forward mind' (Ch. xxv). It is through her eyes, for instance, that we see the almost farcical tension between Lucetta and her two rival lovers, in a domestic tableau which, despite the powerful undercurrent of mixed feelings, retains on the surface a studiously contrived propriety:

They sat stiffly side by side at the darkening table, like some Tuscan painting of the two disciples supping at Emmaus. Lucetta, forming the third and haloed figure, was opposite them; Elizabeth-Jane, being out of the game, and out of the group, could observe all from afar, like the evangelist who had to write it down: that there were long spaces of taciturnity, when all exterior circumstance was subdued to the touch of spoons and china, the click of a heel on the pavement under the window, the passing of a wheelbarrow or cart, the whistling of the carter, the gush of water into householders' buckets at the town-pump opposite; the exchange of greetings among their neighbours, and the rattle of the yokes by which they carried off their evening supply.

'More bread-and-butter?' said Lucetta to Henchard and Farfrae equally . . .

To Elizabeth-Jane, silently watching Lucetta's glances into Farfrae's eyes, it is 'plain as the town-pump that Donald and Lucetta were incipient lovers'—

But Henchard was constructed upon too large a scale to discern such minutiae as these by an evening light, which to him were as the notes of an insect that lie above the compass of the human ear. (Ch. xxvi)

It is largely through Hardy's creation of Elizabeth-Jane as a more or less passive, non-participating character that he is able to hint at a deeper order and meaning underlying the web of confusion and conflict on which the story is founded. From her first sight of Henchard, when she marvels at his unexpected magnificence (' "Did ever anything go more by contraries!" ', she exclaims), to her final wonderment at 'the persistence of the unforeseen' with which Hardy concludes the book, it is by means of her quietly judicious perception that all the contrasts of the novel are unified into a single vision. Similarly, by tracing the reversions and transformations of Henchard's attitude towards Elizabeth-Jane, Hardy is able to indicate in yet another way the strength of man's dependence on his illusions, on what *seems* to be rather than on what *is*. To the deluded eye of fond paternity, Elizabeth-Jane's features reveal unquestioned consanguinity, but with knowledge of her true parentage comes the discovery that ' "the eye sees that which it brings with it the means of seeing" ' (*PRF*, p. 125).[4] Searching for positive proof of his wife's written statement, Henchard steals into the girl's bedroom to look again at the face which he had unsuspectingly assumed to be that of his own daughter:

In sleep there come to the surface buried genealogical facts, ancestral curves, dead men's traits, which the mobility of daytime animation screens and overwhelms. In the present statuesque repose of the young girl's countenance Richard Newson's was unmistakably reflected. He could not endure the sight of her, and hastened away. (Ch. xix)

Yet, to Henchard, the chief mockery is that he has no sooner taught the girl to claim kinship with him and to accept his name than he discovers that, after all, she has no right to it. All instinctual emotion, however falsely based, is crushed by the all-important consideration of public disgrace or public sanction.

Convinced of the scathing damage to his local repute and position that must have been caused by such a fact, though it had never before reached his own ears, Henchard showed a positive distaste for the presence of this girl not his own, whenever he encountered her. (Ch. xx)

Finally, when he comes to be utterly dependent on his step-daughter's love—so much so that he deliberately wrongs her in order to keep that love—Henchard despairingly realizes the massive irony of the situation. All the values on which he has previously attempted to style his existence have been turned upside down.

It was an odd sequence that out of all this tampering with social law came that flower of Nature, Elizabeth. Part of his wish to wash his hands of life arose from his perception of its contrarious inconsistencies —of Nature's jaunty readiness to support unorthodox social principles. (Ch. xliv)

The irony is further accentuated by the reversal of Elizabeth-Jane's affection for Henchard when, discovering that he has wil-fully deceived her true father and accepting the deed for the fact without any extenuation, she decides in a 'revulsion of feeling' that she ' "ought to forget him now" ' (Ch. xliii). And yet, as Hardy has explained earlier,

Henchard was, by original make, the last man to act stealthily, for good or for evil. But the *solicitus timor* of his love—the dependence upon Elizabeth's regard into which he had declined (or, in another sense, to which he had advanced)—denaturalized him. (Ch. xlii)

Two days after he had finished *The Mayor of Casterbridge*, Hardy noted in his diary that 'The business of the poet and novelist is to show the sorriness underlying the grandest things, and the grandeur underlying the sorriest things' (*Life*, p. 171). This, in brief, is the philosophy underlying the story of Michael Henchard. It does not necessarily imply a tragic point of view, but is merely a simple statement of what (to Hardy) is a universal truth. Nothing is consistent. Henchard's love for Elizabeth-Jane can be seen both as a 'decline' and an 'advance': everything is dependent, finally, on the manner in which it is viewed and understood.

Hardy's expression of the inherent contrariness of life is summed up in Henchard's musing that ' "when I was rich I didn't need what I could have, and now I be poor I can't have what I need!" ' (Ch. xxxiii), and in his bitter but resigned conversation with Farfrae when the latter has appropriated both his corn trade and his home:

' 'Tis turn and turn about, isn't it! Do ye mind how we stood like this in the Chalk Walk when I persuaded 'ee to stay? You then stood without a chattel to your name, and I was the master of the house in Corn Street. But now I stand without a stick or a rag, and the master of that house is you.'

'Yes, yes; that's so! It's the way o' the warrld,' said Farfrae.

'Ha, ha, true!' cried Henchard, throwing himself into a mood of jocularity. 'Up and down! I'm used to it. What's the odds after all!' (Ch. xxxii)

It is an attitude to which the consciously pathetic image of the dead goldfinch in its cage (Henchard's wedding-present to Elizabeth-Jane) is only a decorative gesture, a conventional symbol of man's inhumanity—or, rather, of his 'unnaturalness'. Henchard's own death is bounded by the sturdy rationality of Elizabeth-Jane's thoughtful realization, in the face of her own unforeseen happiness, that good fortune is not equally distributed amongst men, and that 'there were others receiving less who had deserved much more' (Ch. xlv).

Artistically, the story of Michael Henchard comes full circle, with what might be termed the 'spherical completeness of perfect art' which Hardy so admired in the parable stories of the Bible (*Life*, p. 170). When the ex-mayor, dressed in the serviceable clothes of a workman, returns resolutely to his former occupation as a hay-trusser, we are urged to take note of the significance of this fact by a naively intrusive authorial aside couched in terms of Elizabeth-Jane's unconscious observation: 'Though she did not know it Henchard formed at this moment much the same picture as he had presented when entering Casterbridge for the first time nearly a quarter of a century before . . .' (Ch. xliii). Partly because of the obviousness of this sort of artistic contrivance, there is undoubtedly a danger of seeing Henchard purely as an allegorical

M

figure: Douglas Brown, for example, does this in advancing his interesting thesis that Henchard represents the decline of agriculture at the time of the repeal of the Corn Laws.[5] Yet, by his inclusion of the novel's subtitle, *A Man of Character*, Hardy emphasizes that it is Henchard himself who is uniquely the subject of the story. Ultimately, Hardy's elaborate methods of staging his characters and arranging his scenes must be seen to relate purely to the attempt to present this one man, and his relationship with his environment, by means of various contrasting perspectives. The contrived synonymity of his entrance into the world of Casterbridge and his exit from it points to the comparative unreality of his existence there. Those past events which vitally affected his life are shown virtually as fantasy or are left completely in obscurity; and yet these hidden episodes are the abiding reality by which all else is judged. In effect, paradoxically, Hardy is saying to us that the twenty-odd years of Henchard's rise and fall have been dream-like and insubstantial. The grotesque furmity-woman, the artificial Lucetta, and the humble Susan, with her fatal 'honesty in dishonesty', are all in a sense reflections of Henchard himself, and yet, significantly, his relationship with them was, in each instance, a relationship forced by his recognition of man-made laws. With their death or disappearance, he is himself again, and the world of men which has governed his way of living becomes finally, in accordance with Hardy's projected vision, 'a mere painted scene to him', an artificial place which he consciously rejects for the reality and anonymity of death.

VII

Tess of the d'Urbervilles

Fortunately . . . *Tess* is a work so great that it could almost afford to have even proportionately great faults . . .

William Watson, *The Academy*, 6 February 1892

In comparison with Hardy's other novels, both *Tess of the d'Urbervilles* and *Jude the Obscure* rely most heavily on symbolism or significant imagery to make a thematic point, yet, surprisingly, these later works also evoke with unparalleled 'realism' the actual qualities of existence. In *Tess of the d'Urbervilles*, particularly, Hardy's preoccupation with the emotional and representational overtones of landscape and environment in their relation to man reaches its greatest intensity: in no other of his novels does visual and tactile imagery play so important a part.

Yet although it is, as Guerard claims, probably 'the most realistic'[1] of his novels, its distinctiveness lies, paradoxically, in Hardy's consistent use of suggestion and implication. In *Tess of the d'Urbervilles*, life is played out predominantly 'as a Mystery'. The depth and intensity of the story derive from the great sensitivity of Hardy's 'abstract imaginings', based on a unique appreciation of the 'meaning' *behind* 'simple optical effects' (*Life*, p. 185). Again, in this novel, the exquisite accuracy of concrete detail is shown to be only the visible manifestation of a larger pattern reflecting the ambiguity and complexity of life itself. With his supreme mastery of this technique in *Tess of the d'Urbervilles*, Hardy achieves most nearly an approximation of the quality which he found in Turner's water-colours—of which he observed, at the time of writing the novel, that 'each is a landscape *plus* a man's soul' (*Life*, p. 216).

As in *Far from the Madding Crowd*, *The Return of the Native* and *The Mayor of Casterbridge*, the structure of the novel is based essentially on contrast, on the balancing of opposites which are yet related to the scheme of the whole. Tess's fundamental purity—according to the system of nature—is, according to social law, blemished by actions which are both sinful and unforgiveable, so in his presentation of her as epitomizing these different values, Hardy must portray her, as he does Henchard, both as she *is* and as she is *seen*. She must be made credible to us as a real, living presence, but she must also be seen objectively, as the representation of an idea. For this reason *Tess of the d'Urbervilles* is less a novel about an individual character than an exploration of a state of being, stated both impressionistically and with categorical explicitness. Henchard's presence, in *The Mayor of Casterbridge*, is almost always concrete and particular; he dominates the story but does not entirely pervade it. His life is the hub around which other characters revolve and his character is specifically moulded by outside events and influences. With *Tess of the d'Urbervilles*, Hardy's concentration on one character expands immensely in significance. To discuss the character of Tess is, in effect, to discuss Hardy's technique in the whole novel, for in a very real sense, as Ian Gregor remarks: 'She is the heart of the novel, giving it all the life it has . . . If an enlargement of the character takes place, it is to increase the force of the character, not to point out its significance.'[2]

The progression and organization of the tale itself are fundamentally straightforward. Although essentially a moral work, it is avowedly 'neither didactic nor aggressive', being merely, as Hardy asserted in his preface of 1892, 'an attempt to give artistic form to a true sequence of things'. At its best, the 'moral' in the story of Tess's life is enacted in physical terms rather than in a consciously psychological or dogmatic framework. Similarly, Hardy's presentation of Tess as a character is, when analysed, seen to be surprisingly restricted to the surface. As the psychological side of her character is generally shown indirectly or in analogy, so, too, the vividness and density of her physical presence is largely pictorial, the result of a painstaking accumulation of concrete and suggestive detail. It would have been easy, one supposes, for Hardy to turn Tess into a symbol as, to some extent and despite her undeniable individuality, Eustacia becomes a symbol in *The Return of the Native*. She does not become overtly symbolic, I feel, because her essential simplicity is so tangibly real and so many-faceted.

One of Hardy's most consistent and effective techniques in his novel-writing is, as I have previously pointed out, his method of showing rather than telling; his tendency to create a picture and then to expound upon the elements of its composition. His characters, depending (partly) upon their significance, tend to become static 'portrait studies', often superbly detailed, but somehow unreal, or larger than life. John Holloway remarks that 'Of set purpose, Hardy's characters often lack rotundity in a literary, figurative sense';[3] they are seen against their environments, as constituent parts of the whole system of nature rather than as individuals. In *Tess of the d'Urbervilles*, however, this method of depicting character takes on a new force. Like the presence of Egdon Heath in *The Return of the Native*, Tess embodies in herself the elements of the natural world in all their ineffable variety. She is not seen against her environment (as, for instance, are Henchard or Bathsheba), but is an intrinsic part of it. If any one aspect of her character dominates, it is simply her basic earthliness, her association with all that is real and living. At the same time, Hardy differentiates her and gives her an historical reality by giving full particulars of her previous life, her place in society and, most notably, in the line of her noble forebears. With her identity thus established, his treatment of her as a being rather than as an individual is given point and solidity, and even in his persistent and deliberate associations of her with the most diverse elements of the natural world, we do not lose sight of her uniqueness or her essential humanity. The impression of her as a part of the natural world is nowhere concentrated, but is scattered through the novel in random hints and references, forming a consistent, all-pervading 'atmosphere' which gives a peculiarly subtle emotional colouring to every aspect of her life.

Immediately after the scene of her seduction, for example, her natural innocence ('She had been made to break an accepted social law, but no law known to the environment [of nature]') is reinforced by Hardy's presentation of her as a part of that environment. During her pregnancy she roams on 'lonely hills and dales', and 'her quiescent glide was of a piece with the element she moved in' (Ch. xiii); after her baby is born and has died, 'some spirit within her rose automatically as the sap in the twigs' (Ch. xv). At Talbothays, she and her fellow milkmaids walking through the mead show 'the bold grace of wild animals—the reckless unchastened motion of women accustomed to limitless space—in which they abandoned themselves to the air as a swimmer to the wave' (Ch. xxvii). She struggles against her love for Angel Clare, but 'Every see-saw of her breath, every wave of her blood, every pulse singing in her ears, was a voice that joined with nature in revolt against her scrupulousness' (Ch. xxviii), and Angel himself woos her

in undertones like that of the purling milk—at the cow's side, at skimmings, at butter-makings, at cheese-makings, among broody poultry, and among farrowing pigs—as no milkmaid was ever wooed before by such a man. (Ch. xxix)

Her physical beauty, too, is described in terms which emphasize her identification with the innocent sensuousness of her lush and fertile environment. She has a 'mobile peony mouth' (Ch. ii); her hair, as a child, is 'earth-coloured' (Ch. v); when she returns from her first visit to Alec d'Urberville she has 'roses at her breast; roses in her hat; roses and strawberries in her basket to the brim' (Ch. vi). At Talbothays, Angel finds that he had 'never before seen a woman's lips and teeth which forced upon his mind with such persistent iteration the old Elizabethan simile of roses filled with snow' (Ch. xxiv). Even her hands, at cheesemaking, show themselves 'amid the immaculate whiteness of the curds . . . of the pinkness of the rose', and her skin is 'as cold and damp to his mouth as a new-gathered mushroom' (Ch. xxviii). After sleep she is 'warm as a sunned cat', and when she yawns, Angel sees 'the red interior of her mouth as if it had been a snake's' (Ch. xxvii).

Hardy's method in building up his composite picture of Tess differs perceptibly and significantly from that with which he draws the character of Michael Henchard in *The Mayor of Caster-bridge*, even though his essential themes and attitudes in the two stories are comparable. When suggesting the inherent strength and solidarity of Henchard's character in terms of natural imagery, Hardy's referents are almost exclusively specific in their emotional connotations: he has the brute power of a bull, the unconscious dignity of a lion; his rages are volcanic, his moods and passions like the lowering of the skies. There is little doubt that Hardy's intention in using such a familiar form of symbolism is to promote an immediate acceptance and understanding on the part of the reader. The two contrasting attitudes towards Henchard's personality are clearly and firmly established. The character of Tess Durbeyfield, on the other hand, is nowhere so consciously categorized. The wealth and diversity of the imagery by which Hardy accentuates her affiliation with the natural processes of the world has purely the effect of emphasizing her intrinsic being; it does not necessarily evoke any particular or spontaneous response until it is seen cumulatively, as part of a much larger pattern. The progression of Tess's life is constantly paralleled by the smallest details of all the other infinitesimal existences with which it is surrounded and of which it is a part. By a scarcely perceptible accumulation of delicately appropriate imagery and material observation, Hardy creates a vast, emotive background which gives to her existence its essential integrality, and which in retrospect has a far deeper significance.

It is surely not accidental, for example, that most of the important stages of her history are highlighted by the sounds of birdsong or by its conspicuous absence. After the fateful death of the horse, Prince, Hardy shows that life carries on regardless of this small tragedy: 'The atmosphere turned pale, the birds shook themselves in the hedges, arose, and twittered . . .' (Ch. iv). On the morning when Tess leaves to work for Alec d'Urberville, she wakes 'at the marginal minute of the dark when the grove is still mute, save for one prophetic bird who sings with a clear-voiced conviction that he at least knows the correct time of day' (Ch. vii), and on her arrival at his home she is set to work looking after his mother's pet fowls and whistling to her bull-finches. At the scene of her seduction the birds are asleep, roosting in the trees above their heads; afterwards, Hardy tells us, 'she had learnt that the serpent hisses where the sweet birds sing' (Ch. xii) even though 'the trees were just as green as before; the birds sang and the sun shone as clearly now as ever' (Ch. xiv). She leaves for Talbothays on a 'thyme-scented, bird-hatching morning in May' (Ch. xvi), and as she walks down into the valley, she feels that 'in every bird's note seemed to lurk a joy'. She is attracted to Angel 'like a fascinated bird' (Ch. xix), but when Dairyman Crick's story reminds her of her past, 'Only a solitary cracked-voiced reed-sparrow greeted her from the bushes by the river, in a sad, machine-made tone, resembling that of a past friend whose friendship she had outworn' (Ch. xxi). When she is happiest, the 'buoyancy of her tread' is 'like the skim of a bird which has not quite alighted' (Ch. xxxi).

Sometimes, Hardy deliberately extends this pervasive imagery so that, without appearing forced or contrived, it functions in a way which is directly symbolic or prophetic. Birds appear with ominous foreboding at crucial moments in the story. A rooster's daylight crow portends ill fortune immediately after Tess's wedding to Angel. After their separation she sleeps alone in a forest and on awakening finds herself surrounded by wounded pheasants slowly dying in agony. Once again, during her exile at Flintcomb-Ash, she and Marian are visited at their work by 'strange birds from behind the North Pole . . . gaunt spectral creatures with tragical eyes—eyes which had witnessed scenes of cataclysmal horror' who come silently to look for food (Ch. xliii). Frequently, too, the suggestion that Tess herself is like a bird reaches almost symbolic proportions. Hardy tells us, for instance, that she has been 'caught in her days of immaturity like a bird in a springe' (Ch. xxxi); and finally, when she is 'caught' again by

Alec d'Urberville, she looks at him 'with the hopeless defiance of the sparrow's gaze before its captor twists its neck' (Ch. xlvii). The power and congruity of these consciously premonitive images derive from the fact that Hardy has drawn them directly from the richly detailed natural world with which Tess is already firmly associated: thus, such apparently obvious symbolic referents seem to be in no way artificial, but are only credible illustrations of the mysterious coincidences always contained in real life.

On this first level, then, our conception of Tess as a living presence is largely based on Hardy's sympathetic association of her with the tangible natural world in all its aspects. In keeping with this imagery of her essential earthliness, Hardy shows her responding to life with the spontaneous, instinctive volition of an animal. She does not belong expressly to any society or to any time in history; she belongs simply to the country, which is timeless. Her elemental quality is shown to be at once perennial and vulnerable in its striking contrast with the unliving representative phenomenon of a modern progressive age:

... there was the hissing of a train, which drew up almost silently on the wet rails, and the milk was rapidly swung can by can into the truck. The light of the engine flashed for a second upon Tess Durbeyfield's figure, motionless under the great holly tree. No object could have looked more foreign to the gleaming cranks and wheels than this unsophisticated girl, with the round bare arms, the rainy face and hair, the suspended attitude of a friendly leopard at pause, the print gown of no date or fashion, and the cotton bonnet drooping on her brow. (Ch. xxx)

By design, she is 'an almost standard woman' (Ch. xiv). Angel sees her in the early morning as 'a visionary essence of woman—a whole sex condensed into one typical form'. Yet she cannot be raised above the common level; it is unnatural to her.

He called her Artemis, Demeter and other fanciful names half teasingly, which she did not like because she did not understand them.

'Call me Tess,' she would say askance; and he did. (Ch. xx)

She is individualized in so far as she is more intelligent and sensitive than her peers, but Hardy continually emphasizes that

in presenting her he is presenting no more than the tragic complexity of ordinary human nature. Her actions and emotions are
fundamentally representative. After her 'fall', Hardy remarks
that

... it had not been in Tess's power—nor is it in anybody's power—to
feel the whole truth of golden opinions while it is possible to profit by
them. She—and how many more—might have ironically said to God
with St. Augustine: 'Thou hast counselled a better course than Thou
hast permitted.' (Ch. xv)

Similarly, her initial recovery from her misfortune is simply 'the
irresistible, universal, automatic tendency to find sweet pleasure
somewhere, which pervades all life' (Ch. xvi).

By means of his detailed, impressionistic technique, Hardy is
able to show Tess as at once a part of her own specific world and as
a part of humanity—the apotheosis of womanhood. Generally, she
appears to us essentially as an abstract figure, a being compounded
of flowers, earth and sunlight, yet she is firmly established as a real,
sensuous woman by her speech and her actions. When Hardy does
give us a graphic, particularized picture of her, it is with quite a
different intention. There is a marked difference between our
conception of Tess as the imaginative embodiment of nature and
our view of her as she is represented objectively.

In the greater part of the novel, Tess's character—or rather,
Hardy's impression of what she *is*—creates the very fabric of the
narrative. Her fundamental presence is conveyed in action and
description and very little happens that is not somehow related to
her. Nevertheless, our view of life as the novel presents it is not
conditioned ostensibly by what Tess thinks or by what she sees,
but by what Hardy chooses to show us. So it is that he selects
moments in her life that are representative, pausing in the flow of
action and impression to give a definite, clear picture in which the
moral or social implication of the tale is made into a detached,
pseudo-symbolic composition with Tess as the illustrative titular
subject.

Tess's automatic feeling of shame and despair at her position as 'a spouseless mother' is, says Hardy, merely 'generated by her conventional aspect, and not by her innate sensations':

She might have seen that what had bowed her head so profoundly— the thought of the world's concern at her situation—was founded on an illusion. She was not an existence, an experience, a passion, a structure of sensations, to anybody but herself. To all humankind besides Tess was only a passing thought. Even to friends she was no more than a frequently passing thought. (Ch. xiv)

For this reason, at all the most important stages of her history, Hardy deliberately shows her as others see her, creating a series of distinctly objective vignettes which unemotionally sum up her situation at each given moment. In our first glimpse of her she appears merely as one of a bevy of white-clad village girls, 'a fine and handsome girl—not handsomer than some others, possibly—', engaged in the traditional May-Day 'club-walking'. She is singled out because she is wearing a red ribbon in her hair, but Hardy is careful at first not to draw too much attention to her. She is still, at this stage, 'a mere vessel of emotion untinctured by experience' (Ch. ii). Momentarily, the author dwells, as if reminiscently, on phases of her appearance and personality; but he quickly reverts to the stance of the simple observer—

. . . few knew, and still fewer considered this. A small minority, mainly strangers, would look at her long in casually passing by, and grow momentarily fascinated by her freshness, and wonder if they would ever see her again: but to almost everybody she was a fine and picturesque country girl, and no more. (Ch. ii)

It is exactly in this manner that Angel Clare, passing by with his brothers, first notices her—'she had looked so soft in her thin white gown'—before dismissing the thought of her from his mind. As yet, Tess's life is undistinguished and unblemished. She is shown to us as an almost anonymous figure, simply 'a beautiful feminine tissue, sensitive as gossamer, and practically blank as snow as yet' (Ch. xi). Yet she is singled out, for no apparent reason, and the 'coarse pattern' traced on her life by Alec d'Urberville alters and colours all our subsequent pictures of her. Although still essentially a part of her world, she is hereafter individualized, set apart and studied with increasing depth and detail.

After her baby has been born, Hardy significantly shows her again as part of a distant picture, one of a crowd of workers in a cornfield:

The women . . . wore drawn cotton bonnets with great flapping curtains to keep off the sun, and gloves to protect their hands being wounded by the stubble. There was one wearing a pale pink jacket, another in a cream-coloured tight-sleeved gown, another in a petticoat as red as the arms of the reaping-machine . . . This morning the eye returns involuntarily to the girl in the pink cotton jacket, she being the most flexuous and finely-drawn figure of them all. But her bonnet is pulled so far over her brow that none of her face is disclosed while she binds, though her complexion may be guessed from a stray twine or two of dark brown hair which extends below the curtain of her bonnet. Perhaps one reason why she seduces casual attention is that she never courts it, through the other women often gaze around them. (Ch.xiv)

This picture and the ensuing description show Tess's situation as something which can be observed and rationalized. She is part of a carefully arranged study, an exquisitely detailed set-piece which can be set apart for contemplation and comparison. The general colouring and organization of this early scene are obviously intended as a companion piece for the drab field at Flintcomb-Ash, where Tess has exiled herself as a result of her 'guilt':

Nobody came near them, and their movements showed a mechanical regularity; their forms standing enshrouded in Hessian 'wroppers'—sleeved brown pinafores, tied behind to the bottom, to keep their gowns from blowing about—scant skirts revealing boots that reached high up the ankles, and yellow sheepskin gloves with gauntlets. The pensive character which the curtained hood lent to their bent heads would have reminded the observer of some early Italian conception of the two Marys. (Ch. xliii)

One might take the first picture of Tess in her virginal white as the subject for the first Book, 'The Maiden', and the second, of the young woman in the harvest-field, as illustrating the title, 'Maiden No More' (Bk II). The last picture, with its cold and dreary atmosphere of harshness and resignation, is the focal point for the fifth Book: 'The Woman Pays'.

Numerous other scenes seem to be peculiarly static and representative, and in most of them the figure of Tess herself is given special emotional or thematic emphasis. We have, for example, the portrait of the young girl as she appears to the 'surprised vision' of her fellow-travellers, loaded with the fruit and flowers of Alec d'Urberville's bounty (Ch. vi), or the dramatically stylized picture of the unwed mother baptizing her child:

Her figure looked singularly tall and imposing as she stood in her long white nightgown, a thick cable of twisted dark hair hanging straight down her back to her waist. The kindly dimness of the weak candle abstracted from her form and features the little blemishes which sunlight might have revealed—the stubble scratches upon her wrists, and the weariness of her eyes—her high enthusiasm having a transfiguring effect upon the face which had been her undoing, showing it as a thing of immaculate beauty, with a touch of dignity which was almost regal. The little ones kneeling round, their sleepy eyes blinking and red, awaited her preparations full of a suspended wonder . . . (Ch. xiv)

To the children she does not appear like 'Sissy' any more, but 'as a being large, towering, and awful—a divine personage with whom they had nothing in common'. There is the same conscious use of artistic structure and lighting in, for instance, the highly symbolic vignette of Tess's confession to Angel (see p. 50 above), or in her meeting with Alec amid the bonfires, where her odd attire of black and white gives her 'the effect . . . of a wedding and funeral guest in one' (Ch. l). Each picture calculatedly epitomizes her situation and orientates our emotional response to it. Details of dress, attitude and colour all convey implicitly allegorical overtones which are systematically reinforced by the graphic and appropriate use of setting or landscape—the rich languorous azure of the Vale of Blackmoor; the intense sunlight and sharp stubble of the harvest-field; the desolate brown of the swede-plain, and the frost and rain and snow.

In nearly all these 'studies' there is a curious blending of the immediate and the distant. The immediacy is almost inevitably the result of the atmospheric richness in which the picture is conceived; Tess herself is simply the focal point to which all the elements relate. In none of these tableaux does Hardy give any hint at the development of Tess's individual thoughts or attitudes. We gain from the picture only a visual, objective impression, so that the 'moral' import comes through to us clearly, with no cross-references. Each scene could well stand alone as a self-sufficient object-lesson, exquisite in its delicacy and precision.[4] It is only at the very end of the novel that Tess becomes solely a symbolic figure; her vitality is lost, and Hardy, in endeavouring to cast her accurately in the role of a fallen woman who is still 'pure', concentrates simply on the picture and the moral. The effect, in its obviousness, is glib and unconvincing.[5] As George Meredith wrote,

... from the moment of the meeting again of Tess and Alec, I grow cold, and should say that there is a depression of power, up to the end save for the short scene on the plain of Stonehenge. If the author's minute method had been sustained, we should have had a finer book. It is marred by the sudden hurry to round the story. And Tess, out of the arms of Alec, into (I suppose) those of the lily necked Clare, and on to the Black Flag waving over her poor body, is a smudge in vapour—she at one time so real to me.[6]

Hardy cannot successfully harmonize his idea of Tess with what she must represent within the context of the story; so that frequently, there is a dichotomy between the showing and the telling. Arnold Kettle points out that 'His art does not quite achieve that sense of the inner movement of life which transcends abstractions. He is constantly weakening his apprehension of this movement by inadequate attitudes and judgements'.[7]

In his portrayal of Tess as a victim of social laws, more sinned against than sinning, he often, as Ian Gregor puts it, 'seems not so much to have his thumb in the scale, as his whole right arm'.[8] Not content with implying the duality of Tess's situation, the contrast between what she appears to be in the eyes of social law, and what she is according to the law of nature, he frequently merges his 'poetical representations' of truth into what can only be called explicit moral allegory. At crucial parts of the narrative, we find that the 'message' implicit in the whole fabric of the novel has been forcibly removed and embodied in concentrated symbolic scenes. One of Hardy's earliest critics, Lionel Johnson, comments on these moments of explicit dogma that: 'At times, they read like quaint modern imitations of those marginal glosses, which adorn the *Pilgrim's Progress* and the *Ancient Mariner*: "Here Tess illustrateth the falling out betwixt Nature and Society," or "In this place did Angel mock at Giant Calvinist, for that he taught an untenable redemptive theolatry." '[9] Thus, for example, the pregnant Tess wandering about the countryside 'looked upon herself as a figure of Guilt intruding into the haunts of Innocence. But all the while she was making a distinction where there was no difference' (Ch. xiii). Sometimes Hardy's commentary is even more blatant, as the irony is embedded in words which are themselves symbolic. Soon after her seduction, Tess meets an artisan who, under the inspiration (as it transpires) of Angel's father, travels the country inscribing religious warnings on stiles and fences, 'placing a comma after each word, as if to give pause while that word was driven well home to the reader's heart'—

THY, DAMNATION, SLUMBERETH, NOT.
2 Pet. ii. 3.

Against the peaceful landscape, the pale, decaying tints of the copses, the blue air of the horizon and the lichened stile-boards, these staring vermilion words shone forth. They seemed to shout themselves out and make the atmosphere ring. Some people might have cried 'Alas, poor Theology!' at the hideous defacement—the last grotesque phase of a creed which had served mankind well in its time. But the words entered Tess with accusatory horror. It was as if this man had known her recent history; yet he was a total stranger. (Ch. xii)

The character of Alec d'Urberville, the direct descendant of Aeneas Manston and William Dare, is born of the same impulse to create an easily recognizable moral fable. His studied artificiality (in direct contrast with Tess's naive innocence) is obviously that of the music-hall villain. 'There he is', says a contemporary critic—who calls himself The Baron de Bookworms—

... and all the perfumes of the Vale of Blackmoor will not suffice for dispelling the strong odour of the footlights which pervades every scene where this unconscionable scoundrel makes his appearance. That he is ultimately disposed of by being struck to the heart with the carving-knife that had been brought in for cold-beef slicing at breakfast, is some satisfaction.[10]

In addition to the twirling 'mistarchers' and rolling eyes, however, Hardy deliberately imbues his character with diabolical properties. He is 'the blood-red ray in the spectrum' of Tess's life; on one occasion he even comes to her in a setting of smoke, flames and pitchforks, saying, ' "You are Eve, and I am the old Other One come to tempt you in the disguise of an inferior animal" ', after which he quotes some appropriate lines from *Paradise Lost* (Ch. l). There is a similar obviousness (and irony) in the name 'Angel' for the man whom Tess worships in the Paradise of Talbothays, and in Alec's transformation—'a ghastly *bizarrerie*'—into a fanatic lay preacher (Ch. xlv). In a very real sense, Tess's wanderings, her relationships with Alec and Angel, and her metaphorical journey from rustic innocence to experience, do constitute a kind of *Pilgrim's Progress*, an historical chronicle worked out in terms of allegory but set in a recognizably real framework.

　　To a large extent, Hardy's boldness in setting up his 'impressions' with such dramatic clarity is justified by his creation of a surrounding other world whose details, while firmly based on solid reality, have overtones of mystery and fantasy. Here again he uses basically the same technique as he employs in many of the earlier novels, but he develops it in *Tess of the d'Urbervilles* more positively and with more striking effect. In *Desperate Remedies*, for example, ghosts and omens were used with almost the sole aim of creating decorative melodramatic overtones, while in *The Return of the Native* the world of witchcraft and black magic is seen as a vital constituent of man's imagination, a grotesque manifestation of his credulous perception of the world which represents, for purposes of art, the other side of an emotional conception of reality. In *Tess of the d'Urbervilles*, on the other hand, magic, so bound up as it is with indigenous history and ballad and folklore, is an inseparable part of everyday living. The medieval legends and superstitions in which Tess believes are an omnipresent reminder of her inescapable position as one of the 'folk', part of a vast lineage stretching backwards into infinity. Her own particular story, in its very ordinariness, is simply that of the traditional 'ruined maid' in ballad and folk legend; Hardy reminds us that some of Tess's 'mailed ancestors rollicking home from a fray' had doubtless 'dealt the same measure even more ruthlessly towards peasant girls of their time' (Ch. xi). The fancies and traditions of the farming community in which she is born abound in her story and relate significantly to almost every aspect of her life. Joan Durbeyfield rocks her youngest child to sleep with 'the favourite ditty of "The Spotted Cow" '—

> I saw her lie do'—own in yon'—der green gro'—ove;
> Come, love!' and I'll tell' you where!' (Ch. iii)

and when Tess reappears out of doors after the birth of her baby, her female companions, singing at their work, 'could not refrain from mischievously throwing in a few verses of the ballad about the maid who went to the merry green wood and came back in a changed state' (Ch. xiv). Throughout the tale the ballad atmosphere is reinforced by the extensive use of references to omens, ghosts and fairies, which belong as much to the countryside as Tess herself. As she passes at night through an uninhabited part of Blackmoor on her way home, the supernatural weaves an almost tangible web around her:

Superstitions linger longest on these heavy soils. Having once been forest, at this shadowy time it seemed to assert something of its old character, the far and the near being blended, and every tree and tall hedge making the most of its presence. The harts that had been hunted here, the witches that had been pricked and ducked, the green-spangled fairies that 'whickered' at you as you passed—the place teemed with beliefs in them still, and they formed an impish multitude now. (Ch. l)

N

It is hard to separate the vivid mythic imagery from the rich and detailed vision of everyday life, so closely are they intermingled. In such an atmosphere of credulity, the natural cause becomes an omen as easily as a lurid sunset can be seen to resemble Purgatory. Hardy forces us to see with the eye of rational truth, but shows us at the same time that the eye of the imagination is equally as powerful in that it can see beneath the obvious physical fact. From the beginning of *Tess of the d'Urbervilles* there are hints which, taken as part of the general pattern, are obviously premonitive: as has been suggested, 'the destiny of Tess comes to us as a cumulation of visible omens'.[11] Many of the images in the book appear to be introduced casually as circumstantial detail, but ramify from chapter to chapter, reappearing with increasing forcefulness at key points of the narrative. The apparently random observation that Tess, dancing in her virginal white with the other village maidens, is the only one amongst them to sport the 'pronounced adornment' of a red ribbon (Ch. ii), is reinforced by the equally slight mentioning that one of the roses given to Tess by Alec d'Urberville pricks her on the chin; now, though, Hardy adds that 'Like all the cottagers . . . Tess was steeped in fancies and prefigurative superstitions; she thought this an ill omen' (Ch. vi). The symbolic connotations of redness and blood as they are to be associated with her life are thus tentatively and then more boldly established. There are many more obvious references to ill-luck, death and murder, gradually and persistently building up in intensity. Tess is splashed with blood when Prince is killed and the luxurious flowers in the garden at the dairy blight her arms with red stains as she creeps along to hear Angel's music. Later, she strangles with her own hands the bleeding and dying pheasants randomly picked off by hunters, and when Alec insults her she strikes him with her heavy threshing-gauntlet, so that his blood drops on to the straw. There is a ballad-type inevitability in the progression and accumulation of such images until the murder of Alec and Tess's own hanging, yet in spite of their seeming obviousness they do not appear extraordinary because each 'omen' appears separately and is firmly placed in a background of mundane experience. In the context of the story, the strangest details are no more than the strangeness of all life, represented with poetic vividness.

The essential feeling of a mythical, magical atmosphere surrounding the natural and earthly extends even into the descriptions of the most ordinary things and experiences. A band of milkmaids and dairymen searching in the field for an elusive blade of garlic are seen as creatures from another world:

As they crept along, stooping low to discern the plant, a soft yellow gleam was reflected from the buttercups into their shaded faces, giving them an elfish, moonlit aspect, though the sun was pouring upon their backs in all the strength of noon. (Ch. xxii)

Tess, in the 'mixed, singular, luminous gloom' of early morning, seems to Angel to shine above the mist with 'a sort of phosphorescence . . . She looked ghostly, as if she were merely a soul at large. In reality her face, without appearing to do so, had caught the cold gleam of day from the north-east' (Ch. xx).

Often this method of imbuing the everyday with an element of fantasy is used in the novel to imply not only the intrinsic strangeness of things, but also the complete deceptiveness of the human imagination, its ability to transform the truth. Tess's heightened perception as she listens to Angel's harp in the garden at Talbothays is magnificently shown:

Tess was conscious of neither time nor space . . . she undulated upon the thin notes of the second-hand harp, and their harmonies passed like breezes through her, bringing tears into her eyes. The floating pollen seemed to be his notes made visible, and the dampness of the garden the weeping of the garden's sensibility. Though near nightfall, the rank-smelling weeds glowed as if they would not close for intentness, and the waves of colour mixed with the waves of sound. (Ch. xix)

Before this, Hardy remarks that 'both instrument and execution were poor; but the relative is all'. The description of the garden and the music, as seen through Tess's eyes, conveys the emotionally heightened tone of her perception. She is caught—again, as Cytherea and Bathsheba and Eustacia were caught—by the bewitching power of her own imagination. Hardy shows us the paltry reality of the damp garden with its rank weeds and floating pollen, but in such a way that we, like Tess, are made relatively unaware of it. The mesmerically beautiful dream—like Angel's love for Tess—has a greater emotional reality than the rather unpleasant fact it conceals. In the same way, earlier in the novel, Hardy describes the visible euphoria of drunken revellers as having a beatific sublimity:

. . . as they went there moved onward with them, around the shadow of each one's head, a circle of opalized light, formed by the moon's rays upon the glistening sheet of dew. Each pedestrian could see no halo but his or her own, which never deserted the head-shadow, whatever its vulgar unsteadiness might be; but adhered to it, and persistently beautified it; till the erratic motions seemed an inherent part of the irradiation, and the fumes of their breathing a component of the night's mist; and the spirit of the scene, and of the moonlight, and of Nature, seemed harmoniously to mingle with the spirit of wine. (Ch. x)

Throughout the novel there is this same suggestion of mysticism, of things appearing to be something other than they are. Often the result is merely a striking pictorial effect which gives strength to the general pattern; sometimes, more specifically, the suggestiveness of dream or enchantment can stand in place of action and explanation, thereby moulding our total response to a particular situation. At the beginning and end of Tess's story, Hardy deliberately evokes an atmosphere of unreality. Her seduction takes place on a night of luminous mists and moonlight:

'Tess!' said d'Urberville.
There was no answer. The obscurity was now so great that he could see absolutely nothing but a pale nebulousness at his feet, which represented the white muslin figure he had left upon the dead leaves . . . D'Urberville stooped; and heard a gentle regular breathing . . . She was sleeping soundly, and upon her eyelashes there lingered tears.
Darkness and silence ruled everywhere around. Above them rose the primeval yews and oaks of The Chase, in which there poised gentle roosting birds in their last nap; and about them stole the hopping rabbits and hares. (Ch. xi)

avenging of this first wrong,

ed in a whisper of the men as

od watching her, as still as the
ent over her . . . her breathing
esser creature than a woman.
es and hands as if they were
, the stones glistening green-
e light was strong, and a ray
ng under her eyelids and

ress of the situation are
e specifically ethereal,
nding dimly beautiful
ch episode as softened
, transformed into something which man
properly understand. The seduction scene is thus glossed
over and yet shown even more poignantly by his insistence on
Tess's dreaming, unknowing simplicity, by the implied comparison of her vulnerability with that of the 'gentle roosting
birds'. Her final capture at the end of the book is presented in
exactly the same way; again, she is shown as a dreaming, half-wild
creature, caught in a twilight world whose brutality does not
really touch her. The two scenes are obviously intended as being
complementary: they represent the beginning and end of Tess's
confused and bewildered acquaintance with the hard fact of life.
She loses her virginity in the haunts of innocence and antiquity,
amongst skipping rabbits and ancient druidical oaks, and sur-
renders her right to life in the sacrificial temple of pagans of
antiquity. The natural progression of her life is the movement
from sleep to sleep.

Throughout the novel there is a continual tension between an
objective and a subjective view, as Tess herself is torn between a
knowledge of material truth and her own imaginative conception
of it. In the description of her marriage to Angel, for example, the

material simply does not exist; to Tess, everything appears through the 'highly charged mental atmosphere' in which she is living, as she moves about 'in a mental cloud of many-coloured idealities', 'glorified by an irradiation not her own' (Ch. xxxiii). Yet afterwards, when she has made her 'confession' to her husband, there is a subtle altering of perspective to show the objective truth of her situation in uncompromising physical terms:

He looked upon her as a species of impostor; a guilty woman in the guise of an innocent one. Terror was upon her white face as she saw it; her cheek was flaccid, and her mouth had almost the aspect of a round little hole. The horrible sense of his view of her so deadened her that she staggered . . . (Ch xxxv)

Tess herself is, as a character, more or less unchangeable. The irony and impact of her story come essentially from the contrasting ways in which she is seen—as innocent but seemingly guilty, or as guilty but seemingly innocent. The various kaleidoscopic reflections of her fundamental being together make up a total vision of actuality with all its curious illogicalities.

Jude the Obscure

There may be books more disgusting, more impious as regards human nature, more foul in detail, in those dark corners where the amateurs of filth find garbage to their taste; but not, we repeat, from any Master's hand.

M.O.W.O. (Mrs Oliphant), *Blackwood's Magazine*, January 1896,
'The Anti-Marriage League'

... read the story how you will, it is manifestly a work of genius ...
The Illustrated London News, 11 January 1896

Like *Tess of the d'Urbervilles* and *The Mayor of Casterbridge, Jude the Obscure* is an exploration of various states of being, showing, in the contrast between the real and the ideal, the tragedy which is 'created by an opposing environment either of things inherent in the universe, or of human institutions' (*Life*, p. 274). Hardy's more explicit aim, as stated in the preface to the first edition of 1895, was 'to tell, without a mincing of words, of a deadly war waged between flesh and spirit', and in the fulfilling of this aim he himself considered that he had differed very little from his customary procedure. 'Like the former productions of this pen', he wrote,

Jude the Obscure is simply an endeavour to give shape and coherence to a series of seemings, or personal impressions, the question of their consistency or their discordance, of their permanence or their transitoriness, being regarded as not of the first moment. (Preface)

Nevertheless, when it was first published in book form, this, the last of Hardy's novels, aroused a storm of violent controversy, and even today—though for rather different reasons—there is still a wide diversity of opinion on its merits. Although now *Jude the Obscure* is more often revered than reviled, it is consistently

considered as being anomalous and extraordinary, a deviation
from Hardy's 'norm'. Douglas Brown, for instance, writes that in
this work 'Hardy's characteristic narrative method is to be virtually
transformed. . . . He enters the lists alongside George Eliot and
Henry James with a tragic psychological fiction. The desire to
develop his art in this way sprang from his seriousness and his
compassion. But the endeavour in fact places that art upon its
weaker resources.'[1] The plain truth, according to this critic, is that
Hardy was incapable of exploring intellectual problems or deep
emotional relationships, or even the processes of the individual
mind. The work is, despite these drawbacks, a bold experiment,
and for this Hardy 'deserves honour'.

Brown's attitude is not unusual. Many critics feel that *Jude the
Obscure* is the most complex and interesting thematically and, at
the same time, possibly the most flawed artistically of all Hardy's
novels. The autobiographical element is so strong that the author
finds difficulty in achieving sufficient artistic dissociation and the
perspective of the whole suffers from the imbalance; the dialogue
(especially that between Sue and Jude) is frequently stilted; and the
symbolic presentation of the dual forces in Jude's character, those
of the flesh and the spirit, is often too obvious and contrived to be
really convincing. John Holloway asserts that the novel does not
'fully represent Hardy' because 'there is . . . no background at all
of nature or of a harmonious common life in accord with it'.
Instead, it portrays 'a whole world of *déracinés* . . . who hurry
from town to town in trains, or live isolated in inns and ex-
temporized lodgings. It is this very restriction of scope which
makes the book so much more agitated and bitter than Hardy's
others. All rectifying stabilities have dropped out of sight; and
nothing is left but a frustrated aggregate of querulous and dis-
orientated individuals.'[2] Holloway obviously sees this as a fatal
weakness in the novel, and it is interesting that he should make the
presence of a stable background his criterion for a value judgement
of the work as a whole. Nevertheless it is a perceptive comment in
that it points out the most obvious difference between *Jude the
Obscure* and the other 'Novels of Character and Environment' and

shows, too, how easy it is to ignore the reasons for this difference.

It is true that in presenting his impression of life and its inherent contradictoriness, Hardy employs in this particular work a technique quite different from that of any of the other novels. In *Jude the Obscure* there is almost no reliance on great heroic or poetic scenes, the spectacular effects of light and colour or the use of richly evocative language which we find in *Far from the Madding Crowd* or *The Woodlanders* or *Tess of the d'Urbervilles*. The whole texture of the writing has become thinner, less substantial; yet the comparatively dry, abstract prose is in its total impact strangely powerful, recreating as it does the apparent ordinariness of everyday life. Mundane, simply reported incidents frequently take on a deeper significance later in the story, and snatches of conversation or half-remembered episodes are seen to be, in context, ironical or premonitive. Irving Howe describes this static, reflective tendency in the novel more specifically as a 'photographic' quality: 'What is essential in *Jude*, surviving and deepening in memory, is a series of moments rather than a series of actions. These moments ... tend to resemble snapshots rather than moving pictures, concentrated vignettes rather than worked-up dramatic scenes.'[3] It is this which gives the book its peculiar flavour, compounded of remoteness and familiarity, and it is, I think, especially noticeable in Hardy's delineation of his characters. Often his presentation of them is false and unconvincing in the extreme, but our total impression—especially of Sue and Jude—is of real, emotional, existing individuals. It is true that they are not given depth and definition in Hardy's customary manner; they are not set against a background of infinite natural processes and human traditions. They do not relate to anything but their own images (significantly, Jude falls in love with his cousin's photograph, and Arabella sells his own studio portrait to a junk shop, while later Phillotson is shown as gazing at a photograph of Sue, 'a duplicate of the one she had given Jude, and would have given to any man' and 'ultimately kissing the dead pasteboard with all the passionateness, and more than all the devotion, of a young man of eighteen') (Pt III, Ch. vi).

Similarly, the surrounding countryside and the towns of the novel's setting are viewed with detachment as scenes, places only dimly connected with human existence. In *Jude the Obscure*, Hardy concentrates on examining the world of each individual mind, with its own ideals and dreams, and on highlighting its intricate subtleties against the starkness of physical reality. The main characters have few associations with earthly things, no stabilizing force of countryside. Arabella leaves England for Australia, and then comes back to London with a new husband; Phillotson leaves Marygreen for Christminster and then moves on, disillusioned, to Shaston. Sue and Jude in particular have no bonds, only a morbid prehistory of broken marriages and mysterious murders (the location of the gibbet where their common ancestor was said to have been hanged recurs symbolically throughout the story). Motifs of wandering and searching dominate the tale. The word '*Thither*', which Jude carves on a road-post pointing to Christminster, at first epitomizes his striving for adventure and fulfilment, but soon it is surrounded by nettles, and finally its hopeful inscription is almost entirely obliterated by moss. The action of the novel is spread thinly over a wide, continually changing landscape; the six parts of the story are labelled each with its particular geographical location—'At Marygreen', 'At Christminster', 'At Melchester'. There is a perpetual sense of rootlessness, of almost trancelike drifting. Sue and Jude spend considerable time in trains, inns and lodging-houses, none of which is identified in detail. Only once is the place itself important, when Jude unwittingly takes Sue to the same inn where he has previously spent a night with Arabella. Otherwise, for the most part, these destinations are featureless and unromanticized, a drab collection of muddy streets, dim shops and cafés and crumbling ruins. It is important to note that at no stage does Hardy describe in any detail the years of domestic happiness that Jude and Sue must have spent together, during which two children were born to them.

Thus it can be seen that the setting of *Jude the Obscure* does reflect Hardy's method of characterization. It is, because of its apparent unfriendliness, a prime motivating force. Hardy's presentation of the novel as spread over a wide rambling landscape reflects the bewilderment and lack of stability in the minds of these characters as surely as the terrain of *The Woodlanders* reflects the characteristics of its inhabitants, or as the differences between Talbothays and Flintcomb-Ash reflect Tess's mental states before and after her marriage. The method is the same, though its execution in *Jude the Obscure* is less concrete, more diffuse and suggestive—in consequence, perhaps, of the greater abstraction of its theme.

Connected with this, too, is the peculiar lack of definite action in the book. All is vague and generalized; deeds are mostly recollected or reported in conversations. We are shocked when Sue jumps out of her bedroom window or when Little Father Time hangs himself and the other children, largely because these precise, symbolic actions jar on the neutral, unequivocal background of the tale. Otherwise, the action consists largely of *seeing*: Jude gazing at buildings, Sue lettering her texts, Jude reading. Life is a series of visions, real or imagined, punctuated with meetings and conversations, journeys and destinations. Yet by the very simplicity of this 'snapshot' method, Hardy can convey most effectively the enormous discrepancy between what actually *happens* and what it *means* subjectively. Thus he shows how Jude first becomes aware, almost by accident, of Phillotson's feeling for Sue:

On turning the corner and entering the village the first sight that greeted his eyes was that of two figures under one umbrella coming out of the vicarage gate. He was too far back for them to notice him, but he knew in a moment that they were Sue and Phillotson. The latter was holding the umbrella over her head, and they had evidently been paying a visit to the vicar—probably on some business connected with the school work. And as they walked along the wet and deserted lane Jude saw Phillotson place his arm around the girl's waist; whereupon she gently removed it; but he replaced it; and she let it remain, looking quickly round her with an air of misgiving. She did not look absolutely behind her, and therefore did not see Jude, who sank into the hedge like one struck with a blight. There he remained hidden till they had reached

Sue's cottage and she had passed in, Phillotson going on to the school hard by.

'O, he's too old for her—too old!' cried Jude in all the terrible sickness of hopeless, handicapped love.

He could not interfere. Was he not Arabella's? He was unable to go on further, and retraced his steps towards Christminster. (Pt II, Ch. v)

We are not directly involved in the actual event as it happened. It is presented to us, with all its irrelevant circumstantial detail, exactly as it appeared to Jude himself, a fleeting glimpse of the truth whose poignancy and immediacy lie in the seeming detachment with which it is shown. Always there is an ironic dichotomy between the calm progression of events as they actually occur and as they appear to one who is emotionally involved.

All through the novel Hardy's method is to point the difference between objective and subjective truth, the real and the imagined ideal. 'The tragedy of unfulfilled aims' (Preface) depends on the discrepancy between the consistency of an illusion and the inconsistency of life as it really is. Neither Jude nor Sue can accept what is actually *there*. To Jude, as a child, the distant Christminster is a shining vision, while the tangible countryside around him consists only of dark 'chimaeras' (Pt I, Ch. iii). Yet, once alienated from the fields and lanes of Marygreen, he is equally disconcerted by the venerable college buildings of Christminster. Reality always proves inferior to the vision:

. . . he found that the colleges had treacherously changed their sympathetic countenances: some were pompous; some had put on the look of family vaults above ground; something barbaric loomed in the masonries of all. The spirits of the great men had disappeared.

. . . What at night had been perfect and ideal was by day the more or less defective real. (Pt II, Ch. ii)

Later, Sue and Jude are in their imagination scorned even by the statues around the University Theatre:

. . . the quaint and frost-eaten stone busts encircling the building looked with pallid grimness on the proceedings, and in particular at the bedraggled Jude, Sue and their children, as at ludicrous persons who had no business there. (Pt VI, Ch. i)

From the very beginning, the outside world is depicted as if seen through Jude's eyes. Its unromantic, unsympathetic drabness is epitomized first by the solitary field where, as a child, he is set to scare the rooks:

'How ugly it is here,' he murmured.
The fresh harrow-lines seemed to stretch like the channellings in a piece of new corduroy, lending a meanly utilitarian air to the expanse, taking away its gradations, and depriving it of all history beyond that of the few recent months, though to every clod and stone there really attached associations enough and to spare—echoes of songs from ancient harvest-days, of spoken words, and of sturdy deeds. Every inch of ground had been the site, first or last, of energy, gaiety, horse-play, bickerings, weariness. Groups of gleaners had squatted in the sun on every square yard. (Pt I, Ch. ii)

In this passage, Hardy is careful to point out the contrast between Jude's subjective, imperfect view and the objective fact as he, the author, sees it. Yet perhaps Hardy is too careful, too eager to disclaim that his perspective and that of his character are practically synonymous. Never, either here or in the subsequent action, are we led to believe that Jude's attitudes are invalid, or that the opposite to what he sees is anything other than slightly coarse and meaningless. The ordinary lives of lesser human beings are shown as having a rather uncouth and ridiculous flavour:

Under the hedge which divided the field from a distant plantation girls had given themselves to lovers who would not turn their heads to look at them by next harvest; and in that ancient corn-field many a man had made love-promises to a woman at whose voice he had trembled by the next seed-time after fulfilling them in the church adjoining. (Pt I, Ch. ii)

Here there is a distinctly satirical analogy between natural processes and man's perversion of them, and Jude's contrasting ignorance of life is shown implicitly as a high-minded quality. We are prepared later to believe that Arabella's 'seduction' of his innocence is vulgar and animal and Hardy does little to show us (as D. H. Lawrence would like to believe)[4] that she is vital and heroic. By stressing her artificiality and insensitivity, Hardy continually implies a complete, non-ironic, esoteric sympathy for Jude. It is a sympathy which is entirely different from his artistic involvement with Henchard or Tess, and it dominates the orientation of the entire story, giving it the subjective top-heaviness which is at once its greatest strength and its greatest flaw.

William Marshall makes the comment that Jude's vision 'may be, at certain times, and within the limit of his capacities, *ironic*, but that Hardy's art emphasizes not irony but absurdity, the essential quality of a universe that necessarily excludes the possibility for irony'.[5] Almost inevitably, the stern reality which intrudes into Jude's consciousness, his dream-world of ideals, is seen as either crude and indifferent or as absurd, with something of the grotesque caricature verging on nightmare which one finds in Dickens. As a character, Jude appears most convincingly to us when he is alone. Hardy frequently describes his thoughts and actions with a clarity against which the real world, in its random detail, is seen only as a dreamlike part of his mind. Hardy's concern with the perspective of Jude's consciousness and its isolation from physical actuality is clearly brought out in his description of the boy drawing water from the well, soon after Phillotson's departure from Marygreen:

There was a quiver in his lip now, and after opening the well-cover to begin lowering the bucket he paused and leant with his forehead and arms against the framework, his face wearing the fixity of a thoughtful child's who has felt the pricks of life somewhat before his time. The well into which he was looking was as ancient as the village itself, and from his present position appeared as a long circular perspective ending in a shining disk of quivering water at a distance of a hundred feet down. There was a lining of green moss near the top, and nearer still the hart's-tongue fern.

He said to himself, in the melodramatic tones of a whimsical boy, that the schoolmaster had drawn at that well scores of times on a morning like this, and would never draw there any more...

A tear rolled from his eye into the depths of the well. The morning was a little foggy, and the boy's breathing unfurled itself as a thicker fog upon the still and heavy air. His thoughts were interrupted by a sudden outcry:

'Bring on that water, will ye, you idle young harlican!' (Pt 1, Ch. i)

Everything outside Jude's peculiarly orientated vision intrudes on it sharply and unpleasantly. His altruistic pleasure in watching the rooks feed on the corn is rudely shattered by 'a smart blow on his buttocks, followed by a loud clack' and the sudden presence of the farmer, 'the great Troutham himself, his red face glaring down upon Jude's cowering frame, the clacker swinging in his hand' (Pt 1, Ch. ii). Later, he is jerked into a recognition of Arabella's presence ironically as he is dreaming of his future, 'looking at the ground as though it were thrown thereon by a magic lantern'. Suddenly 'something smacked him sharply in the ear'; his dream is broken and he is made to discover 'what was simmering in the minds around him' (Pt 1, Ch. vi). Throughout his progressive disillusionment (from his well-intentioned but unrewarded concern for the hungry rooks and his credulous attitude towards Arabella, to his final realization of Sue's fallibility), each ideal is shattered by practical reality, only to be replaced by another vision, even more difficult to attain.

Significantly, Hardy's descriptions of Jude's solitary, self-enclosed world are almost invariably shown with unemotional, detached clarity, simply depicted without explanation or philosophizing. Yet, whereas Tess or Eustacia or Henchard, for example, are shown objectively as constituent parts of a larger pattern, the exploration of Jude's character is entirely derived from within: in a sense, object and subject are one. So completely does the perspective of Jude's mind dominate the structure of the novel that it provides the chief, if not the only, point of comparison against which the sordid or absurd phantasmagoria of the outside world is judged. What Jude thinks and feels is the simple logical truth; the rest is complex and inexplicable. The crucial moments of his life are presented, usually, as brief masterpieces of understatement. In his attempted suicide, for instance, the young Jude's determined confrontation with the supposed mysteries of life and death is given with the methodical restraint of a scientific report:

In the dusk of that evening Jude walked away from his old aunt's as if to go home. But as soon as he reached the open down he struck out upon it till he came to a large round pond. The frost continued, though it was not particularly sharp, and the larger stars overhead came out slow and flickering. Jude put one foot on the edge of the ice, and then the other: it cracked under his weight; but this did not deter him. He ploughed his way inward to the centre, the ice making sharp noises as he went. When just about the middle he looked around him and gave a jump. The cracking repeated itself; but he did not go down. He jumped again, but the cracking had ceased. Jude went back to the edge, and stepped upon the ground.

It was curious, he thought. What was he reserved for? He supposed he was not a sufficiently dignified person for suicide. (Pt I, Ch. xi)

Thought and action are completely mingled so that the enigmatic arbitrariness of life is stressed perfectly by Jude's almost ludicrous determination, and then by his defeated bewilderment. So it is, too, when he receives Sue's letter telling him of her impending marriage to Phillotson:

Jude staggered under the news; could eat no breakfast; and kept on drinking tea because his mouth was so dry. Then presently he went back to his work and laughed the usual bitter laugh of a man so confronted. Everything seemed turning to satire. And yet, what could the poor girl do? he asked himself: and felt worse than shedding tears.

'O Susanna Florence Mary!' he said as he worked. 'You don't know what marriage means!' (Pt III, Ch. vi)

The same technique, on a rather lower emotional level, can be seen in Jude's almost mesmerized reaction to his first sight of Arabella:

He gazed from her eyes to her mouth, thence to her bosom, and to her full round naked arms, wet, mottled with the chill of the water, and firm as marble.

'What a nice-looking girl you are!' he murmured, though the words had not been necessary to express his sense of her magnetism. (Pt I, Ch. vi)

The novel gains its intense psychological verisimilitude from many short scenes such as these, episodes in which the abstractions of feeling and emotion are transcribed into observable actions and events. For all their symbolic differences (Alvarez describes Sue and Arabella as being like 'the white and black horses, the noble and base instincts, which drew Plato's chariot of the soul'),[6] the main characters are not just constituent parts of a moral treatise. Hardy firmly establishes their identities as familiar, 'historically true' contemporaries at the same time as he develops their symbolic or allegorical significance. The success with which he does this is largely determined by the way in which he uses Jude's idiosyncratic interpretation of events as a base for his own 'series of seemings'. Whereas in his previous novels Hardy's method is to demonstrate the contrast between the obvious truth and the different shades of meaning which may be found in it, in *Jude the Obscure* the dividing line between what really exists and what appears to the imagination as truth is far less clear-cut. The rigid contrasts and the detailed contrivance of the symbolic episodes (the pig sticking; Jude's killing of the trapped rabbit whose agonies resemble those of his own futile love for Sue; the birth to Sue of a still-born child after the deaths of the other children) are made significant and credible, to a greater or lesser extent, by occurring within a framework where the particular mental apprehension of an event is shown to be more important than the event itself. For this reason, writes F. P. McDowell: 'The novel is, as it were, a kind of kaleidoscope; the pattern formed by image, event, character and idea continually changes with the angle from which it is viewed. The fluid contours of the novel form and reshape to furnish changing vistas of meaning; new impressions of the whole which are yet related to our previous impressions continually emerge.'[7] The seemingly unbridgeable gap between the mundane flow of incident and the sudden, glaringly magnified tableaux is spanned throughout the novel by an element of psychological fantasy, a knowledge that all we see as 'real' is governed by the illogical impressionism of an individual consciousness. Hardy's creation of this limiting framework, together with

o

his careful selection and presentation of details and situations, is constantly geared towards showing that life, despite its surface ordinariness, is in fact a bitter and inexplicable mystery.

At the beginning of the novel, the contrasts between what Jude expects from life and what he is likely to find are hinted at more or less humorously. As a child, he sees Christminster as a nebulous but glorious shining light, a fairy vision, an answer to a prayer:

> Suddenly there came along this wind something towards him—a message from the place—from some soul residing there, it seemed. Surely it was the sound of the bells, the voice of the city, faint and musical, calling to him, 'We are happy here!'
> He had become entirely lost to his bodily situation during this mental leap, and only got back to it by a rough recalling. (Pt I, Ch. iii)

His simple credulity is countered by the rational earthiness of the rustic carter, whom he asks for information about this magical town:

> ' 'Tis all learning there—nothing but learning, except religion. And that's learning too, for I never could understand it. Yes, 'tis a serious-minded place. Not but there's wenches in the streets o' nights. . . . You know, I suppose, that they raise pa'sons there like radishes in a bed? And though it do take—how many years, Bob?—five years to turn a lirruping hobble-de-hoy chap into a solemn preaching man with no corrupt passions, they'll do it, if it can be done, and polish un off like the workmen they be, and turn un out wi' a long face, and a long black coat and waistcoat, and a religious collar and hat, same as they used to wear in the Scriptures, so that his own mother wouldn't know un sometimes . . .' (Pt I, Ch. iii)

More fascinating details are imparted to Jude by other journeymen and itinerants and by some mysterious hunchbacked old woman, who 'told him more yet of the romantic charms of the city of light and love'. (Pt I, Ch. iii).

In this first section, Jude's slowly increasing awareness is shown as a sort of moral fable, a war of rather less-than-deadly sins against an inspired but naive dreamer whose only fault is that he lives for a non-existent ideal. We are shown in panoramic succes-

sion the long line of characters to whom his beliefs and aspirations
are foolish or incomprehensible. Some are wise in ignorance, like
the carter to whom prostitute and academic may be mentioned in
the same breath; others, like Arabella and the cunning Vilbert,
whose faked medical skill disguises a lack of knowledge in anything except practical self-advancement, deliberately set out to
dupe him. Each of these characters, with the exception of Arabella,
comes briefly into Jude's life like a figure in a dream and drifts out
again, being immortalized, like an object lesson, in a vivid self-
contained picture—that of Farmer Troutham beating Jude with
the clacker, with the vision of the church spire ('to which he had
largely subscribed, to testify his love for God and man') shown
with heavy irony in the distance; that of Jude and Arabella
drinking beer beneath a large painting of Samson and Delilah; the
fanciful caricature that is Vilbert—

. . . a light-footed pedestrian . . . wearing an extraordinarily tall hat, a
swallow-tailed coat, and a watch-chain that danced madly and threw
around scintillations of sky-light as its owner swung along upon a pair
of thin legs and noiseless boots. (Pt 1, Ch. iv)

Throughout the novel, Jude (and later, Sue) retain a more or
less childlike comprehension of the world in which the distasteful
or unsympathetic elements are visualized as exaggerated and
artificial or as grotesquely frightening.[8] Like Little Father Time,
they see 'life' in all its bustling and often unattractive reality as
something in which they have no part. Hardy epitomizes the vast-
ness and loneliness of the world as Jude and Sue see it in his
description of the prematurely aged child of Jude's first marriage:

The boy seemed to have begun with the generals of life, and never to
have concerned himself with the particulars. To him the houses, the
willows, the obscure fields beyond, were apparently regarded not as
brick residences, pollards, meadows; but as human dwellings in the
abstract, vegetation, and the wide dark world. (Pt v, Ch. iii)

In a scene which exactly parallels an incident in Hardy's own childhood (Life, pp. 15-16), the boy Jude is shown lying on his back

with a straw hat over his face as he ponders the problems of existence:

He ... peered through the interstices of the plaiting at the white brightness, vaguely reflecting. Growing up brought responsibilities, he found. Events did not rhyme quite as he had thought. . . . As you got older, and felt yourself to be at the centre of your time, and not at a point in its circumference, as you had felt when you were little, you were seized with a sort of shuddering, he perceived. All around you there seemed to be something glaring, garish, rattling, and the noises and glares hit upon the little cell called your life, and shook it, and warped it.

If he could only prevent himself growing up! He did not want to be a man. (Pt I, Ch. ii)

Similarly, Sue at one stage wishes that she was still a child, and Hardy continually stresses her childish, sexless appearance, her abnormal fear of things physical—as when she meets Arabella for the first time:

'Good morning!—I must go,' said Sue hastily.

'And I, too, must be up and off!' replied the other, springing out of bed so suddenly that the soft parts of her person shook. Sue jumped aside in trepidation. 'Lord, I am only a woman—not a six-foot sojer!...' (Pt v, Ch. ii)

Arabella sees the couple as ' "Silly fools—like two children" ', and always Hardy shows them as onlookers, wary of life and yet eager to play with it. Even at moments of intense pleasure, their fantasy world is tinged with irrational timidity, as when, at the Agricultural Exhibition, they linger in the pavilion of flowers. To them it is 'an enchanted palace'.

Sue's usually pale cheeks reflect[ed] the pink of the tinted roses at which she gazed; for the gay sights, the air, the music, and the excitement of the day's outing ... had quickened her blood and made her eyes sparkle with vivacity ...

'I should like to push my face quite into them—the dears!' she had said. 'But I suppose it is against the rules to touch them—isn't it, Jude?'

'Yes, you baby,' said he: and then playfully gave her a little push, so that her nose went among the petals.

'The policeman will be down on us, and I shall say it was my husband's fault!' (Pt v, Ch. v)

At crucial moments, when they grapple with the real 'rules' which society has laid down for them, they hang back and watch the progression of events with misgiving. When, for instance, they finally decide to be married, they linger to watch, as if in a series of tableaux, the couples who are signing the register before them. Here again, Hardy arranges the spectacle to fit an exaggerated didactic purpose, giving undue weight to the plight of the innocent couple by painting these grosser human types with lurid Hogarthian relish:

The soldier was sullen and reluctant: the bride sad and timid: she was soon, obviously, to become a mother, and she had a black eye. Their little business was soon done, and the twain and their friends straggled out, one of the witnesses saying casually to Sue and Jude in passing . . . 'See the couple just come in? Ha, ha! That fellow is just out of gaol this morning. She met him at the gaol gates, and brought him straight here. She's paying for everything.'
Sue turned her head and saw an ill-favoured man, closely-cropped, with a broad-faced, pock-marked woman on his arm, ruddy with liquor and the satisfaction of being on the brink of a gratified desire. They jocosely saluted the outgoing couple, and went forward in front of Jude and Sue . . . (Pt v, Ch. iv)

It is worth noting that Hardy rationalizes the histrionic brutality of the scene by previously describing the office, with its musty books and its wooden floor, 'stained by previous visitors', as appearing dreary and frightening *to them* (that is, to Sue and Jude) —'though to its usual frequenters it doubtless seemed ordinary enough'. The lesson is learnt, however. To Sue the whole process of marriage is sordid and vulgar; she turns to Jude, 'her mouth shaping itself like that of a child about to give way to grief', and soon they leave the place, 'stealthily and guiltily, as if they had committed a misdemeanour, closing the door without noise'.

Increasingly towards the end of the story, the view of the outside world as a farce or a nightmare does not come from within

Jude's consciousness but is imposed from without by Hardy himself, and there is consequently a greater conflict between the subjective and the objective presentation of scene and character. There is an overdrawn comparison, for example, in the two contrasting portraits of Arabella and Sue at the Agricultural Exhibition. The first is slightly jocular, almost mocking in tone:

... from the London train alights a couple; a short, rather bloated man, with a globular stomach and small legs, resembling a top on two pegs, accompanied by a woman of fine figure and rather red face, dressed in black material, and covered with beads from bonnet to skirt, that made her glisten as if clad in chain-mail. (Pt v, Ch. v)

In the second, the particular attention to detail is lovingly sympathetic, and the total impression is of *feeling* more than of objective vision:

Sue, in her new summer clothes, flexible and light as a bird, her little thumb stuck up by the stem of her white cotton sunshade, went along as if she hardly touched ground, and as if a moderately strong puff of wind would float her over the hedge into the next field. Jude, in his light grey holiday-suit, was really proud of her companionship, not more for her external attractiveness than for her sympathetic words and ways. (Pt v, Ch. v)

The picture of Sue gains in realism, conveying something of her character as well as her appearance, by being shown through Jude's eyes; Arabella, on the other hand, is purely an imaginative creation, a crudely drawn, glittering pantomime figure. It is the same difference as that between a photograph and a caricature. This disparity is evident all through the book, but only becomes really contrived in the latter part. Hardy's descriptions take on an emotional honesty when their limitations and exaggerations are also the valid and credible products of Jude's particular imagination. It is when he moves out of this frame of reference that the pictures tend to become forced and unnatural, and we feel irritated by his authorial intrusions and manipulations. There is the same annoying duality of approach in the presentation of the characters themselves. Throughout the novel there is a constant tension, not

only between Sue's image of fragile defencelessness and her cold
academic mind, but also between Hardy's artistic presentation of
her as an individual character and his using of her as a philosophical
mouthpiece. Because of his own ambivalent attitude, it is impossible for us to think that Hardy intended Sue to be simply the
incarnation of half of Jude's soul. Her greatest reality lies in her
inconsistency and the most vividly realized pictures of her all
show her lack of conventionality and her spontaneity: her buying
of the forbidden idols; her escape from college; her appearance in
Jude's clothes; her marriage to Phillotson; her leaping from her
window to escape from him; her illicit releasing of the pet pigeons;
her appearance at the graveside of her children, where '[her]
coloured clothing . . . suggested to the eye a deeper grief than the
conventional garb of bereavement could express' (Pt vi, Ch. ii).

These pictures convey, far more than her unreal philosophizings,
the image of Sue which Hardy must have intended to project. Yet
the connection between Sue as Jude sees her and as Hardy explains
her is in many ways a strained and artificial one and unfortunately,
towards the end of the novel, the idea almost completely over-
shadows the imaginative representation.

Up until the death of Little Father Time, Hardy's blending of
the real and pseudo-symbolic in a carefully stated imaginative
framework has been, for the most part, consistent and successful.
After it, however, the elements of fantasy and reality become
sharply differentiated and distorted, ranging from pedantic, stilted
debates on morality to actions of the most incongruous melodrama. Sue, in particular, is transformed into the embodiment of
an idea, over-rhetorically expressed. After the deaths of the
children, she cries out,

'Our life has been a vain attempt at self-delight. But self-abnegation is
the higher road. We should mortify the flesh—the terrible flesh—the
curse of Adam!' (Pt vi, Ch. iii)

The unconvincingness of such an outburst is reinforced by Hardy's
showing of her soon afterwards in the traditional stance of a
penitent. Jude finds her in church, beneath 'a huge, solidly

constructed Latin cross'. Hardy explicitly shows it as being a symbol of all that is mysterious and foreboding, an oppressive and invincible power:

It seemed to be suspended in the air by invisible wires; it was set with large jewels, which faintly glimmered in some weak ray caught from outside, as the cross swayed to and fro in a silent and scarcely perceptible motion. Underneath, upon the floor, lay what appeared to be a heap of black clothes, and from this was repeated the sobbing that he had heard before. It was his Sue's form, prostrate upon the paving. (Pt VI, Ch. iii)

The brilliantly imaginative impact of the cross, with its seemingly magical qualities and its air of weighty mysticism, underlines the superstitious blindness of Sue's return to orthodox Christianity. (' "I see marriage differently now. My babies have been taken from me to show me this! Arabella's child killing mine was a judgment—the right slaying the wrong." ') Jude, representing the other side of the argument, rises to similar heights of unconvincing passion, in which Hardy must necessarily simplify the issues at hand:

'. . . do not do an immoral thing for moral reasons! You have been my social salvation. Stay with me for humanity's sake! You know what a weak fellow I am. My two Arch Enemies you know—my weakness for womankind and my impulse to strong liquor. Don't abandon me to them, Sue, to save your own soul only! . . . Isn't my safety worth a little sacrifice of dogmatic principle? I am in terror lest, if you leave me, it will be with me another case of the pig that was washed turning back to his wallowing in the mire!' (Pt VI, Ch. iii)

When, after this oratorical injunction, he finally succumbs to her will, he symbolically dissolves their union with a dramatic gesture, the prosaic reality of which rather detracts from its intended effect:

'Perhaps—perhaps I spoilt one of the highest and purest loves that ever existed between man and woman! . . . Then let the veil of our temple be rent in two from this hour!'
    He went to the bed, removed one of the pair of pillows thereon, and flung it to the floor. (Pt VI, Ch. iii)

Hereafter, neither Sue nor Jude is a real, living character; they act their parts mechanically and unconvincingly. They become part of the structural argument, a pair of puppets acting out their roles for the conclusion. Speedily, Arabella, in the role of *dea ex machina*, gives the news to Phillotson, makes Jude drunk, remarries him, lets him die (preferring Vilbert, whom she has 'caught' with his own love potion) and writes his epitaph (' "He's a 'andsome corpse" ') and Sue's (' "She's never found peace since she left his arms, and never will again till she's as he is now!" ') (Pt VI, Ch. xi).

All this, taking place in some eighty pages, comprises about one-fifth of the total story. On the surface, at least, it appears that in his conclusion to the tale Hardy has abandoned his aim of giving 'a series of seemings or . . . impressions': there is little here but alternate starkness and contrivance. The grotesque improbability of Little Father Time's 'crucifixion' to save the souls of his parents is blatantly symbolic—to the extent that neither of the other children is ever given a name or a place of birth. They have their importance not as characters but simply as parts of a symbol, unrecognized and unidentified. As with Tess's baby, 'Sorrow', their death is their prime reason for existing. Similarly Sue, after this cataclysmic event, becomes an embodiment of penitence in the same way as Tess, the 'fallen woman', is shown in Alec d'Urberville's room merely as a wooden and mechanical figure in a melodrama.

It is, of course, possible to see this exaggeration of technique simply as an intensification of Hardy's artistic aim to show the difference between the world as it is and as it seems to his protagonists. This, doubtless, is what he originally intended. The startling *grotesquerie* of the mass suicide in *Jude the Obscure* is the sort of fanciful vision which might logically fit into the perspective of an overstrained imagination, a dream or nightmare turned reality, of the sort which perpetrated Lucetta's death in *The Mayor of Casterbridge* or showed the sleep-walking Angel's instinctive feeling for the woman whom he had abandoned on a principle. Hardy's success or failure in the presentation of such incidents lies principally in his ability to reconcile the incorporeal, or the mental state of his protagonist, with the visible reality as he chooses to depict it. Lucetta's death and Angel's sleep-walking are not simply the transmogrification of the real; for the purposes of the story, they *are* the real. It is essential that we be convinced that such events could have taken place. Yet, just as in *A Laodicean* Hardy's blasé introduction of patently 'unreal' characters into a recognizably 'real' world promulgates total disbelief, so, too, the neatly rationalized slaughter of the innocents in *Jude the Obscure* (' "Done because we are too menny" ') jars on the imagination, even though we may admit Hardy's reasons for this sort of contrivance. Whatever his intention, the sudden intrusion of this deliberately stylized tableau effectively shatters our acceptance of his world as it is projected through Jude's imaginative vision: it comes, too obviously, 'from the outside'. It is interesting to note, parenthetically, that Hardy drew the line at presenting us with the actual execution of the deed; such an omission points at once to the purely dogmatic function of this little scene and also, perhaps, to Hardy's own lack of conviction in its emotional or practical acceptability.

It has frequently been suggested that, at crucial stages of his narratives, Hardy seems to be incapable of conveying successfully the deepest emotions of humanity, and that his lapses into melodramatic stylization and directly symbolic representation are merely the self-conscious betrayals of this weakness. Yet there is ample proof that this is not so. Elsewhere in *Jude the Obscure*, and often in *Tess of the d'Urbervilles*, he has shown how intensely and vividly the essence of feeling can be conveyed by understatement, allusion, the evocative use of language. In *Jude the Obscure*, particularly, he makes the most subtle and effective use of prosaic and ordinary circumstance to suggest, by contrast, the drama of human relations; for instance, there is the masterly scene of Sue's parting with Phillotson:

Some days passed, and the evening of their last meal together had come—a cloudy evening with wind—which indeed was very seldom absent in this elevated place. How permanently it was imprinted upon his vision; that look of her as she glided into the parlour for tea; a slim, flexible figure; a face, strained from its roundness, and marked by the pallors of restless days and nights, suggesting tragic possibilities quite at variance with her times of buoyancy; a trying of this morsel and that, and an inability to eat either. Her nervous manner, begotten by a fear lest he should be injured by her course, might have been interpreted by a stranger as displeasure that Phillotson intruded his presence on her for the few brief minutes that remained.

'You had better have a slice of ham, or an egg, or something with your tea? You can't travel on a mouthful of bread and butter.'

She took the slice he helped her to; and they discussed as they sat trivial questions of housekeeping, such as where he would find the key of this or that cupboard, what little bills were paid, and what not.

'I am a bachelor by nature, as you know, Sue,' he said in a heroic attempt to put her at her ease . . . (Pt IV, Ch. iv)

The immediacy and unstressed pathos of this picture compare well with the presentation of the break between Sue and Jude, which takes place, rather too appropriately, beside the grave of their children:

'It is here—I should like to part,' said she.

'So be it!'

'Don't think me hard because I have acted on conviction. Your generous devotion to me is unparalleled, Jude! Your wordly failure, if you have failed, is to your credit rather than to your blame. . . . Every successful man is more or less a selfish man. The devoted fail. . . . "Charity seeketh not her own." '

'In that chapter we are at one, ever beloved darling, and on it we'll part friends. Its verses will stand fast when all the rest that you call religion has passed away!'

'Well—don't discuss it. Goodbye, Jude; my fellow-sinner, and kindest friend!'

'Goodbye, my mistaken wife. Goodbye!' (Pt VI, Ch. iv)

It is all too obvious that Hardy is trying to make a point and that the drama of the moment is geared towards its dogmatic purpose. There is none of the fleeting, 'living' quality of the former scene, which depends on a quiet juxtaposition of general impression and individual perception, and which gains in impact from its completeness as a picture. The difference between the two episodes is almost solely one of perspective. In the earlier description, the emotions of the characters arise naturally from their material situation and are seen essentially as a part of it; the whole scene is shown as a complete, miniature fragment of 'real' life. The parting between Sue and Jude, in comparison, is made up solely of abstractions: Sue's sorrow and Jude's anguish can scarcely be seen as anything other than the deliberately heightened expression of the author's own argument.

In the last section of *Jude the Obscure*, the 'rules' of living form the dominant pattern. The chief formalistic device of the novel (the contrast between imagined reality and the world as it exists) can only operate in terms of conscious rationalization:

Vague and quaint imaginings had haunted Sue in the days when her intellect scintillated like a star, that the world resembled a stanza or melody composed in a dream; it was wonderfully excellent to the half-aroused intelligence, but hopelessly absurd at the full waking . . .

. . . 'We must conform!' she said mournfully. 'All the ancient wrath of the Power above us has been vented upon us, His poor creatures, and we must submit. There is no choice. We must. It is no use fighting against God!'

'It is only against man and senseless circumstance,' said Jude. (Pt VI, Ch. iii)

Sue, in finding the necessary order by obeying what she considers to be the will of 'God', ultimately destroys the natural harmony which Jude imagined he had found in his relationship with her. Accordingly, Hardy must rearrange the perspective of the novel to show, objectively, what happens to them both. His attempt to relate the differing worlds of Sue and Jude to a larger social and moral perspective inevitably results in the collapse of the artistic balance which depended on Jude's imaginative vision. Psychic reality or 'intuitive conviction' gives way to a comparatively crude representation of 'fact' which Hardy is constrained to eke out by authorial explanations, often issuing learnedly from the mouths of the characters themselves.

The partial breakdown of *Jude the Obscure* is primarily the result of Hardy's inability to transfer his point of view from the particular to the general. In his effort to mould the implied truth of his 'seemings' into a graphic dramatization of their universal significance, he is, in effect, turning against his own original intentions. Yet there is no doubt that Hardy intended his work to be explicit in its meaning, despite his explanatory comment offered in the preface to the first edition. 'Of course,' he wrote, soon after the publication of the novel, 'the book is all contrasts— or was meant to be in its original conception' (*Life*, p. 272). The treatment of the marriage laws, the frank realism of which shocked many of his original readers, was, according to the postscript Hardy added to the preface in 1912, initially developed simply as

... a good foundation for the fable of a tragedy, told for its own sake as a presentation of particulars containing a good deal that was universal, and not without a hope that certain cathartic, Aristotelian qualities might be found therein.

Nowadays, of course, the fortuity or otherwise of his choice of subject is scarcely relevant, and the basic problem is whether or not the novel *Jude the Obscure* as Hardy finally presented it was the right vehicle for the ideas he wanted to express. Arthur Mizener claims that the tragedy which Hardy originally envisaged needed a form 'which is consciously an artifice', and that, in creating a realistic framework for his idea, he finally succeeded only in writing '... a novel which is formally neither fish, flesh nor good red herring, a novel whose tremendous verisimilar life is consistently being sapped by a series of irrelevant devices and yet remains, as a systematic artifice, "a paradise of loose ends" '.[9] According to Mizener, Hardy was a hopeless adherent of the old 'naturalistic assumption that narrative must be significant historically rather than fabulously', and, further, he 'never really faced the possibility that a great work of art aims at a kind of truth superior ... to a scientific and historical verisimilitude'. To quote this is to show how ambivalent a novel this is; how precariously it is balanced between representative fable and conscious realism. The geometrical construction of plot, the frequent, often bold use of symbolism and the stilted conversations between the main characters often seem to be completely at variance with the precise, austere presentation of contemporary life which is the fabric of the novel, and which caused some of Hardy's early critics to believe that he intended an essay in the style of Zola or Tolstoy 'the decadent sociologist'.[10]

What has not often been realized, I think, is that the story of *Jude the Obscure* is deliberately compounded of both 'social realism'—the facts as Hardy sees them objectively, and 'fable'—the world as it appears to Jude. For the most part, Hardy has reconciled these seemingly irreconcilable opposites simply by showing life as an impression through the eyes of his protagonist. In most of the novel, as I have shown, there is a striking contrast between Hardy's presentation of life as it is and as it appears imaginatively. The harshness and artifice of the world of oppressive laws and conventions is not shown as 'fact', but as an exaggerated impression in Jude's mind, deliberately depicted as alien and unreal to increase the effect of allegory. The 'fabulous' significance of *Jude the Obscure* is in fact a part of its historical truth in so far as the distortion of the real can be seen to be simply the expression of idiosyncratic human perception. Thus, the tentative method first explored in *Desperate Remedies* reaches its greatest heights of artistry in Hardy's last novel, where fantasy and reality are shown as being almost completely fused. Hardy's vision of the world, as depicted in Jude's imagination, embraces both sides of the truth to show, finally, the complexity of the illusion which is man's only possible conception of ultimate truth.

Conclusion

Hardy's pervasive theme in all his novels—the contrast between appearance and reality—is also, consistently, the most important factor in their artistic construction. In accordance with what he called his own 'idiosyncratic mode of regard'—his individual impression of the world—his work is based largely on a method of showing rather than telling, whereby plot and structure depend to a great extent on varying states of perception. There is a continual tension between objective 'reality' and an imaginative or romanticized vision, between the projected viewpoints of the characters themselves and the larger, contrasting perspectives of the author. By deliberately exaggerating or highlighting his subject, Hardy manages to present a picture which is consciously an artifice but which aims at an impression of greater verisimilitude than the simple transcription of fact. The art of each of his novels is, in the broadest sense, essentially a way of looking at things in order to reveal the strangeness of man's position in the world and to show that, in fact, 'nothing is as it appears'.

Undeniably, the imaginative depth and richness of Hardy's vision is largely a result of his use of varying perspective and visual effects which are firmly based on the recognizably real. The ephemeral, often artificial validity of man's world as it appears to him must be contrasted with some kind of absolute, some abstract force which gives it its special definition. In *Under the Greenwood Tree*, for example, the lives of human beings are seen almost as two-dimensional shapes within a larger perspective of time, while in *Far from the Madding Crowd* the vagaries and vanities of man's existence relate finally to the vast unalterable pattern of natural processes. The heath in *The Return of the Native* itself epitomizes the continual flux and metamorphosis of life which make up the permanence of infinity. In the earlier novels, particularly, man's relationship to his environment and to society is shown within a larger framework, and this contrast creates the underlying order of the story; each detail and incident takes on a different significance when seen against the totality of existence.

As an extension of this method Hardy also shows, with increasing emphasis in his later novels, how every aspect of life may be distorted and transmuted by the processes of the mind. The life of each individual character is thus frequently shown in terms of differing mental perspectives and contrasts of emotional and factual perception. Probably the most considerable development in his technique as a novelist is in his use of this method. In *Desperate Remedies*, for instance, a particular emotional viewpoint can sometimes be used to give a striking artistic effect: in *Tess of the d'Urbervilles*, on the other hand, the different views of Tess's situation form in themselves much of the structure of the novel. The intricate combinations of contrasting perspectives shape the progression of the whole story, as mood, fantasy and personal vision are made to be more important, thematically, than the physical realities themselves. People act and behave, says Hardy, according to what they *see*, but what they see is not necessarily the truth. Throughout his works, we find that his characters are forced to make judgements and decisions specifically on the conventional or imagined representations of reality. The smallest shred of evidence becomes the fact, while the facts themselves are lost. It is not, I think, accidental that Hardy relies so frequently on the outward, 'pictorial' evocation of incident and emotion. Supposedly 'important' events are glossed over or summarized briefly simply because events, in themselves, are relatively unimportant in comparison with man's interpretation of them. Rather, the action in the novels hangs on illusions and deceptions, on inability to communicate, on misinterpretation of the facts. Tess's note to Angel is lost before it can save her; Boldwood falls in love with Bathsheba on the strength of a Valentine; Paula Power judges Somerset to be unworthy of her on the flimsy evidence of a distorted photograph. Characters are deluded by pictures in their minds, and use words as talismans against their actions. The imagination is stronger than the physical truth and can mould reality according to its whim, but always there is the shock of discovery, or realisation, and the destruction of the dream.

It is in his later concentration on individual characters and individual social or moral problems as the bases for his novels that Hardy tends to move away from the relative simplicity of structure and the rich confusion of images and visual effects that characterize *Far from the Madding Crowd* and *The Return of the Native*. His approach to his subject becomes increasingly fabulistic, and his selection of detail is almost wholly orientated towards a particular theme. In his transferring of life to art he begins to show us not only what man sees but also what he *ought* to see. In the earlier novels, Hardy's use of emotive language and imagery is aesthetic rather than dogmatic; he is primarily concerned with displaying all the elements of his picture of life to illustrate his basic concept of contradictoriness. In *Tess of the d'Urbervilles* or *Jude the Obscure*, however, the 'impression' of fluctuating real life includes a far greater emphasis on symbolic detail at crucial stages of the story, and on a view of the characters which is directed towards a specific judgement of them.

It is important to realize, however, that in all his novels, Hardy's selection and ordering of his material is based on what Barbara Hardy calls 'an error or a partiality or a blindness or a fantasy';[1] his work cannot be judged as 'realistic' or 'unrealistic' because it is essentially an exaggeration or a distortion of fact. Hardy himself was primarily concerned that his readers should recognize his art for what it was: an illusion of reality. Long after he had done with novel-writing, he remarked that he should have put, at the beginning of each new romance, 'Understand that however true this book may be in essence, in fact it is utterly untrue' (*Life*, p. 392). When he is most deeply concerned with the problems of humanity, his picture of 'truth' gains in force from its conjunction with deliberately artificial representations of caricature and fantasy.

P

At its best, even his creation of an explicitly moral parable is simply an intensification of his characteristic artistic method—the juxtaposition of the weird and the ordinary, of fact and fiction against a background of the wholly inexplicable.

Certainly, in all his novels Hardy was more preoccupied with the expression of his art than with the propounding of any deep underlying philosophy. On 23 December 1920, he wrote protestingly:

I have no philosophy—merely what I have often explained to be only a confused heap of impressions, like those of a bewildered child at a conjuring show . . . It is my misfortune that people *will* treat all my mood-dictated writing as a single scientific theory. (*Life*, pp. 410-11)

Always his intention is to show the contrasts and irrationalities inherent in the smallest details of existence. 'The Scheme of Things', he once wrote, 'is, indeed, incomprehensible; and there I suppose we must leave it—perhaps for the best. Knowledge might be terrible' (*Life*, p. 410). So it is that even in *Jude the Obscure*, his most thought-provoking work, he avowedly creates not an explanation or an indictment of the tragedy of life, but rather a complex statement of the forces of that life as man may interpret them. He offers no solution; he merely gives an impression, an artist's view which displays the distortions and illusions and absurdities in man's vision as accurately as possible. The neat formulae of his plots and the deliberately conspicuous patterns of image and symbol give only a semblance of order to what he sees as the entirely contradictory mystery of living.

It is for this reason that the world he portrays in his novels is credible, often exquisitely accurate as to detail, but consciously distanced from our normal experience so that it may be regarded objectively as a picture or as an impression, something disproportionate to material fact. We are led to feel not that 'this is life' but that 'life *is like* this'; the slight credibility gap makes us at once more critical and more aware of his vision and of its importance.

NOTES

INTRODUCTION: HARDY'S CONCEPT
OF HIS ART

1 John Wain, review in *The Observer* (13 December 1959).
2 Ian Gregor and Brian Nicholas, *The Moral and the Story* (London, 1962), p. 125.
3 Morton Dauwen Zabel, 'Hardy in Defense of His Art: The Aesthetic of Incongruity', *Southern Review*, vi (Summer 1940), pp. 125-49.
4 David Lodge, *The Language of Fiction* (London, 1966), p. 164.
5 Frank Chapman, 'Revaluations: (IV) Hardy the Novelist', *Scrutiny*, III, i (June 1934), p. 36.
6 Thomas Hardy, 'The Profitable Reading of Fiction', in Harold Orel, ed., *Thomas Hardy's Personal Writings* (Lawrence, University of Kansas Press, 1966), p. 114. (Hereafter referred to as *PRF*.)
7 Philip Larkin, 'Wanted: Good Hardy Critic', *Critical Quarterly* (Summer 1966), p. 174.
8 See R. L. Purdy, *Thomas Hardy: A Bibliographical Study* (London, 1954), pp. 265-7.
9 Thomas Hardy, *Life and Art: Essays, Notes and Letters*, ed. Ernest Brennecke, Jr. (New York, 1924; reprinted 1966), Introduction, p. 4.
10 Florence Emily Hardy, *The Life of Thomas Hardy* (London, 1962), p. 153. (Hereafter referred to as *Life*). This work contains in one volume the two works originally published separately as *The Early Life of Thomas Hardy, 1840-1891* (London, 1928) and *The Later Years of Thomas Hardy, 1892-1928* (London, 1930).
11 Lodge, op. cit., p. 76.
12 Henry James, letter to Hugh Walpole (17 May 1912), as quoted in Miriam Allott, *Novelists on the Novel* (London, 1959; 1965), p. 235.
13 Barbara Hardy, *The Appropriate Form: An Essay on the Novel* (London, 1964; 1971), pp. 4-5.
14 E. M. Forster, *Aspects of the Novel* (London, 1927; 1949), p. 125.
15 Albert J. Guerard, *Thomas Hardy: The Novels and Stories* (Cambridge, Mass., Harvard University Press, 1949), p. 10.
16 Thomas Hardy, 'The Science of Fiction', Orel, op. cit., p. 137. (Hereafter referred to as *SF*.)
17 S. F. Johnson, 'Hardy and Burke's "Sublime" '. In Harold C. Martin, ed., *Style in Prose Fiction: English Institute Essays 1958* (New York, 1959), p. 57.
18 T. S. Eliot, from *After Strange Gods*, in *T. S. Eliot: Selected Prose* (penguin Books), p. 185.

CHAPTER I: THE TECHNIQUE OF THE NOVELS

1 Virginia Woolf, *A Writer's Diary* (London, 1953), p. 92.

2 Katherine Anne Porter, 'Notes on a Criticism of Thomas Hardy', *Southern Review*, vi (Summer 1940), p. 161.

3 Donald Davidson, 'The Traditional Basis of Thomas Hardy's Fiction', *Southern Review*, vi (Summer 1940), pp. 162-178.

4 Ibid., p. 168.

5 J. I. M. Stewart, *English Studies* (Essays and studies collected for the English Association), i (1948), p. 6.

6 See Carl J. Weber, *Hardy of Wessex* (New York, Columbia University Press, 1940), Ch. iii, 'Studies in Painting and Poetry', pp. 26-7 and Appendix 3, pp. 236-7; also F. B. Pinion, *A Hardy Companion* (London, 1968), 'Influences and Recollections of Painting', pp. 193-200.

7 R. C. Carpenter, 'Hardy and the Old Masters', *Boston University Studies in English*, v (1961), p. 18.

8 Henry James, 'The Art of Fiction', as quoted in Susanne Langer, *Feeling and Form* (London, 1953), p. 290.

9 W. M. Thackeray, letter to David Masson (6 May 1851), as quoted in Allott, *Novelists on the Novel*, p. 67.

10 Mario Praz, *The Hero in Eclipse in Victorian Fiction* (London, 1956), Introduction, p. 29.

11 George Eliot, *Adam Bede*, Bk II, Ch. xvii.

12 Frank O'Connor, *The Mirror in the Roadway: A Study of the Modern Novel* (London, 1957), p. 241.

13 Geoffrey Grigson, 'Thomas Hardy', in *The Harp of Aeolus and other Essays on Art, Literature and Nature* (London, 1948), p. 124.

14 John Ruskin, from *Modern Painters*, Vol. v, Pt IX, Ch. xi, as quoted in Kenneth Clark, *Ruskin Today* (London, 1964), p. 221.

15 T. S. Eliot, *After Strange Gods*, p. 185.

16 Alistair Smart, 'Pictorial Imagery in the Novels of Thomas Hardy', *Review of English Studies*, new ser., xii (1961), p. 262.

17 Cf. the description of Thomasin in *The Return of the Native*, Bk II, Ch. ii: 'the pigeon-hole admitted the sunlight so directly upon her brown hair and transparent tissues that it almost seemed to shine through her'.

18 See, e.g., David Cecil, *Hardy the Novelist: An Essay in Criticism* (London, 1943), especially Ch. iii.

19 Frank O'Connor, *The Mirror in the Roadway*, pp. 249-50.

20 Dorothy Van Ghent, 'On *Tess of the d'Urbervilles*', in *The English Novel: Form and Function* (New York, 1953), p. 201.

21 A. J. Guerard, *Thomas Hardy*, p. 157.

22 Grigson, 'The Preraphaelite Myth', in *The Harp of Aeolus*, p. 87.

23 Ibid., p. 90.

24 Samuel C. Chew, *Thomas Hardy: Poet and Novelist* (New York, 1921, 1928; reissued 1964), p. 86.

25 Guerard, op. cit., p. 48.
26 Richard C. Carpenter, 'Hardy's "Gurgoyles"', *Modern Fiction Studies*, vi (Autumn 1960), p. 231.
27 Guerard, op. cit., p. 86.
28 Ibid., p. 84.
29 See S. F. Johnson, 'Hardy and Burke's "Sublime"', loc. cit.
30 Cecil, *Hardy the Novelist*, p. 51.

CHAPTER II: EXPERIMENTS AND MISTAKES

1 See 'General Preface to the Novels and Poems' (Wessex Edition, Vol. i, *Tess of the d'Urbervilles*, 1912); also R. L. Purdy, *Thomas Hardy: A Bibliographical Study*, p. 286. The 'Wessex' edition was divided as follows:

I *Novels of Character and Environment: Tess of the d'Urbervilles; Far from the Madding Crowd; Jude the Obscure; The Return of the Native; The Mayor of Casterbridge; The Woodlanders; Under the Greenwood Tree; Life's Little Ironies; Wessex Tales.*

II *Romances and Fantasies: A Pair of Blue Eyes; The Trumpet-Major; Two on a Tower; The Well-Beloved; A Group of Noble Dames.*

III *Novels of Ingenuity: Desperate Remedies; The Hand of Ethelberta; A Laodicean.*
The above were all reprinted by Macmillan for this edition in 1912. In 1914 a fourth section, *Mixed Novels*, was added for the inclusion of another volume of short stories, *A Changed Man*.

2 Joseph Warren Beach, *The Technique of Thomas Hardy* (Chicago, 1922; reprinted New York, 1962), p. 109.
3 See the 'General Preface to the Novels and Poems'.
4 Donald Davidson, 'The Traditional Basis of Thomas Hardy's Fiction', loc. cit., p. 168.
5 John Holloway, *The Victorian Sage: Studies in Argument* (London, 1953), p. 288.
6 Virginia Woolf, 'The Novels of E. M. Forster', in *The Death of the Moth* (London, 1942), pp. 106-7.
7 Irving Howe, *Thomas Hardy* (London, 1966), p. 34.
8 It is worth noting that Hardy uses this same description, almost word for word, in *The Return of the Native* (Bk III, 'The Fascination', Ch. v). The scene is a love-meeting between Clym and Eustacia, and the chapter ends with yet another direct quotation from *Desperate Remedies*: Clym, left alone in the 'oppressive horizontality' of the marshy countryside, is 'too much reminded of the arena of life; it gave him a sense of bare equality with, and no superiority to, a single living thing under the sun'. F. R. Southerington examines the similarities between these passages in his study, *Hardy's Vision of Man* (London, 1971), pp. 82-3.
9 Carpenter, 'Hardy's "Gurgoyles"', loc. cit., p. 224.
10 Holloway, op. cit., p. 249.
11 J. Hillis Miller, *Thomas Hardy: Distance and Desire* (London, 1970), Preface, p. xiv.

CHAPTER III: *UNDER THE GREENWOOD TREE* AND *THE TRUMPET-MAJOR*

1 Emma Hardy, quoted in Weber, *Hardy of Wessex*, p. 162.
2 Joseph Warren Beach, *The Technique of Thomas Hardy*, p. 69.
3 Ibid., p. 117.
4 Q. D. Leavis, 'Hardy and Criticism', *Scrutiny*, xi (Spring 1943), p. 231.
5 Cecil, *Hardy the Novelist*, p. 142.
6 John F. Danby, '*Under the Greenwood Tree*', *Critical Quarterly*, i (Spring 1959), p. 5.
7 Douglas Brown, *Thomas Hardy* (London, 1954), p. 114.

CHAPTER IV: *FAR FROM THE MADDING CROWD*

1 Critic in *The Observer* (3 January 1875), quoted in L. Lerner and J. Holmstrom, eds., *Thomas Hardy and his Readers* (London, 1968), p. 33.
2 Roy Morrell, *Thomas Hardy: The Will and the Way* (Kuala Lumpur, 1965), p. 59.
3 Irving Howe, *Thomas Hardy*, p. 57.
4 Holloway, *The Victorian Sage*, pp. 255-6.
5 See Weber, *Hardy of Wessex*, pp. 9-10, and Pinion, *A Hardy Companion*, p. 154.
6 Harrison Ainsworth, *Rookwood* (1834), Bk II, Ch. i.
7 Henry James, *The Nation* (New York, 24 December 1874), quoted in Lerner and Holmstrom, p. 30.

CHAPTER V: *THE RETURN OF THE NATIVE*

1 Walter Allen, *The English Novel: A Short Critical History* (London, 1954), p. 238.
2 Edwin Muir, *The Structure of the Novel* (London, 1928), p. 91.
3 M. A. Goldberg, 'Hardy's Double-visioned Universe', *Essays in Criticism*, vii (October 1957), pp. 376-7.
4 Lloyd Fernando, 'Thomas Hardy's Rhetoric of Painting', *Review of English Literature*, vi (October 1965), pp. 72-3.
5 Ibid., p. 65.
6 See John Paterson, 'The "Poetics" of *The Return of the Native*', *Modern Fiction Studies*, vi (Autumn 1960), pp. 214-22, for a detailed analysis of Hardy's interest in Greek and Roman literature and mythology, and the effect of this on the novel.
7 Book VI exceeds this time limit, but was added by Hardy to the original five books of the novel as an 'afterthought' dictated by serial requirements for a 'happy ending'. (See note on p. 473, Macmillan's Wessex edition, 1912.)

8 G. D. Klingopulos, 'Hardy's Tales Ancient and Modern', in Boris Ford, ed., *The Pelican Guide to English Literature, VI: From Dickens to Hardy* (Penguin Books, 1958), p. 415.

CHAPTER VI: *THE MAYOR OF CASTERBRIDGE*

1 See John Paterson, '*The Mayor of Casterbridge* as Tragedy', *Victorian Studies*, iii (December 1959), pp. 151-72.
2 Thomas Hardy, 'Candour in English Fiction', in Orel, op. cit., p. 127.
3 D. H. Lawrence, 'Study of Thomas Hardy', from *Phoenix*, (pub. 1936). Reprinted in Anthony Beal, ed., D. H. Lawrence: *Selected Literary Criticism* (Mercury Books, London, 1956; 1964), p. 167.
4 This quotation, Orel notes, is from Thomas Carlyle, *The French Revolution*, Pt i, Bk i, Ch. ii: 'Realized Ideals'.
5 See Douglas Brown, *Thomas Hardy: 'The Mayor of Casterbridge'*, Studies in English Literature No. 7 (London, 1962; 1966), esp. pp. 37-44.

CHAPTER VII: *TESS OF THE D'URBERVILLES*

1 A. J. Guerard, *Thomas Hardy*, p. 61.
2 Ian Gregor and Brian Nicholas, *The Moral and the Story*, p. 137.
3 J. Holloway, *The Victorian Sage*, p. 268.
4 Two episodes of the serial version of *Tess of the d'Urbervilles* 'proved unacceptable' to the editor of the *Graphic* and were printed separately elsewhere. These, notably, were Chs x and xi, which described the story of Tess's seduction; and Ch. xiv, the baptism and death of her baby, which was printed under the title of 'The Midnight Baptism, A Study in Christianity', in the *Fortnightly Review* (May 1891). (See R. L. Purdy, *Thomas Hardy: A Bibliographical Study*, p. 69.)
5 Cf. pp. 42-3 above.
6 George Meredith, Letter to Frederick Greenwood, 11 January 1892, quoted in Lerner and Holmstrom, *Thomas Hardy and his Readers*, p. 65.
7 Arnold Kettle, *An Introduction to the English Novel* (London, 1953; 1962), ii, p. 64.
8 Gregor and Nicholas, op. cit., p. 145.
9 Lionel Johnson, *The Art of Thomas Hardy* (London, 1895), p. 219.
10 Review in *Punch*, (17 February 1892), quoted in Lerner and Holmstrom, op. cit., p. 84.
11 Tony Tanner, 'Colour and Movement in Hardy's *Tess of the d'Urbervilles*' *Critical Quarterly*, x (Autumn 1968), p. 227.

CHAPTER VIII: *JUDE THE OBSCURE*

1 Douglas Brown, *Thomas Hardy* (London, 1954), pp. 89-90.
2 Holloway, *The Victorian Sage*, p. 288.

3 Howe, *Thomas Hardy*, p. 145.

4 See D. H. Lawrence, *Study of Thomas Hardy* in Anthony Beal, ed., *D. H. Lawrence: Selected Literary Criticism*, pp. 198 ff.

5 William Marshall, *The World of the Victorian Novel* (New York, 1967), p. 405.

6 A. Alvarez, '*Jude the Obscure*', originally '*Jude the Obscure:* Afterword', New American Library Edition (New York, 1961), reprinted in A. J. Guerard, ed., *Hardy: A Collection of Critical Essays* (New Jersey, 1963), p. 116.

7 Frederick P. McDowell, 'Hardy's "Seemings or personal impressions": The Symbolical Use of Image and Contrast in *Jude the Obscure*', *Modern Fiction Studies*, vi (Autumn 1960), p. 250.

8 See Emma Clifford, 'The Child: the Circus: and *Jude the Obscure*', *Cambridge Journal*, vii (June 1954), pp. 531-46.

9 Arthur Mizener, '*Jude the Obscure* as a tragedy', *The Southern Review*, vi (Summer 1940), p. 198.

10 See, e.g., Jeannette L. Gilder, *The World* (13 November 1895), as quoted in Lerner and Holmstrom, *Thomas Hardy and his Readers*, p. 113.

CONCLUSION

1 Barbara Hardy, *The Appropriate Form*, p. 6.

INDEX

Note. References in italic type indicate sustained discussion of a novel or character.

Ainsworth, Harrison, 56, 69, 120; *Rookwood*, 120
Allen, Walter, 125
Alvarez, A., 199
Art, in relation to Hardy's novels, 8, 14-25, 33, 41-3, 44, 126; Dutch and Flemish *genre* painting, 16, 19, 41, 88; French Impressionist school, 22, 24, 26, 43; Pre-raphaelite school, 41, 43, 136. *See also individual artists*

'Baron de Bookworms, The', 182
Beach, Joseph Warren, 59, 60-1, 85
Bellini, 25
Boldini, 48
Brown, Douglas, 95, 168, 190
Burke, E., *Enquiry into the Sublime and Beautiful*, 56
Burne-Jones, Sir E., 41

'Candour in English Fiction', 4, 147
Carpenter, Richard C., 17, 66, 67
Cecil, Lord David, 56, 85
Chapman, Frank, 2
Chew, S. C., 45
Coleridge, Hartley, 57
Coleridge, S. T., *Biographia Literaria*, 23
Collins, Wilkie, 61
Conrad, Joseph, *The Nigger of the 'Narcissus'*, 34
Correggio, 16
Crivelli, 25

Danby, John F., 86
Davidson, Donald, 14, 60
Desperate Remedies, 15, 16, 22, 57, 58, 59, *61-71*, 72, 73, 83, 101, 102, 104, 109, 114, 117, 182, 212, 214
Aldclyffe, Miss, 16, 62, 63-4, 68, 70
Graye, Ambrose, 65-6
Graye, Cytherea, 14, 16, 54, *65-71*, 109, 185
Manston, Aeneas, 63, 66-70, 109, 181
Seaway, Ann, 63
Springrove, Edward, 67-9
Springrove, Farmer, 64-5
Dickens, Charles, 13, 196
Dostoevsky, Feodor, 44
Douw, Gerard, 16
Dumas, Alexandre (*père*), 20, 56

Eliot, George, 13, 19, 101, 190; *Adam Bede*, 19
Eliot, T. S., 11, 12, 23

Far from the Madding Crowd, 15, 16, 26, 35, 39, 42, 49, 58, 59, 60, 69-70, 81, *101-24*, 135, 151, 155, 170, 191, 213, 215
Boldwood, Farmer, 102, 114-17, 118, 121, 123, 214
Everdene, Bathsheba, 14, 80-1, *103-123*, 135, 171, 185, 214
Oak, Gabriel, 35, 36, 51, *102-23*, 135

Far from the Madding Crowd (*cont.*)
  Robin, Fanny, 42, 46, 81, 110-11, 113
  Smallbury, Liddy, 16
  Troy, Sergeant, 46, 81, *102-23*, 135
Fernando, Lloyd, 136
Fielding, Henry, *Tom Jones*, 44
Forster, E. M., 7, 61, 136

'General Preface to the Novels and Poems', 58
Gérôme, 44
Goldberg, M. A., 133-4
Gothic, influence of on Hardy's novels, 9, 51, 55-6, 62, 69, 76, 114, 120
Gregor, Ian, 21, 170, 180
Greuze, 16
Grigson, Geoffrey, 21
Guerard, A. J., 7, 8, 41, 45, 54, 55, 60, 169

Hand of Ethelberta, The, 1, 59, 72, 81, 146
Hardy, Barbara, 6, 7, 215
Hobbema, 48
Holbein, 16, 76
Holloway, John, 10, 60, 71, 118, 171, 190-1
Howe, Irving, 102, 191
Hunt, W. Holman, 41, 42-3

James, Henry, 1, 6-7, 18, 123, 190
Johnson, Lionel, 181
Johnson, S. F., 11
Jude the Obscure, 2, 9, 15, 23, 25, 40, 54, 59, 60, 62, 83, 86, 116, 146, 147, 169, *189-212*, 215, 216
  Bridehead, Sue, 9, *190-210*
  Fawley, Arabella (Donn), 191-207
  Fawley, Jude, 9, *190-212*

'Little Father Time', 40, 193, 201, 205, 207-8
Phillotson, Arthur, 191-209
Troutham, Farmer, 197, 201
Vilbert, 201, 207

Kettle, Arnold, 4, 180

Laodicean, A, 1, 15, 55, 59, 60, *71-84*, 208
  Dare, William, 71, *77-83*, 181
  De Stancy, Charlotte, 16, 80
  De Stancy, Captain William, *77-82*
  Havill, James, 79, 83
  Power, Abner, 71, 77, 81, 83
  Power, Paula, 55, 60, *73-82*, 214-15
  Somerset, George, 16, *73-82*, 214-15
Larkin, Philip, 3
Lawrence, D. H., 1, 147, 196
Leavis, Q. D., 85
Life of Thomas Hardy, The, 4, 5, 9, 11, 19, 20, 21, 22, 23, 25, 26, 44, 46, 48, 52, 53, 56, 58, 59, 72, 128, 129, 146, 166, 167, 169, 189, 201, 211, 215, 216
Lodge, David, 1, 2, 5

McDowell, F. P., 199
Marshall, William, 196
Mayor of Casterbridge, The, 13, 38, 39, 40, 49, 55, 59, 71, 144, *146-68*, 170, 173, 189, 207-8
  Farfrae, Donald, 38-9, 148-67
  'Furmity-woman, the', 148, 157, 160, 168
  Henchard, Elizabeth-Jane (Newson), 38-9, 55, *148-67*
  Henchard, Michael, 10, 14, 38, 39, 55-6, 71, *146-68*, 170, 171, 173, 196, 197
  Henchard, Susan (Newson), 148, 151, 152, 156-7, 162, 168

Mayor of Casterbridge (*cont.*)
Le Sueur, Lucetta, 49, 54, 148, 150-1, 153, 161-4, 168, 207-8
Meredith, George, 180
Millais, 41, 43
Mizener, Arthur, 211
Moroni, 89
Morrell, Roy, 102
Moule, Horace, 85
Muir, Edwin, 126

O'Connor, Frank, 20, 37
Oliphant, Mrs (M.O.W.O.), 189

Pair of Blue Eyes, A, 40, 47, 59, 101, 102, 135
Knight, Henry, 40, 46, 47, 51, 135
Smith, Stephen, 46, 47
Swancourt, Elfride, 10, 40, 46, 47
Paterson, John, 138, 146
Poe, Edgar Allen, 69
Poor Man and the Lady, The, 52, 61
Porter, Katherine Anne, 13, 24
Praz, Mario, 19
'Profitable Reading of Fiction, The', 2, 3, 4, 8, 11, 20, 72, 75, 165

Radcliffe, Mrs, 20
Rembrandt, 17, 89
Return of the Native, The, 1, 10, 17, 24, 26, 34, 39, 40, 48, 54, 59, 60, 71, *125-45*, 148, 149, 151, 155, 170, 171, 182, 213, 215, 219 n8
Nunsuch, Susan, 142, 143, 148
Venn, Diggory, 126-7, 128, 130, 143, 144
Vye, Eustacia, 10, 15, 17, 34, 39-40, 45, 54, 71, 126-8, 130-1, *134-45*, 148, 155, 171, 185, 197
Wildeve, Damon, 45, 130, 131, 132, 139-42, 144, 145

Yeobright, Clym, 10, 17, 39, 54, 127, 128, 130-2, *134-44*, 155
Yeobright, Mrs, 16, 51, 128, 130, 131-3, 135, 142, 144
Yeobright, Thomasin, 10, 144, 218 n17
Rossetti, 41, 136
Ruskin, John, 22, 41, 42

Sallaert, 16
'Science of Fiction, The', 4, 8, 11, 20, 152
Scott, Sir Walter, 55, 56; *The Bride of Lammermoor*, 3
Smart, Alistair, 24-5
Stewart, J. I. M., 16

Taine, H. A., 20
Tess of the d'Urbervilles, 1, 2, 4, 8, 9, 15, 25, 34, 40, 46-7, 47-8, 55, 58, 60, 67, 146, 147, *169-88*, 189, 191, 208, 214, 215
Clare, Angel, 9, 40-1, 50, 172-88, 207-8, 214
d'Urberville, Alec, 42, 45, 47-8, 81, *172-84*, 207
Durbeyfield, Tess, 10, 14, 15, 40, 42-3, 46-7, 50-1, 67, *170-88*, 196, 197, 207, 214
'Sorrow' (Tess's baby), 207
Thackeray, W. M., 18, 19
Terburg, 16
Tolstoy, Count Leo, 13, 212
Trumpet-Major, The, 15, 39, 85-8, *94-100*
Ball, Cainy, 39
Derriman, Festus, 96-7
Garland, Anne, 97-9
Garland, Widow, 98
Loveday, John, 99
Loveday, Miller, 96-7
'Uncle Benjy', 99

Turner, J. M. W., 22-3, 41, 169
Two on a Tower, 59, 60, 72

Under the Greenwood Tree, 15, 60, 85-
    94, 95, 99-100, 101, 144, 213
    Day, Fancy, 89-94
    Day, Geoffrey, 93
    Day, Mrs, 89-90
    Dewy, Dick, 89-91, 93
    Dewy family, the, 14
    Endorfield, Elizabeth, 93
    Maybold, Parson, 91, 92
    Shiner, Farmer, 89, 91

Van Alsloot, 16
Van Ghent, Dorothy, 40

Wain, John, 1
Wallis, H., 41
Watson, William, 169

Well-Beloved, The, 15, 59, 72
Wellek, Réné, and Warren, Austin,
    34
'Wessex', use of the name, 52, 111
Woodlanders, The, 17, 25, 26-33, 49,
    64, 129, 151, 164, 191, 193
    Charmond, Felice, 28-33
    Damson, Suke, 29, 31, 32, 33
    Fitzpiers, Edred, 16, 28-33, 49, 54
    'Grammer Oliver', 30-1
    Melbury, George, 30, 31, 32
    Melbury, Grace, 17, 29-33, 49
    South, Marty, 27-30, 33, 164
    South, Mr, 49
Woolf, Virginia, 13, 61
Wordsworth, William, 23, 41; Lyrical
    Ballads, 23
Wouvermans, 16

Zabel, M. D., 2, 4
Zola, Emile, 20, 212